PAN AM

AN AIRLINE AND ITS AIRCRAFT

PAN AM

AN AIRLINE AND ITS AIRCRAFT

By R.E.G. DAVIES

Illustrated By MIKE MACHAT

ORION BOOKS / NEW YORK

Dedication

This book is dedicated to Althea ''Gerry'' Lister, whose unstinting efforts as Pan American's historian and record keeper throughout most of Pan American's industrious life have set a standard of excellence which I hope this book can aspire to.

Published by Orion Books, a division of Crown Publishers, Inc., 225 Park Avenue South, New York, N.Y. 10003, and represented in Canada by the Canadian MANDA Group.

ORION and Colophon are trademarks of Crown Publishers, Inc.

Manufactured in Japan

Designed by Mike Machat

Library of Congress Cataloging-in-Publication Data

Davies, R. E. G. (Ronald Edward George)
    Pan American: An Airline and Its Aircraft

    1. Pan American Airways, Inc.—History. 2. Aeronautics, Commercial—United States—History. 3. Airlines —United States—History. I. Title.
HE9803.P36D38   1987   387.7'065'73   87-5581
ISBN 0-517-56639-7

10 9 8 7 6 5 4 3 2 1

First Edition

Contents

Prelude to Pan Am   2-3

The Formative Years

The Formation of
  Pan American Airways   The Fortuitous First Service   4-5

The First Pan American Service   Fokker F-VIIa/3m   6-7

West Indian Aerial Express   Keystone Pathfinder   8-9

Cia Mexicana de Aviación   Fairchild 71   10-11

Encircling the Caribbean   Sikorsky S-38   12-13

Pan American-Grace Airways   Fairchild FC-2W2   14-15

Pan Am's
  Latin American Workhorse   Pan Am's Fords   16-17

A Versatile Metal Airplane   Ford Tri-Motor   18-19

New York, Rio and
  Buenos Aires Line   Consolidated Commodore   20-21

The SCADTA Story   Pan Am's Covert Connections   22-23

Mexican Maneuvering   Caribbean Consolidation   24-25

The First Atlantic Sortie   Fokker F-10A   26-27

The Flying Boat Era

The First Clipper Ship   Sikorsky S-40   28-29

Transoceanic Problems   Planning for the Pacific   30-31

Operations in Alaska   Lockheed L-10 Electra   32-33

China National Aviation Corp.   Douglas Dolphin   34-35

An Airliner Before Its Time   Sikorsky S-41   36-37

Conquest of the Pacific   Martin M-130   38-39

Competition for
  Atlantic Supremacy   The Contenders   40-41

The Greatest Flying Boat   Boeing 314   42-43

The Great Piston-Engined Landplanes

The Modern Airliner   Douglas DC-2   44-45

The Old Indestructible   Douglas DC-3   46-47

Flying ''Above the Weather''   Boeing 307 Stratoliner   48-49

They Also Served   Sikorsky S-43   50-51

Transocean Landplane   Douglas DC-4   52-53

Efficient Elegance   Lockheed 049 Constellation   54-55

Luxury Aloft   Boeing 377 Stratocruiser   56-57

The Second Level   Convair 240   58-59

Lest We Forget…   Curtiss C-46   60-61

The Thoroughbred Airliner   Douglas DC-6B   62-63

Nonstop Trans-Atlantic at Last   Douglas DC-7C''Seven Seas''   64-65

The Jet Age

The Jet Age Begins   Boeing 707-120   66-67

Change of Allegiance   Douglas DC-8-32   68-69

The Era of Domination   Boeing 707-320C   70-71

Variations on a Theme   Boeing 720B   72-73

The Most Successful Airliner   Boeing 727   74-75

Permutations on the Pedigree   Boeing 737   76-77

The Wide-Bodied Era

The Ultimate Airliner   Boeing 747   78-79

The Ultimate Range   Boeing 747SP   80-81

Domestic Routes at Last   McDonnell Douglas DC-10   82-83

Trijet Quandary   Lockheed L-1011 TriStar   84-85

The Wind of Change   Airbus A300B4 and D.H.
                              (Canada) Dash Seven   86-87

Appendices

Associates and Subsidiaries   88

Pan Am's Flying Boats in Perspective   89

Index   90

The Airline of 1,000 Airplanes

In this book 982 Pan American aircraft are listed individually by registration and constructor's numbers, and with their Clipper names. Pan American also took possession of 20 or more SCADTA aircraft and so the total has exceeded 1,000. There were 103 flying boats, including 38 S-38s. Exactly 100 DC-2s and DC-3s are accounted for, as well as 92 DC-4s. So far Pan Am has operated 381 jets.

To provide every aircraft detail would require a much larger volume than this. Some Clippers, for example, had as many as five different names but only the first and best known is listed here.

Among the modern types, fuel capacity and payload have been traded off depending upon the mission required of each individual type. Here, the range and seating quoted have been selected as those normally used to comply with the majority of the missions demanded by Pan American. Weights quoted are in short tons (2,000 lb.); dimensions are rounded off to the nearest foot; and dates are stated according to international practice, i.e., day, month, year, in that order. Number of seats is mixed class.

Further Reading

I hope that the contents of this book will stimulate readers to seek more detailed reading material on the fascinating story of Pan American Airways. For this purpose, I recommend other books of mine and the following specialist works on Pan American Airways:

The Struggle for Airlines in Latin America, by William Burden (New York Council on Foreign Relations, (1943)

Empire of the Air, by Matthew Josephson (Harcourt, Brace, 1943)

Airways Abroad, by Henry Ladd Smith (University of Wisconsin Press, 1950)

An American Saga—Juan Trippe and his Pan Am Empire, by Robert Daley (Random House, 1980)

The Chosen Instrument, by Marylin Bender and Selig Altschul

The Perilous Sky, by Wesley Philips Newton (University of Miami Press, 1978)

Acknowledgments

In compiling the material in this book, I am indebted to many sources, notably to Pan American's own records, patiently established by veteran keeper of the books Althea Lister and continued since 1974 by Ann Whyte. These have been supplemented by comprehensive contributions from many sources: Harry Gann of Douglas, Dr. Peter van Driel of Boeing, Harvey Lippincott of United Technologies, Theron Reinhart of Fairchild, and many contributors from the American Aviation Historical Society, notably Bill Larkins, world authority on the Ford Tri-Motor, and Richard Allen, specialist on Lockheed and much else, and Don Thomas.

Most of the photographs were from Pan American's voluminous files—also established by "Gerry" Lister—or from those of the National Air and Space Museum. Those of the early German aircraft and airships came from Lufthansa, most of the Mexican aircraft from the files of Ing. José Villela-Gómez, and the fine Shorts S-23 picture from the Rudy Arnold collection at NASM. The early Chinese aircraft of CNAC were from Mrs. Price, courtesy of Dr. Bill Leary, and one or two photographs were from Mike Machat's or my own collections.

Finally I would like to thank Bob van der Linden for helping me to select the photographs and for acting as my technical conscience throughout the preparation of the book, and to Donna Corbett for the index.

R.E.G.D.

Artist's Notes — Aircraft Color Schemes

After thirty years of researching aircraft color schemes, I have discovered "Machat's Law" — "*The only consistency in aircraft color schemes is their inconsistency.*" The corollary states, "*Upon review of five examples of one type of aircraft, all five will have color-scheme variations.*"

With this in mind, I faced the formidable challenge of depicting Pan Am's aircraft in their correct markings, only to discover Machat's Law at work again. The aircraft shown are the first examples of each type **delivered** to Pan American unless noted otherwise. The criterion for each choice was, therefore, the delivery date published in official Pan Am records, and not necessarily the first aircraft in service.

There was, however, some consistency: the colors. From the 1930s until 1958, Pan American used a dark blue trim (PMS 289) and a light/medium blue (PMS 299) thereafter. The insignia was in black until the late 1920s.

M.M.

Author

I had just finished my contribution to John Wegg's immaculate book on Finnair, to which endeavor Mike Machat, my former colleague at Douglas, had also supplied his meticulous aircraft drawings. I was on a Pan American trans-Atlantic flight and the idea of a new kind of aviation book occurred to me. I hastily scribbled down some notes on the back of an envelope, which I still have as a souvenir of how *Pan Am—An Airline and Its Aircraft* started.

During 40 years of reading—and sometimes writing—about airlines and airliners, I had observed that aviation literature seemed to fall broadly into two categories. On the one hand were the scholarly works. These trace the development of aircraft or an aspect of aviation in the customary academic style. Often the text is relieved only by hundreds of footnotes, while some have a few token illustrations or exhibits. Such books have usually remained on the shelf until needed by its owner to check a fact or figure. And they are usually expensive.

The other type of aviation book is of the so-called "coffee table" variety, too often consisting of a random collection of photographs, poorly—and sometimes incorrectly—captioned. These touch only superficially upon the selected subject. Nevertheless, many of these books are artistically produced, often in full color. They are widely distributed, because of their eye-catching attractiveness, and their typically lower price.

This led me to identify a paradox: the latter variety of books usually reaches a much larger audience; yet the former type should be more widely read if the fascinating story of the development of the air transport industry is to be disseminated to generate more interest.

I therefore decided to try to combine the best qualities of both types of book in a well-illustrated airline history. A key element would be fine aircraft drawings, supplemented by well selected photographs, concise explanatory text, maps, charts, statistics, and tabular data. This would be an exciting way to tell an exciting story, and reasonably priced, might thus reach a bigger readership.

The back of my envelope chose Pan American as a model. During the 60 years of its brilliant history, it pioneered transocean and intercontinental air routes; it sponsored airplane types which were in the van of technical progress, and as the Chosen Instrument of commercial aviation policy overseas, it became a powerful political force. Without Pan American the course of air transport, even some nations' destinies, would have been different.

Mike Machat's artistry and the enthusiastic cooperation of the publishers have helped me to tell Pan American's story in a new way. I hope that together we have been able to portray vividly and accurately its role in the global development of air transport.

R. E. G. Davies

Artist

I agreed with great pleasure and expectation to join forces with Ron Davies, one of aviation's leading writers and historians, to produce this unique work. Ron's tireless interest and enthusiasm (not to mention his ocasional slave-driving tendencies) have been an inspiration as these pages emerged from a congenial writer-artist partnership.

To me, the name PAN AMERICAN has always symbolized the future. In October, 1958, at the age of eleven, I had been one of a crowd of onlookers at New York International Airport on the historic occasion when the world's first two jetliners parked next to one another on the ramp that crisp autumn afternoon, pausing for breath as they vied for pride of place in starting the Jet Age.

B.O.A.C.'s Comet 4 seemed dwarfed by Pan Am's 707 but both looked like machines from another galaxy compared to the prop-driven Stratocruisers and Constellations parked nearby. The scene is as vivid in my memory today as it was then. A year later, I was thrilled to sit in the left-hand cockpit seat of a Pan Am DC-7C, and watch the new 707s at the gates. I was a youthful witness to the "changing of the guard" as a new era unfolded before my eyes.

Nothing has revived the memory of that moment more than to prepare the drawings for this book on Pan American's history. Equally, I enjoyed the challenge of undertaking the thorough research needed to ensure the standards of accuracy that I know will be demanded by author, publisher, and reader alike.

Many others have helped directly or indirectly to make this project a reality. John Wegg set a standard to which we could all aspire with his magnificent books on Finnair and the Caravelle—in both of which I was honored to participate. Fellow enthusiasts Jon Proctor and Craig Kodera offered research material specifically for my artistic needs. Lenny Pustilnick, backed by Fred Digby and the able crew of typesetters at Anthony Type, lent his design expertise to help create the style of text and page layouts. I should mention also that Ron himself pitched in with the maps.

Production Assistant Michelle Grisanti served as my proverbial right hand in keeping the studio under control, and I thank especially my wife Sheri and my daughter Melissa (who, at two, can identify a "Super Eighty") for enduring the hectic months of frenetic activity necessary to produce a work of this kind.

Mike Machat

Publisher

The name Pan American has for sixty years been synonomous with all our daydreams of what flying should be—adventurous, romantic, and a force for peace in bringing peoples and nations together. During the pioneering decades of the 1920s and 1930s, Pan American was led by one of the airline industry's giants, Juan Trippe, and advised by, among others, the immortal Charles Lindbergh. They created a world airline network by developing long range navigational and logistical techniques. These were later to assume such immense importance in World War II that Pan Am could be classified as a national asset. Its largely self-taught operational and engineering skills led to ocean-spanning achievements which established the United States as pre-eminent in global air transportation, almost, at the height of the Juan Trippe era, to a position of world dominance.

The Martin Clipper's piston-engined radials that drove the propellers through the ocean spray and the Pacific skies have given way to the enormous jet engines of the world-embracing Boeing 747s. The trim but austere paint schemes of a bygone conservative era have given way to the brilliant blue and white of Pan American's contemporary insignia, to symbolize the technological miracle of global airline service.

The Crown Publishing Group has been privileged to work with the noted specialist on air transport and airline history, R. E. G. Davies, whose partnership with the meticulous artist Mike Machat, has produced this evocative presentation of the truly remarkable Pan American story.

The Publisher

Prelude To Pan Am

Florida–The Cradle of Air Transport in the United States

Although sustained for only three months, the **St. Petersburg—Tampa Airboat Line** could justly claim to be the world's first airline. Percival Fansler, the founder, chose a Benoist XIV flying boat as his equipment, and one of the famous aviators of the day, Tony Jannus, as his pilot. Daily operations began on 1 January 1914 on the 18-mile route across Tampa Bay. The fare was $5.00, or the same amount for 100 lb. of freight, for the one-way trip.

This pioneer company carried 1204 passengers and some air express packages until the first week in April, when it ceased operations, partly because of the wane of the tourist season, and partly because of Jannus's desire to seek other adventures. He eventually found these in the Great War in Europe, and was killed while training Russian pilots in 1917.

Fansler's initiative proved that passengers and packages could be carried safely by air, and that an airline could pay its way under special circumstances. True, the St. Petersburg city fathers subsidized the operation, but Fansler paid back most of the loan from earnings. One lesson to be learned was that an overwater route offered an excellent opportunity for airplanes to compete with surface transport, because ships were slow by comparison. A natural assumption was that waterborne aircraft were safer in the event of a forced landing. Also, in the case of the route between St. Petersburg and Tampa, the surface journey at that time was circuitous, adding time, expense, and inconvenience to an otherwise simple journey.

The conclusion was widely drawn, therefore, that flying boats or floatplanes were suitable for commercial airplane operations. Four years later, after the first

World War had ended, the next airline to start regular service in the United States was also based in Florida, offered competition with shipping, and also used flying boats instead of land planes.

Aeromarine–The First Foreign Air Mail Contract

One of the most under-recognized pioneer airlines in the United States was Aeromarine, a company started at the end of World War I by Inglis M. Uppercu, a former New York automobile distributor, and founder of the Aeromarine Plane and Motor Corporation at Keyport, New Jersey. Uppercu bought some ex-Navy Curtiss F-5L coastal patrol flying boats and converted them to carry as many as fourteen passengers.

At about the same time, a small company, Florida West Indies Airways, had received a foreign air mail contract from the U.S. Post Office on 15 October 1920. But it was unable to begin service and Aeromarine took over the operation as **Aeromarine West Indies Airways.** The contract was the first of its kind to be issued, but Aeromarine was the second to begin service on 1 November. Another operation, Eddie Hubbard's Seattle-Victoria (British Columbia) line got under way first, although his was the second contract to be issued. The third was granted to Merrill Riddick, who opened a route from New Orleans to Pilottown.

Aeromarine's was easily the most extensive operation of the three, even though it was seasonal. The big Curtiss boats, weighing seven tons, fully loaded, with a cruising range of four hours, were impressive for their time. Unlike the other two mail lines, Aeromarine also carried passengers. On 1 November 1921 they began two regular daily services, Key West-Havana and Miami-Nassau. The 105-mile Havana trip took between 1½ and 2 hours and cost $50 one way, compared with $19 for an all-day voyage by ship. A similar ratio applied to the $85 flight on the 185-mile Nassau route.

Uppercu showed remarkable ingenuity in utilizing his aircraft. When the Florida winter vacation ended, he moved the fleet north to New York and the Great Lakes and operated services there during the summer. This seasonal routine, incidentally, was repeated half a century later by the Provincetown-Boston Airline.

Nevertheless, in spite of carrying almost 20,000 passengers in perfect safety in a little more than two years, Aeromarine could not pay its way. It folded up in 1923, and its mail contract lapsed. By this time the Key West-Havana route had presumably been designated as FAM 1. When Pan American took it over in 1927, it was designated FAM 4, the original number having been reallocated to Colonial Airways.

Aeromarine's **Curtiss F-5L** carried passengers and mail as early as 1920.

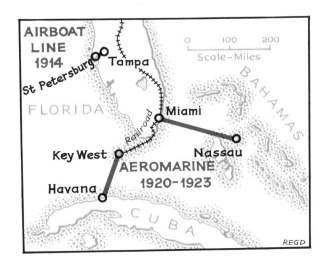

The **Benoist XIV**—first scheduled airline flight in the world.

The Colombian Challenge

During the early 1920s, the United States lagged behind Europe and other areas of the world in the development of air transport. The Germans particularly had been remarkably enterprising in overcoming the restrictions of the Treaty of Versailles by designing some fine aircraft, building and operating them if necessary in foreign countries. In South America, a group of Colombian and German businessmen founded the **Sociedad Colombo-Alemana de Transportes Aéreos (SCADTA)** on 5 December 1919.

Demonstrating remarkable initiative, the company imported some Junkers-F 13 metal aircraft, fitted with floats, to operate along the Magdalena River. The line opened on 19 September 1921 and has continued to operate ever since. Today's AVIANCA, Colombia's national airline, is SCADTA's direct descendant, and is thus the oldest airline in the Americas.

Peter Paul von Bauer, head of SCADTA, consolidated a Colombian domestic network and then cast his eyes northwards. A German master salesman, Fritz Hammer, representing the Condor Syndikat, arranged for two Dornier Wal flying boats, the *Atlántico* and the *Pacífico*,

to be shipped to Colombia. They were owned by Condor and leased to SCADTA.

Von Bauer then embarked on a bold venture. He led a delegation to the United States in the two Wals, leaving Barranquilla on 18 August 1925 and arriving in Havana on 1 April. After some U.S. prevarication, only the *Pacífico* was allowed to fly to Florida. Hammer went to New York, to enlist business support, while von Bauer went to Washington, and obtained an audience with President Coolidge. But he received little encouragement, and only the Commerce Department showed any real interest.

The delegation had to return, frustrated, to Colombia. Had the negotiations succeeded, SCADTA could have started a trans-Caribbean service, and the chronicle of airline history would have been very different.

Von Bauer's expedition certainly gave food for thought in the U.S.A. Within a few weeks, on 8 January 1926, the State Department called an interdepartmental conference. The Air Commerce Act and the Foreign Air Mail Act were passed shortly afterwards. The U.S.A. was about to enter the international commercial airline arena. All it needed was an airline.

The Dornier Wal *Pacífico* at Lake Amatitlan, Guatemala.

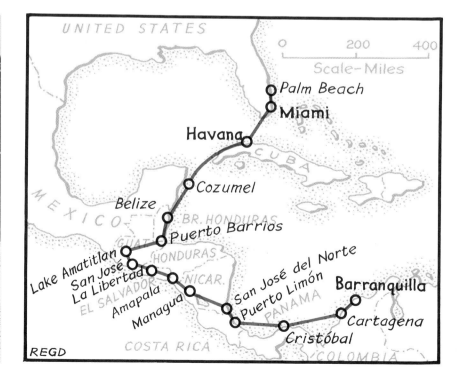

The Formation Of Pan American Airways

When the United States finally decided to enter the international aviation scene in the mid-1920s, three different groups of investors displayed interest in starting international air services from Florida. One of these was influenced by Peter Paul von Bauer, of the Colombian airline, SCADTA, which had been unsuccessful in 1925 in obtaining landing and traffic rights in the U.S.A. One of von Bauer's associates, Captain J.K. Montgomery, continued to promote the idea of a trans-Caribbean service. He enlisted banking support through Richard Bevier and George Grant Mason, and opened discussions with President Machado of Cuba on 8 March 1927. The group incorporated in New York on 14 March as **Pan American Airways.**

Previously, two former American air aces from World War I, Reed Chambers and Eddie Rickenbacker, had formed **Florida Airways,** opening a mail route from Atlanta to Miami on 1 April 1926. The two pilots were backed by an impressive banking group, with names such as Percy Rockefeller, Charles Stone, Charles Hayden, George Mixter, Richard Hoyt, and Anne Morgan representing the elite of Wall Street. But after less than a year, and losing its aircraft through crashes, Florida

Airways had gone into bankruptcy. Nevertheless, the original intent had been to extend southwards into the Caribbean, with Havana as the first objective, and the idea was kept alive by the promoters, even though Rickenbacker departed for other ventures.

The third group was spearheaded by Juan Trippe, a young man from an influential New England family. He had a consuming interest in airplanes and their potential as transport vehicles, and operated **Long Island Airways** from 1923 until 1925 as a rich man's charter service. He then formed Eastern Air Transport (not the same company as the forerunner of Eastern Air Lines) to bid for the new U.S. Post Office contract, CAM 1, from Boston to New York. The competitor was **Colonial Airways,** but Trippe quickly organized a merger of the two rival bidders.

Always a visionary, Trippe was responsible for creating associated Colonial companies, Colonial Western and Canadian Colonial, the former with ambitions to fly westwards at least as far as Chicago, the latter to serve Canada. But his visions were clouded by the parochial views of his New England associates, and together with John Hambleton and Cornelius Vanderbilt, his original backers, Trippe parted company with Colonial and went south. He linked up with Anthony Fokker, the Dutch aircraft designer and constructor who had established Atlantic Aviation as a U.S. subsidiary, and made a trial flight to Havana, where he contemplated the broad horizons of the potential Latin American commercial airline market.

Trippe's group formed the **Aviation Corporation of America** on 2 June 1927. The initial capital, put up by Hambleton, C.V. Whitney, Trippe, and their friends, was $300,000, equivalent to perhaps $5,000,000 in today's money. André Priester, another Dutchman, was hired as operations and engineering specialist.

Sparring began between the three competing groups. In a flurry of corporate maneuvering during the summer of 1927, the Chambers-Hoyt group formed **Southeastern Air Lines** on 1 July, Trippe formed **Southern Air Lines** on 8 July, and Montgomery's Pan American won the coveted U.S. Post Office Foreign Air Mail Contract (FAM 4) on 16 July. Southeastern Airlines was reincorporated as **Atlantic, Gulf and Caribbean Airways** on 11 October.

Trippe proposed to merge the three groups into an amalgamated company to be called Pan American Airways. Performing an outflanking movement of dubious ethics, an activity which was to characterize his entire career, he played his trump card. He and

Hambleton flew to Havana and persuaded Cuba's President Machado to grant landing rights in Cuba exclusively to the Aviation Corporation. Montgomery's mail contract thus became no more than a piece of paper, no longer useful as a bargaining chip.

With Trippe no doubt displaying his ability to procrastinate patiently, politely, but unyielding, however long the wrangling continued, an agreement was finally reached. Hoyt produced an acceptable formula: 40% shareholding to be held each by Trippe's and Hoyt's groups, 20% by Montgomery's. No single party was to control, and everything must be paid for in cash. Total capital was to be $500,000.

On 23 June the resultant merger, the **Aviation Corporation of the Americas**—a subtle change of name from Trippe's company—was completed. **Pan American Airways Inc.** was the operating subsidiary. From the date of its formation, there was no doubt as to who ran the show. Juan Terry Trippe embarked on a career that was, within barely a single decade, to build on a 90-mile route to Cuba to fashion the largest and most influential airline in the world.

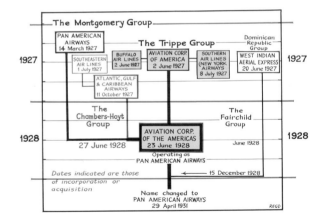

Juan Trippe while at Yale University. The photograph suggests the determination that was to characterize his later career.

The Fortuitous First Service

While the complex corporate and financial negotiations proceeded throughout 1927, serious operational problems confronted Pan American Airways, the company which nominally held the precious FAM 4 mail contract. Under the terms, at risk of default, Pan American had to demonstrate its ability to fly aircraft according to a regular schedule over the designated route no later than 19 October 1927.

Unfortunately, the Fokker F VII aircraft selected for the occasion had only been ordered on 19 August and delivery did not take place until 30 September. Although flown to Miami, they could not perform their appointed mission from Key West to Havana because Key West's Meacham Field was not yet completed. The Fokkers, and for that matter, Pan American and its ambitions, were stranded in Miami.

There followed one of the most remarkable episodes in the history of air transport, not solely because of the series of coincidences which permitted the event, but because of the far-reaching consequences. Had Trippe and his co-negotiators failed to meet the terms of the contract, he would have had problems in obtaining an extension, as other aspiring interests would have been eager to allege collusion, if not conspiracy.

Almost unbelievably, at the proverbial eleventh hour, on the eve of the deadline date to be exact, Jack Whitbeck, Pan American's representative in Miami, learned that a Fairchild FC-2 single-engined monoplane had arrived at Key West, and was awaiting reports of a threatened hurricane before taking off on a delivery flight to the Dominican Republic, via Havana. The aircraft was owned by West Indian Aerial Express, an airline which had already started service from Barahona, in the Republic.

Whitbeck offered to pay $145.50 to the pilot, Cy Caldwell, if he would fly to Havana, on charter from Pan American, with seven sacks containing 13,000 letters from Key West and 15,000 more that had just arrived on the *Havana Special* of the Florida East Coast-Atlantic Coast Line railroads. At that time, the trains still ran through to Key West by a remarkable "railroad that went to sea," via the small islands south of Florida.

Not wishing to turn aside some easy money, Cy Caldwell complied. He took the 251-lb load on the FC-2, *La Niña*, temporarily fitted with floats for the ferry flight, from Key West to Havana, taking one hour to complete the 90 miles, flying at a altitude of 1000 feet, arriving at 9:25 a.m. The hurricane did not materialize. The Pan American Flight Report, meticulously completed to ensure legitimacy, recorded "unlimited visibility."

Thanks to this accidental opportunity—for Caldwell would not have tarried in Key West, had there not been a hurricane warning—and had a potential rival airline not chosen that moment to take delivery of an aircraft, and had the weather not improved, Pan American might never have got off the ground—literally. Murphy and his Law had been sabotaged by Juan Trippe, whose prospects could now well be described as echoing the words of the flight report: unlimited visibility.

The **Fairchild FC-2** *La Niña* of **West Indian Aerial Express**—Something borrowed...

The First Pan American Services

One of Pan American's three **Fokker F-VII/3m's**.

Pan American's first Miami base at **36th Street**

Cabin service on board the **Fokker F-VII/3m**.

Meacham Field, Key West, in 1928.

Having overcome the crisis of qualifying for the U.S. Post Office mail contract, and with negotiations proceeding towards an eventual amalgamation of the three rival groups, Pan American Airways set about the task of establishing itself in Florida. For reasons of convenience related to its unusual geographical position, Key West did not rate highly as a potential permanent base. A small island at the end of the chain of reefs known as the Florida Keys, it was connected with the mainland by a railroad which was itself an impressive feat of engineering.

The original choice of Key West was simply because it was the nearest U.S. point to Cuba, and aircraft could not fly for much more than a hundred miles with an adequate payload over water where there was no landing ground. Single-engined aircraft had an alarming tendency to need emergency fields because of the unreliability of the engines at that time. When the trimotored Fokker came along, therefore, with better range and with a reserve of power in the event of an engine failure, Key West's strategic position was redundant. It could not match the advantages of a big city like Miami, which could provide the services and resources that a company with big ambitions would need, if it was to establish an airline gateway of substance to the Caribbean and beyond.

When the Fokker F VIIa entered service on 28 October 1927, therefore, its route from Key West to Havana was short-lived. Nevertheless, the inaugural flights were performed with a certain sense of history. Piloted by Hugh Wells, with Ed Musick as navigator, the *General Machado* set off from Meacham Field at 8:25 a.m. with 772 lb of mail. The flight took 1 hr 20 min, and Musick piloted the return leg later that day.

Pan American completed the necessary arrangements to be able to open passenger service from Key West on 16 January 1928. It received the permanent FAM 4 air mail contract, at $2.00 per mile, on 29 May. A few months later, on 15 September, the *General Machado*, and its sister ship, the *General New*, transferred from Key West to Miami, when the 36th Street airfield was completed. Pan American established its base at Miami on 29 October and terminated all service at Key West on 3 December 1928.

The Fokker F VIIa's days were numbered, however. The need for a waterborne aircraft to serve the islands of the Caribbean had become obvious even to André Priester, who predictably favored landplanes. Only three Fokkers were delivered, the third one in fact replacing one which had already sunk in the Gulf of Mexico. When the Sikorsky S 38s took over, the remaining two were transferred to Mexico, where Juan Trippe was establishing a foothold.

André Priester, a Dutchman who came to America with Anthony Fokker, was recruited by Juan Trippe as his chief technical adviser.

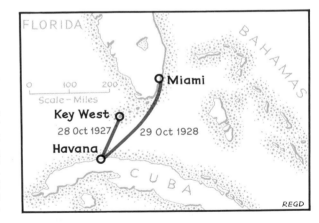

Fokker F-VIIa/3m

8 seats • 118 mph

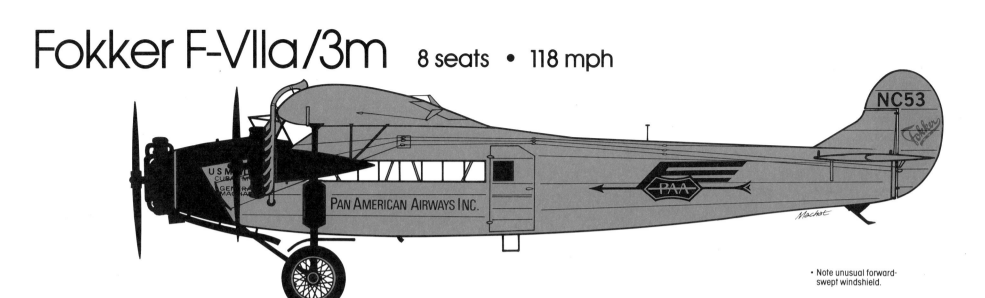

• Note unusual forward-swept windshield.

Wright Whirlwind (240 hp) x 3 • 8,800 lb. max. gross take-off weight • 600 statute miles range

Pan American's first service airplane—the term airliner had not yet come into use—was a model of one of the most important series of commercial aircraft produced during the first decade following the end of World War II and the beginning of air transport. The Fokker F-VIIa/3m was the first three-engined version of the single-engined F-VII, which had first flown in April 1924 and had entered service with the famous Dutch airline, K.L.M., on 1 July of that year.

The basic method of Fokker construction was to construct a welded tubular steel frame fuselage, and cover this with plywood or fabric, while the thick wing was built entirely of wood. This latter was the best available that combined strength with light weight, the Dutch factory preferring Lithuanian birch. As was customary at the time, with engines normally attached to the front end of the fuselage or hung on the wings, power plants varied, but the first **F-VII** had one Rolls-Royce Eagle engine. The aircraft weighed a little over 2½ tons, fully loaded, and cruised at about 85 mph. Napier Lion engines added about 10 mph to the speed.

The **F-VIIA**, with Bristol Jupiter engines, was a cleaned up version, with neater landing gear and rounded wingtips, and the 480 hp engine permitted a speed of up to 118 mph, and more than 1½ tons additional gross weight. Then, while on a visit to the U.S.A., Anthony Fokker sent word back to the factory in Amsterdam to produce a three-engined version, so as to enter the Ford Reliability Trials competition. Powered by three Wright Whirlwind engines, with an all-up weight of 8800 lb. (almost 4½ tons) the aircraft was an immediate success.

By this time, Fokker had founded the Atlantic Aircraft Corporation in May 1924, and this became the Fokker Aircraft Corporation, based at Hasbrouck Heights, in New Jersey. At first the aircraft were built in Europe, then the wings were imported into the U.S., and finally the whole aircraft was built in New Jersey. By the time Pan American became interested, the **F-VIIa/3m** had fine credentials. Entering service with K.L.M. in the summer of 1926, it had been used on several record-breaking long distance flights, including the Maitland-Hegenberger California-Hawaii "first," the Ford-sponsored Byrd Arctic Expedition, and the Kingsford-Smith trans-Pacific flight in the summer of 1928. It had put up some impressive performances for K.L.M., with special flights to Batavia (now Jakarta) in impressive demonstrations of reliability,

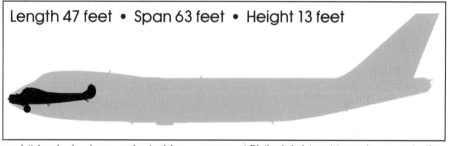

Length 47 feet • Span 63 feet • Height 13 feet

and it had also been selected by a group of Philadelphia citizens to operate the Philadelphia Rapid Transit Service, or P.R.T. Line, during the latter half of 1926, to mark the Sesquicentennial (150th) anniversary of the United States by a service to Washington. The U.S.-built version was known as the Fokker Trimotor.

P.R.T.'s chief engineer was André Priester, and when Juan Trippe obtained the Fokkers, he obtained the services of Priester too. The F-VIIA/3m's life with Pan American was brief, but the aircraft was an undoubted success, especially in Europe. Including the finest of the series, the higher-powered, faster, and heavier **F-VIIb/3m**, 170 of the 600 airline aircraft in Europe in 1933 were Fokkers, and most of these were exported to foreign countries. By comparison, in that year, there were 114 Junkers, of which 70 were used in Germany.

FLEET LIST

Regist. No.	Const. No.	Name	Delivery Date	Disposal
NC 53	703	*General Machado*	30.9.27	Sank in Gulf of Mexico, 15.8.28
NC 3314	612	*General New*	30.9.27	Transferred to CMA (Mexico). Sold 1.4.32
NC 5192	614		31.8.28	Transferred to CMA (Mexico). Crashed 21.4.30

West Indian Aerial Express

The story of how Pan American managed to qualify for its first airmail contract by an incredible piece of luck has been recounted earlier as the Fortuitous First Service, involving the delivery of an aircraft to a new airline based in the Dominican Republic. This was the **West Indian Aerial Express, C por A (WIAX)** which was itself the result of a happy coincidence. Basil Rowe, one of the carefree fraternity of barnstorming pilots of the period, arrived in the Republic early in 1927, seeking suitable venues for the customary displays of stunt flying and a little joyriding business. He visited the small town of Barahona, where some U.S. sugar planters found themselves almost isolated, and the idea of an airline was born.

WIAX was promoted mainly by H.L. Harper, with other local businessmen. Rowe was the chief pilot, and his two Waco 9 biplanes constituted the fleet. The capital was $50,000. The embryo airline made experimental flights to Port-au-Prince, Haiti, on 14 July 1927, and back to the Dominican capital, Santo Domingo, the next day. The company was smart enough to obtain mail contracts from these two countries of the island of Hispaniola and from Cuba.

While Cy Caldwell was inadvertently letting Pan American through the back door by his Good Samaritan act on the Fairchild FC-2 delivery, Basil Rowe delivered the Keystone Pathfinder, *Santa Maria*. West Indian Aerial Express began scheduled services on 1 December 1927, from Santo Domingo to San Juan, Puerto Rico, thrice a week, and to Port-au-Prince, once a week. Typical fares on the Keystone were $50 one way San Juan-Santo Domingo, and $85 San Juan-Port-au-Prince. The large aircraft was also able to carry cargo at 25¢ per pound, and mail at $2.50 per pound.

One interesting interlude was when, on 6/7 February 1928, Charles Lindbergh passed through on his goodwill tour around the Caribbean, he carried some mail for WIAX over its route and through to Havana in *The Spirit of St. Louis*. This is almost certainly the only time the famous aircraft was used for commercial purposes, and there must have been a unique moment when it was parked alongside its erstwhile rival, the Keystone, which had formerly been a transatlantic contender.

On 20 February West Indian extended its route at both ends, to Santiago de Cuba and to St. Thomas and St. Croix. Two weeks later, on 8 March, the United States passed the Foreign Air Mail Act, and on 31 May bids were advertised for FAM 6, Miami-San Juan. Basil Rowe and WIAX suddenly found themselves in Pan American's way. Ostensibly this would not have appeared to be a problem, as Pan American at the time was actually smaller and its line experience was less. To ensure beyond any doubt that, to comply with the clause in the law which required that a majority of shares should be U.S.-owned, an affiliated company, West Indian Aerial Express Inc., was formed in the U.S. in June 1928 as a holding company. The capital was now $92,000, with additional investment by Sherman Fairchild, who became president, and Graham Grosvenor.

When the bids were opened on 14 July, Pan American Airways won the contract at the top rate, $2.00 per mile, a procedure which became a habit for Juan Trippe during the formative years of his Latin American and transocean empire during the next eleven years. Basil Rowe and Cy Caldwell might have regretted the *La Niña* incident, but Rowe recognized the facts of business life and pragmatically went on to a distinguished career with Pan American, when, on 16 October, WIAX C por A sold its assets to the holding company, which was in turn absorbed by Juan Trippe's little airline on 22 December 1928.

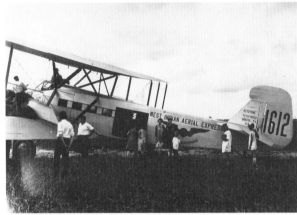

West Indian Aerial Express's flagship is seen here boarding passengers at an airfield in Santo Domingo early in 1928.

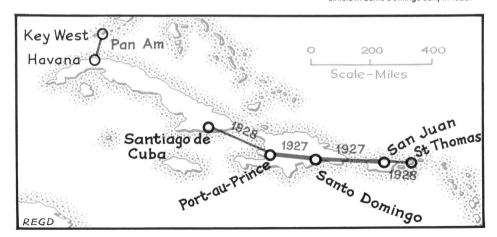

Keystone Pathfinder

10 seats • 85 mph

Basil Rowe, WIAX.

The **Keystone Pathfinder,** flagship of a forgotten airline.

Wright Whirlwind (220 hp) x 3 • 10,900 lb. max. gross take-off weight • 750 statute miles range

This large three-engined transport was selected by Basil Rowe, the Chief Pilot of West Indian Aerial Express, of the Dominican Republic. This particular aircraft, one of only three built, was originally prepared to enter the famous prize competition for the first transatlantic crossing, subsequently won by Charles Lindbergh. Equipped with two Liberty engines, and named the *American Legion,* it had come to grief during a test flight, killing its two pilots.

Rowe's selection was presumably made partly because, as a reconstructed aircraft, it was probably going cheap. But another factor was that, in spite of its ungainly appearance, its three Wright Whirlwinds apparently enabled it to take off and land in what Rowe termed "dollar bill-sized airfields." In his words, describing the limited terrain available "I could readily understand why there was such a scarcity of birds as they had probably all broken their necks in forced landings."

Re-christened the *Santa Maria,* it went into service when West Indian Aerial Express began scheduled operations on 1 December 1927, the first airline to do so in the entire Caribbean area, if an isolated experiment in Cuba in 1920 is excluded from the reckoning. It was handed over to Pan American on 20 September 1928, actually before the acquisition of West Indian had been completed.

Although Pan American soon disposed of it, flying it to Miami in 1929 en route back to the Keystone factory at Bristol, Pennsylvania, it was subsequently rebuilt and sold again, and by all accounts had a long, useful, and sometimes interesting life.

Length 45 feet • Span 75 feet • Height 16 feet

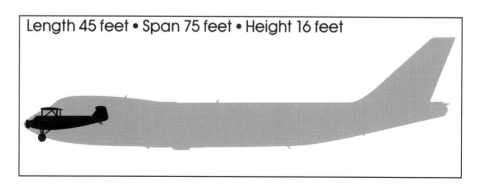

FLEET LIST

Regist. No.	Const. No.	Name	Delivery Date	Disposal
1612	3137	*Santa Maria*	20.9.28	Sold in 1929

9

Compañía Mexicana de Aviación (C.M.A.)

Pre-History of Mexicana

The first airline Concession (Contract Number 1) to be issued by the Secretariat of Communications and Public Works (Secretaria de Comunicaciones y Obras Publicas, or SCOP) under the supervision of Ing. Juan Guillermo Villasana, was to a company called **Compañía Mexicana de Transportación, S.A. (C.M.T.A.)** on July 1921. This was a small operation started by two U.S. citizens resident in Mexico, L.A. Winship and Harry J. Lawson. They had purchased two Lincoln Standard biplanes and at first intended to fly them on a route from the Mexican capital to the U.S. border at Ciudad Juarez.

They soon discovered, however, that a more lucrative use for their fleet was to provide a service to the Gulf Coast region near Tampico, where the Mexican oilfields were booming. During the first year of operations, C.M.T.A. carried 1,248 passengers, of whom 289 were on regular and inter-city flights. Business dropped off in 1922 and 1923, but some further Lincoln Standards were acquired, and the company apparently survived as a nominal, if not an operational entity.

One of Mexicana's **Lincoln Standards,** carrying payrolls to the Tampico oil fields.

Foundation of Mexicana

The oilfield business attracted other competitors for the Mexico City-Tampico route, for which there seems to have been a great demand. Three more Concessions were granted. Number 2, to Mario Bulnes, was never used; Number 3 went to a pilot, William "Slim" Mallory; Number 4 to a businessman, George Rihl. Mallory and Rihl pooled their interests, and with other investors founded **Compañía Mexicana de Aviación (C.M.A.)** on 24 August 1924. Lic Gustavo Espinosa Mireles was the first president of the new company.

C.M.A. then bought C.M.T.A. This amounted simply to purchasing the small fleet of Lincoln Standards, believed to number as many as ten. The goodwill of the route was worth nothing, as all the Concessions were for the same route. Thus C.M.A. can trace its history back to 1921 by taking account of its purchase—an historical device used by many of the world's airlines to claim ancient ancestry.

George Rihl, founder of **Compañía Mexicana de Aviación.**

Sherman Fairchild

Fairchild Interest

In 1925 the prominent U.S. industrialist, Sherman Fairchild, whose main interest at the time was aerial photography, but who was becoming intrigued with other aviation enterprises, purchased a 20% shareholding in C.M.A. and undertook to supply all equipment, including aircraft, at cost. On 16 August 1926, C.M.A. signed a ten-year contract with SCOP, and on 9 December of the same year, made a survey flight to Matamoros, on the U.S. frontier opposite Brownsville, stopping at Tampico, using a Lincoln Standard.

Having been granted a more comprehensive contract, for scheduled services for passengers and mail, C.M.A. started a thrice-weekly service from Mexico City to Tampico, via Tuxpan, on 15 April 1928. By this time, the first Fairchild FC-2s had been delivered and these little utility aircraft were to serve C.M.A. well, even after the arrival of the larger Ford Tri-Motors in 1929. *Ciudad de México* (M-SCOE) had opened the Tampico route, and *Ciudad de Mérida* (M-SCOZ) and *Ciudad de Veracruz* (M-SCOY) inaugurated a second route to the Yucatán on 15 October 1928.

Pan American Takes Over

On 2 January 1929 the U.S. Post Office advertised for bids on Foreign Air Mail Route (FAM) No 8, from Brownsville, Texas, to Mexico City, via Tampico. Although there were six other bidders, Pan American Airways received the contract at the top rate of $2.00 per mile. On 23 January, Juan Trippe of Pan American purchased the entire stock of the incumbent Mexican airline C.M.A. from George Rihl for 300,000 pesos, which at that time were worth $150,000—somewhat more than the equivalent value today. The transaction was made by an exchange of stock through Pan American's parent corporation, the Aviation Corporation of the Americas, and Sherman Fairchild acquired a substantial interest thereby, to add to his holdings made through the West Indian Aerial Express deal.

As the map shows, the acquisition of C.M.A. did more for Pan American than simply provide a link to the Mexican capital. It helped to consolidate its influence throughout the area and enabled Juan Trippe to control the entire air route system to and through Central America.

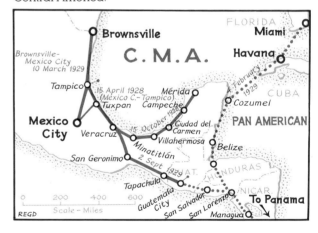

Fairchild 71

Identifying the Mexican Fairchilds

To unravel the numbering system employed by the Mexican aircraft registration authorities during the late 1920s would defy the best efforts of the wartime mathematicians who solved the mystery of the fiendishly clever German Enigma device. The earliest numbering system started with the letter M, followed by a hyphen and four letters, of which the first three were SCO, for **S**ecretaria de **C**ommunicaciones y **O**bras Publicas. Defying all logic, the same registration was given to different aircraft, while the same aircraft was often given more than one registration.

The M-SCO system gave way to another in 1928, at about the time when the Fairchild FC-2s and Model 71s appeared on the scene. The prefix X was substituted for the M, followed by the hyphen and then by the letter A as the first of four letters if it was a commercial aircraft. A letter B after the hyphen indicated an aircraft used for general aviation, and a C for government or official aircraft. After 1944 the hyphen was moved so that the prefixes were XA, XB, and XC respectively.

In the table of Mexican Fairchilds on this page, a valiant attempt has been made to restore order from the numerical chaos. Although several sources have suggested that C.M.A. had a larger number, only four FC-2s have been positively identifed from Fairchild records. As with the Model 71s, only some of the details can be ascertained with a reasonable degree of certainty. Where the registration numbers are shown in parentheses, this indicates a little inspired guesswork.

Not shown in this list of Fairchild aircraft, either owned by C.M.A. or assigned to it by Pan American, are two which were diverted there temporarily in 1932 as part of a substantial batch of Fairchild 71s purchased for Pacific Alaska, plus the FC-2W2s with which PANAGRA opened service. These are shown in the sections of this book devoted to those airlines.

FAIRCHILD FC-2 FLEET LIST (MEXICO)

Regist. No.	Const. No.	Name	Delivery Date	Disposal
(X-ABCL) M-SCOE	9	*Cuidad de México*	Aug 27	To Pan Am as NC 998. Retired 1933
X-ABCM (M-SCOY)	30	*Cuidad de Veracruz*	Oct 27	To Pan Am as NC 3432. Retired 1933
X-ABCN M-SCOH	41		Dec 27	To Pan Am as NC 3899, May 1929
X-ABCO (M-SCOZ)	143	*Ciudad de Mérida*	May 28	To Pan Am as NC 6803. Retired 1933

Development of the Model 71

During the latter 1920s, the Fairchild Airplane Manufacturing Corporation of Farmingdale, Long Island, together with its associated branches in Canada, was the leading manufacturer of utility aircraft in the western hemisphere. Fairchild built the aerial equivalent of the small pickup truck, and these were of inestimable benefit to many small airlines, from the deserts of Peru to the frozen wastes of Alaska.

The first production model, the **FC-2** (Fairchild Cabin Model 2) was powered by one Wright J-5 Whirlwind engine, of 220 horsepower. It made its first flight on 20 June 1927. Its wings, with a span of 44 feet, could be folded back, permitting easy transport by road, rail, or ship. The FC-2C was a version built for the Curtiss Flying service, with Curtiss engines.

The **FC-2W**, first flown in the fall of 1927, was better known and more widely used. The 410 horsepower of its Pratt & Whitney engine provided a marked improvement in performance over the FC-2, and the wing span was increased to 50 feet. Production of the FC-2 and FC-2W totalled about 175, of which perhaps 15 were of the latter model. Exact numbers are difficult to assess, as many aircraft were converted from one model to another, not a difficult process in those days.

A further production version, the **FC-2W2**, was a FC-2W stretched by two feet. This provided space for six passenger seats instead of the predecessors' four. About 35 FC-2W2s were produced. PANAGRA was an important customer, and full details are shown on page 15.

This remarkable photograph of a **Fairchild FC2W2**, flying in the Andes, shows an earlier acronym of Pan American-Grace Airways Corp.

Best known of the Fairchild utility range was the **Model 71**, introduced towards the end of 1928. This was a cleaned-up version of the FC-2W2, with oval rear windows and a smoother-looking fuselage. The new designation was derived from a numbering system adopted in 1929, and was at first intended to indicate the number of seats, including the pilot. It did not represent a new design. The significant change in the series was from the FC-2W to the FC-2W2. The Fairchild 71 retained the same Pratt & Whitney Wasp engines as the FC-2W2 and almost 100 were built.

One of Mexicana's **Fairchild 71s**.

FAIRCHILD 71 FLEET LIST (MEXICO)

Regist. No.	Const. No.	Name	Delivery Date	Disposal
(X-ABCF)	602	–	31.1.29	NC 9726. Crashed at Panama, June 29
(X-ABCG)	606	–	10.8.30	NC 9737. Written off 14.8.30
X-ABCH	618	–	4.29	NC 9777. Transferred to Alaska, 1933
X-ABCI	603	–	3.29	NC 9727. To **Aerovias Centrales** as X-ABEF, 24.4.33
(X-ABCJ)	611	–	7.3.30	NC 3172. Formerly Colonial Air Transport. Sold Aug 33
X-ABCK	601	–	28.8.29	NC 9709. To **Aerovias Centrales** as X-ABEE, 9.12.32. Alaska 1936

Encircling the Caribbean

Having established his credentials with the U.S. Post Office almost as a God-given right, Juan Trippe lost no time in expanding Pan American's Caribbean bridgehead, astutely purloined from West Indian Aerial Express. A succession of additional foreign air mail contracts quickly followed his coup and the dates of air mail service inauguration are shown on the map on this page.

The year 1929 witnessed an intense effort. A preliminary survey had already been made by Charles Lindbergh, in *The Spirit of St. Louis,* in a two-month circular tour beginning on 13 December 1927, in Washington, D.C., through Mexico to the Canal Zone, then along the Spanish Main and back through the Antilles and Cuba. Lindbergh favored landplanes but was forced to conclude that, for this region, amphibians were the logical choice. Partly acting on the "Lone Eagle's" advice, Trippe turned to Igor Sikorsky.

The great Russian designer had built large aircraft in Russia before the first World War, and had tried to do the same in the United States with the S-37 landplane. But this was too big for the airline traffic of the time and he turned to smaller amphibians, producing the single-boomed **S-36** in December 1927. Powered by two 220 hp Wright Whirlwinds, this was not satisfactory, and Sikorsky modified the design and completed the first twin-boomed **S-38** in May 1928.

Like the S-36, the wooden-framed hull and the lower sesquiplane were covered in aluminum. The wings were of wood and metal, covered with doped fabric. Each S-38 varied slightly in price, averaging between $50,000 and $54,000. Powered by Pratt & Whitney Wasps, with twice the horsepower of the Whirlwinds, the type was an immediate success. The prototype went into service with the New York, Rio, and Buenos Aires Line (NYRBA) in July 1928. Pan American took the second one off the line and introduced it on 31 October of the same year.

The first three production aircraft, together with the prototype, were **S38A**s. All the others were **S-38B**s. The S38As and the first five S38B's had vertical windshields, but all the others were more elegantly sloped.

Laying aside previous convictions, Lindbergh put in some solid work as a Pan Am pilot, accompanying Basil Rowe on many an inaugural flight. Pan American went on to buy a total of 38 Sikorsky S-38s, mostly for the Caribbean, but many allocated to Latin American associates or subsidiaries, as shown in the table opposite. Three of the S-38Bs, from a later production batch in 1933, went to China. Most of the fleet, other than as indicated in the table, were eventually sold or retired, the last one in 1940.

This versatile aircraft, equally at home as an amphibian on land or water, was the backbone of Pan American's fleet during a critical period, laying the foundations of the Caribbean and Central American network in 1929 and 1930.

Interior of a **Sikorsky S-38.**

Sikorsky S-38

8 seats • 110 mph

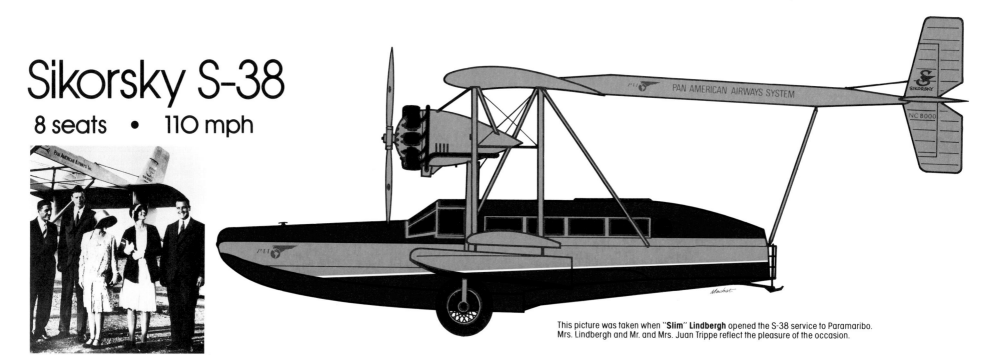

This picture was taken when "**Slim**" **Lindbergh** opened the S-38 service to Paramaribo.
Mrs. Lindbergh and Mr. and Mrs. Juan Trippe reflect the pleasure of the occasion.

Pratt & Whitney Wasp (410-450 hp) x 2 • 10,480 lb. max. gross take-off weight • 595 statute miles range

Reg. No.	Const. No.	Pan Am Delivery	Area or User	Remarks
S-36				
NC 3699		7.12.27	—	Returned to Sikorsky, February 1928
S-38 Prototype				
NC 5933	14A	15.9.30	NYRBA	Originally into service with NYRBA, July 1928; To Pan Am 15.9.30; scrapped 7.10.31
S-38A				
NC 8000	14.1	31.10.28	Caribbean	Operated Pan Am's first S-38 service, 31.10.28
NC 8020	14.4	30.12.29	Caribbean	Damaged beyond repair, 30.12.29
NC 8044	14.10	31.12.28	Caribbean	Damaged beyond repair, 26.5.33
S-38B (vertical windshield)				
NC 9775	114-2	25.4.29	Caribbean	
NC 9776	114-3	19.5.29	Caribbean	Survey flight (Lindbergh-Rowe) Canal Zone-Jamaica, 1.5.30
NC 9107	114-6	7.5.29	Caribbean	Transferred to SCADTA as *Von Krohn*. Crashed 10.3.34
NC 9137	114-9R	30.6.29	Caribbean	Survey flight (Rowe) to Paramaribo, 17.7.29
NC 9151	114-10	7.5.29	Caribbean	
S-38B (sloping windshield)				
NC 197H	214-1	16.8.29	Caribbean	Crashed 19.9.29, soon after delivery
NC 73K	214-4	15.9.30	NYRBA	Transferred to Pan Am's subsidiary, Panair do Brasil
NC 74K	214-5	3.31	Caribbean	Pan Am second owner. Allocated to Cía Naciônal Cubana de Aviación. Rescued Gen. Machado after revolution
NC 75K	214-6	28.8.29	Caribbean	First air mail flight (Lindbergh-Rowe) to Paramaribo. Then to Panair do Brasil as PP-PAM. Crashed 1938
NC 113M	214-9	15.9.30	NYRBA	Stolen at Rio de Janeiro, 25.9.32 and crashed
NC 142M	214-13	16.9.29	Caribbean	First air mail, Miami-Canal Zone, via Havana, Puerto Cabezas (Lindbergh-Rowe) 26.4.30
NC 143M	214-14	1934	Caribbean	Pan Am third owner
NC 144M	214-15	30.9.29	PANAGRA	First air mail (Schultz, Terletzky) to Managua, 21.5.30
NC 145M	214-16	10.10.29	Caribbean	Transferred to UMCA as *Marichu*, then to Panair do Brasil as PP-PAL. Crashed 1933
NC 146M	214-17	16.10.29	Caribbean	
NC 300N	214-18	22.10.29	PANAGRA	Transferred to SCADTA
NC 301N	214-19	15.9.30	NYRBA	Transferred to SCADTA

Length 40 feet • Span 72 feet • Height 14 feet

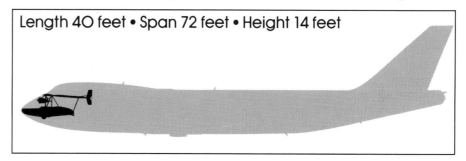

Reg. No.	Const. No.	Pan Am Delivery	Area or User	Remarks
NC 302N	214-20	15.9.30	NYRBA	Dismantled, December 1930
NC 943M	314-1	15.9.30	NYRBA	Transferred to UMCA
NC 944M	314-2	15.9.30	NYRBA	Transferred to New York Airways, 26.5.31. Crashed 14.6.32
NC 945M	314-3	16.1.30	PANAGRA	*San Juan*
NC 946M	314-4	15.9.30	NYRBA	Scrapped 1933
NC 3V	314-7	27.8.34	SCADTA	Used by Pratt & Whitney before Pan Am purchase
NC 16V	314-20	8.5.33	CNAC	Allocated to China. Crashed 24.11.33, Chusan I
NC 304N	414-2	11.12.29	Caribbean	First air mail (Rowe) Miami-Mérida, via Havana, Cozumel, 12.11.29. To Panair do Brasil as PP-PAK, 1931
NC 306N	414-4	22.11.29	PANAGRA	Crashed Ecuador, 7.2.31
NC 308N	414-6	15.9.30	NYRBA	Operated with NYRBA do Brasil, then Panair as PP-PAB
NC 309-N	414-7	22.1.30	Canal Zone	Transferred to SCADTA. Crashed April 1931
NC 17V	414-8	8.5.33	CNAC	Allocated to China. Crashed near Hangchow, 10.4.34
NC 18V	414-9	4.33	PANAGRA	
NC 19V	414-10	4.33	PANAGRA	
NC 21V	414-12	1934	(not known)	Destroyed at Biscayne Bay, Florida, 11.12.41
NC 22V	414-13	2.33	PANAGRA	*San Blas*
NC 40V	514-4	31.1.33	CNAC	Owned by Sikorsky before Pan Am to China. Destroyed Hankow, 13.8.35

Pan American-Grace Airways (PANAGRA)

Before extending further southwards from the Caribbean into South America, Juan Trippe had to overcome stiff opposition. His most important destination was Buenos Aires, the "Paris of South America," and the shortest route was via the west coast. But the way was barred by the **W.R. Grace Corporation,** the powerful United States trading organization whose conglomerate power, from Panamá to Santiago, exceeded that of many of the small nations in its sphere of influence.

At first Trippe sought to exercise a political flanking movement, by establishing airlines in Peru and Chile. In Peru, there was already a sitting tenant. **Huff-Daland Dusters** had originally gone to Peru as a crop-dusting specialist, and on 28 May 1928, on the initiative of Harold Harris and C.E. Woolman, its local representatives, had obtained full Peruvian air traffic rights.

On 16 September of the same year, Trippe's Aviation Corporation of the Americas bought a half-interest in **Peruvian Airways,** founded twelve days previously by the Hayden Stone group. Peruvian had started a token service on 13 September, flying a Fairchild FC-2 from Lima to Talara. On 28 November, Trippe acquired all the vital Peruvian air permits held by Huff-Daland/Dusters.

Chilean Airways, founded on 21 December 1928, never operated, but the tactical move put additional pressure on W.R. Grace. The two sides reached a compromise on 25 January 1929, and formed the **Pan American-Grace Corporation (PANAGRA),** each side contributing $1,000,000 of stock. PANAGRA purchased Peruvian Airways exactly one month later, and the U.S. foreign airmail contract (FAM-9) predictably followed a few days later on 2 March, allowing Trippe to secure the west coast route.

PANAGRA started service under its own name on 15 May, with a Sikorsky S-38 leased from Pan American. It picked up the incoming mail from Miami at Cristobal and carried it to Talara, Peru, whence a Fairchild FC-2 took it to Mollendo on 19 May. The route was extended to Santiago on 21 July, 1929 and to Buenos Aires, for mail only, on 12 October of that year.

The PANAGRA 50:50 partnership, however, was never a happy one, and there was constant bickering at boardroom level. But the rank and file and the flying crews retained a strong *esprit de corps* throughout the almost forty years of its existence before it was sold to Braniff in 1968.

The **FC-2** PANAGRA's first aircraft.

Fairchild FC-2

6 seats • 104 mph

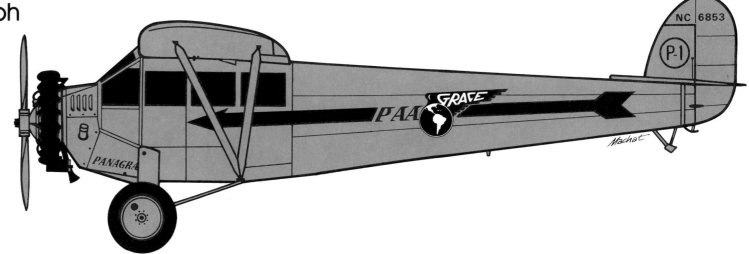

1 Pratt & Whitney Wasp (410-450 hp) • 5500 lb. max. gross take-off weight • 700 statute miles range

Most of PANAGRA's Fairchilds were the 450 hp Pratt & Whitney Wasp-powered **FC-2W2** version of the earlier **FC-2**, whose 220 hp Wright Whirlwind was not up to the stringent operating performance standards required in South America. The aircraft which inaugurated the first service, from Lima to Talara, was an FC-2, of **Peruvian Airways**, but the remainder were of the second series of the FC-2W. This was a "stretched" version, designated the FC-2W2, and was fitted with six passenger seats instead of four. The better-known **Fairchild 71**, incidentally, was a neater version of the FC-2W2, and not, as is sometimes assumed, a different design.

Length 33 feet • Span 50 feet • Height 9½ feet

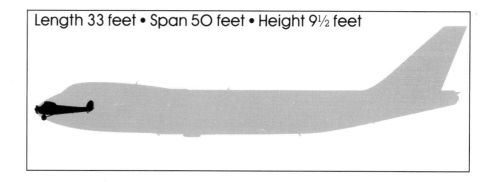

FAIRCHILD UTILITY AIRCRAFT

| Type | Dimensions | | | Pass. Seats | Max. Payload (lb) | Engines | | | Max. Gross to W (lb) | Cruise Speed (mph) | Normal Range (st. miles) |
	Length	Span	Height			No.	Type	hp			
FC-2	30'11"	44'0"	9'0"	4	820	1	Wright Whirlwind	220	3600	103	710
FC-2W	30'11"	50'0"	9'0"	4	970	1	P & W Wasp	425	4600	120	1050
FC-2W2	33'2"	50'0"	9'6"	6	1526	1	P & W Wasp	410-450	5500	104	700
Type 71	33'0"	50'0"	9'6"	6	1427	1	P & W Wasp	410-450	5500	110	770

PANAGRA'S FAIRCHILD FLEET

Type	PANAGRA No.	Regist. No.	Const. No.	Delivery Date	Disposal
FC-2	P 1	NC 6853	139	25.2.29	This aircraft is now displayed at the National Air and Space Museum, in Washington, D.C.
FC-2W2	P 2	NC 8026	519	25.2.29	Crashed in Chile, Feb., 1931
FC-2W2	P 3	NC 9723	527	25.2.29	Crashed at Mendoza, March, 1932
FC-2W2	P 4	NC 9715	532	25.2.29	Sold to Peruvian Government, Oct., 1932
FC-2W2	P 5	NC 8039	529	3.29	
Type 71	P 6	NC 9798	619	3.29	

Pan Am's Latin American Workhorse

Although the Ford Tri-Motors of such airlines as T.A.T. or Maddux are better known among aviation historians, more Fords flew in the colors of Pan American than for any other airline—with the possible exception of TACA, the Central American carrier which bought up every used Ford it could find when other airlines had moved on to modern airliners. Most of Pan Am's Fords were flown by its subsidiaries or associates in Latin America, and most of them were the so-called heavy-duty models, with Pratt & Whitney Wasp engines. These were various series of the 5-AT, although in 1933 Pan Am acquired some of the Whirlwind-powered 4-ATs for operations in Cuba.

The Ford Tri-Motor first went into service in the United States on 2 August 1926. Pan American chose it for its mainline routes in Latin America in 1928. Charles Lindbergh piloted the inaugural flight under **C.M.A.**s colors, from Brownsville to Mexico City on 10 March 1929. Unfortunately the delivery of the mail on this occasion was delayed, as it was left, undiscovered for three weeks, in the luggage compartment situated in the thick wing. Access was by a special hand-operated cranking tool, and the local ground staff did not know of its existence until later.

The first **PANAGRA** Fords were assembled at Guayaquil in August 1929 and started work along the South American west coast to Buenos Aires in October, flying through to Montevideo in November. Throughout its faithful service with the Pan American organization, it was subjected to severe punishment, not only by the terrain but also by the stringent demands made on its load-carrying capabilities, which sometimes entailed cutting large holes in the fuselage to permit awkward-sized cargoes. The Fords had their fair share of the accidents characteristic of the period, but happily a large number of them carried the newspaper report: "no casualties," a tribute to their rugged construction.

The Ford Tri-Motor's first service to Pan American preceded its deployment over the route network. On 21 November 1928, Mrs. Calvin Coolidge was supposed to have christened a Fokker tri-motor, but this had been damaged the day before. Juan Trippe promptly leased a Ford from his friends in Colonial Air Transport as a substitute. Although reported in the press, there is no record that Pan American's image suffered thereby.

This kind of treatment to a **PANAGRA Ford** during an airlift operation in Peru was conducted before the question of torture came before the United Nations.

This photograph shows a Pan American **Ford Tri-Motor** during the early 1930s.

This **Ford 5-AT** was fitted with floats for the operations of **SCADTA** along coastal routes in Colombia and along the Magdalena River.

Pan American's Ford Tri-Motors

Const. No.	Regist. No.	Delivery Date to Pan Am	Initial Pan Am Deployment	Remarks
Model 4-AT-E (Total 4)				
36	NC 7582	June 33	Cubana	Formerly Maddux-TAT-TWA
63	NC 8401	6 May 32	Cubana	Formerly with Pitcairn, Eastern Air Tpt. Sold to Costa Rica, 1934
69	NC 8407	6 May 32	Cubana	Formerly with Eastern. Sold to Dominican Republic, then to U.S.A.
70	NC 7582	6 May 32	Cubana	Formerly with Eastern. Sold to Costa Rica
Model 5-AT-B (Total 10)				
11	NC 9637	31 Dec 28	Mexico	The first Ford delivered to Pan Am. To CMA as XA-BCC; 1938 to Cubana as NM-22; LANICA 1942 as AN-AAJ; back to Mexico (TATSA) as XA-HIL 1949
12	NC 9661	Jan. 29	Mexico	To CMA as M-SCAN, later XA-BCB and XA-BCO. Crashed at Amameca, 26.3.36, with party of German tourists photographing Popocatapetl
17	NC 9639	5 July 34	PANAGRA (Aerovias Peruanas)	Formerly to Maddux, then TWA before sale to Pan Am With PANAGRA as San Fernando (p. 27)
22	NC 9672	31 Aug 29	Mexico	To CMA as XA-BCA, then to PANAGRA in 1935, as San Antonio later to Colombia and Venezuela
23	NC 9664	31 Mar 29	Central America	Fate unknown
27	NC 9670	7 Dec 29	Mexico	To CMA as XA-BCD, later XA-BCU
30	NC 9685	31 Mar 29	Central America	Flew first commercial mail through Central America
31	NC 9673	29 Mar 29	Mexico	To CMA as XA-BCE, later XA-BCV, then to Nicaragua as AN-AAE, back to Mexico, crashed at Actopan, 13.6.46 (no casualties)
40	NC 9684	May 29	Mexico	To CMA as XA-BCF. Aircraft eventually passed to Island Airlines, Port Clinton, Ohio, finally to Johnson Flying Service, Montana. Crashed there 17.8.53 (no casualties)
45	NC 9688	1932	Mexico	To CMA 17.11.34 as XA-BCW. Crashed at San Martin volcano, 5.3.40 (no casualties)

Const. No.	Regist. No.	Delivery Date to Pan Am	Initial Pan Am Deployment	Remarks
Model 5-AT-C (Total 8)				
54	NC 8416	July 29	PANAGRA	Santa Rosa (p. 8) Sold in Colombia to ARCO; then to AVIANCA, finally AVENSA, Venezuela, 1940s
55	NC 8417	15 Sep 29	PANAGRA	San Pedro (p. 18) Ex NYRBA. Crashed at Lima, 21.3.34
56	NC 8418	July 29	PANAGRA	San Cristobal (p. 10) Crashed Ovalle, Chile, 1.4.31 (no casualties)
59	NC 400H	July 29	PANAGRA	Santa Mariana (p. 9) Crashed at Junin, Argentina, 11.6.34, but rebuilt in 1938. Fate unknown
61	NC 402H	15 Sep 29	PANAGRA	San Pablo (p. 19) Ex NYRBA. Sold to various owners in South America until passing to AVENSA, 1940s
62	NC 403H	July 29	PANAGRA	San José Crashed in snowstorm in the Argentine Andes, 16.7.32. All nine occupants killed.
66	NC 407H	31 Mar 29	PANAGRA	Crashed at Lima, 22.3.34 (no fatalities)
74	NC 414H	Nov 32	Mexico	Formerly operated by Ford Motor Co. To Pan Am in 1932 and allocated to CMA as XA-BKS in 1940. Later to AVIATECA, Guatemala, before various owners in the U.S.
Model 5-AT-D (Total 6)				
100	NC 433H	Sep 32	PANAGRA	San Felipe (p. 22) Crashed at Lima, 25.12.35, on test
111	NC 434H	27 Aug 34	SCADTA	Formerly with Ford and National Air Transport
112	NC 438H	27 Aug 34	SCADTA	Formerly with Ford
114	NC 9657	May 34	SCADTA	Formerly with NAT, Pacific Air Transport, United Air Lines. Specially fitted with Edo floats
115	NC 9658	Apr 33	PANAGRA	Fate unknown
116	NC 9659	Jun 33	PANAGRA	This was the last Ford Tri-Motor to be manufactured

SUMMARY OF PAN AMERICAN'S FORD TRI-MOTORS
(Original Deliveries)

Period	Allocated Airline or Region	Number	Model(s)
1929-32	CMA, Mexico	7	5-AT-B
		1	5-AT-C
1929	Central America	2	5-AT-B
1929-33	PANAGRA	1	5-AT-B
		7	5-AT-C
		3	5-AT-D
1933	Cubana	4	4-AT-E
1934	SCADTA, Colombia	3	5-AT-D
	TOTAL	28	

Seventeen were purchased new, nine from other operators, and two came with the NYRBA purchase.

A Versatile Metal Airplane

This was the first **Ford Tri-Motor** delivered to Pan American and was used on **Mexicana's** trunk route from Brownsville to Mexico City.

Cockpit of the **Ford 5-AT** Tri-Motor.

Passenger cabin of the **Ford 5-AT** Tri-Motor.

A **PANAGRA Ford Tri-Motor** at a desert (and almost deserted) outpost in Peru.

THE FORD FAMILY OF METAL AIRLINERS

Model	No. Built	Length	Span	Height	Seats	No.	Type	hp	Cruise Speed	Remarks
Stout 2-AT	11	45'8"	58'4"	11'10"	6	1	Liberty	400	100	Eleven built, of which 5 went to the Ford airline and 4 to Florida Airways
4-AT-A 4-AT-B 4-AT-E 4-AT-F	14 39 24 1 ___ 78	49'10"	74'0"	11'9"	11	3 3	Wright Whirlwind (later) Wright J6-9	220 300	100 107	Typical price: $42,000. Earlier ones had sloping windshield and tail skid Later ones had vertical windshield and tail wheel. Last few had squarecut windows, standard thereafter
5-AT-A 5-AT-B 5-AT-C 5-AT-D	3 42 48 24 ___ 117	49'10"	77'10"	13'8"	14	3	Pratt & Whitney Wasp	420-450	115	Typical price: $55,000. Length and height varied slightly. 5-AT-D was "high-wing" Ford, with square cabin door. Last few had new sloping windshield
8-AT-A	1	53'6"	77'10"	12'10"	—	1	(various)		110	The only single-engined Ford (other than the early Stouts).

A total of 199 of the Ford Tri-Motor family are estimated to have been built. Thirteen were built for the U.S. Army Air Corps, nine for the U.S. Navy, all included in the numbers of 5-ATs summarized above. Additionally there was one AT-6 built for Canada, and a giant 40-seat version, the Model 14, which never flew. Several other models, numbered 7 thru 13, were variations and conversions of the basic 4-ATs and 5-ATs.

Ford Tri-Motor 5-AT

12 seats • 115 mph

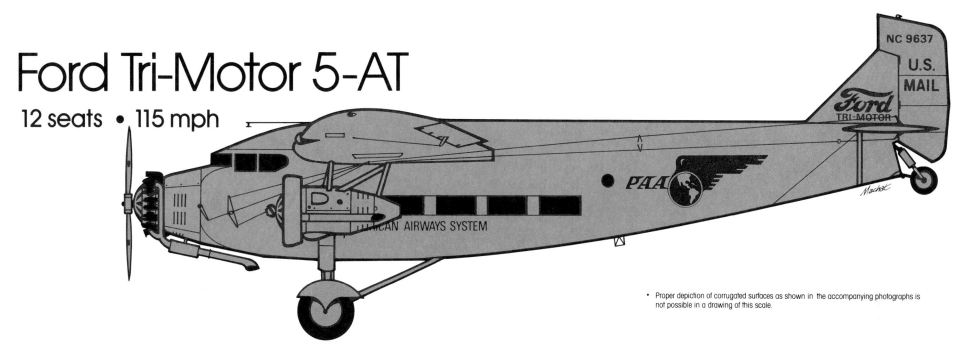

• Proper depiction of corrugated surfaces as shown in the accompanying photographs is not possible in a drawing of this scale.

Pratt & Whitney Wasp (420-450 hp) x 3 • 13,500 lb. max. gross take-off weight • 560 statute miles range

Development of a Classic Transport Airplane

Prelude–A Stout Effort

Almost certainly deriving inspiration from the German Junkers metal airplane method of construction, William B. Stout, of the Stout Metal Airplane Company, produced a small three-seat airplane in 1923. Powered by a 90 horsepower OX-5 engine, the Stout 1-AS "Air Sedan" made its first flight on 17 February from Selfridge Field, Detroit, and was successful enough to encourage Stout further.

This design was considerably modified to produce a transport airplane. The result was the Stout 2-AT, whose 400 hp Liberty engine permitted a fuselage big enough to hold eight people. At first called the "Air Pullman," this was changed to "Air Transport," the abbreviation for which remained throughout the subsequent series of aircraft derived from it. Much of the design work was done by George Prudden, and the metal aircraft began to attract attention after its first flight in 1924.

Ford Takes Over

Edsel Ford took a lively interest in Stout's activity and their two companies began to cooperate. The Ford company quickly built an airport at Dearborn, near Detroit, to prepare for series production of aircraft. Opened on 15 October 1924, the Ford airport was ahead of its time, boasting two concrete runways, measuring 3400 feet and 3700 feet, probably the first of their kind in the world. The Ford Motor Company established its own private airline, which started service between Detroit and Chicago with the Stout 2-AT *Maiden Dearborn*, on 13 April 1925.

On 31 July Ford purchased the Stout Metal Airplane Company. George Prudden left and Stout himself started an airline with three of the remaining 2-ATs in September. Eleven of the Stout transports had been built, of which five served the Ford airline, with four going to Florida Airways, the company which had been started by Eddie Rickenbacker, and which was one of the original aspirants for a foreign air mail contract to the Caribbean and beyond.

A Tri-Motor is Born

In 1925, the lightweight Wright Whirlwind radial engine became available and

Length 50 feet • Span 78 feet • Height 12 feet

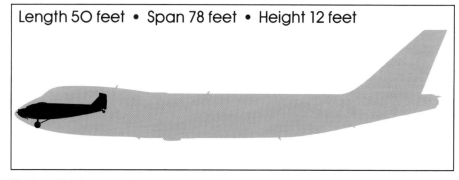

Stout and his team modified the Liberty-powered 2-AT design into the first tri-motor, the 3-AT. Cumbersome in appearance, by the standards of later developments, it made a few test flights, but was destroyed at Dearborn on 17 January 1926.

Inspired, however, by the apparent soundness of the three-engined idea, and under the direction of the Chief Engineer of the Ford Motor Company, William B. Mayo, a new factory and a new airplane were quickly forthcoming. The first Ford 4-AT flew on 11 June 1926. Under the general design direction of Thomas Towle, with assistance by John Lee, Otto Koppen, and H.A. Hicks, the prototype appears to have been hand built. At the insistence of the test pilot, Major "Shorty" Shroeder, it had an open cockpit, but this was soon modified.

Thus began the production of one of the most important commercial airplanes in the history of air transport. Although there were quite a few variants, two basic series emerged: the 4-AT, with Wright Whirlwind engines, suitable for most domestic uses, and the 5-AT, equipped with the 420 horsepower Pratt & Whitney Wasp engines, for heavy duty work such as in South America. The last Ford Tri-Motor came off the line in September 1932, and at least three are still in flying condition today.

New York, Rio and Buenos Aires Line (NYRBA)

In parallel with facing a powerful rival in the W.R. Grace Corporation on the west coast of South America, Juan Trippe also met stern competition on the east coast route to Buenos Aires. The west coast route may have been the shortest to the Argentine capital but the coastal route via Brazil was potentially the most lucrative. Inspired by a man of great vision, a former Boeing marketing representative named Ralph O'Neill, the **New York, Rio and Buenos Aires Line (NYRBA)** was founded on 17 March 1929. It was backed by substantial investors such as James Rand, of Remington Rand, Reuben Fleet, of Consolidated Aircraft, and others to the sum of $8,500,000. In addition to the Commodore flying boats promised by Fleet, six Ford Tri-Motors were ordered in May 1929. These were specifically destined to fly across the high Andes between Buenos Aires and Santiago, Chile.

Anxious to take advantage of the mail contracts granted by the governments of Argentina, Uruguay, and Venezuela, NYRBA also obtained some Sikorsky S-38 amphibians, and with these versatile machines conducted proving flights along the east coast route during the summer of 1929. The S-38 had the honor of inaugurating the first scheduled service by NYRBA, between Buenos Aires and Montevideo, on 21 August 1929. A Ford Tri-Motor followed shortly afterwards, on 1 September, by opening service to Santiago.

O'Neill received Brazilian authority to open operations along the long coast of that country on 15 October. He also established bases at key points, including Rio de Janeiro, where the Ponto do Calabouco landfill was later to become one of the world's most famous airports, Santos Dumont. Between 19 and 25 February 1930 NYRBA made its historic inaugural flight from Buenos Aires to Miami. Although the elegant Commodore *Rio de Janeiro* departed from Buenos Aires, and the equally attractive Commodore *Cuba* brought the mail into Miami, no less than six different Sikorsky S-38s, working in relays, had carried it from Porto Alegre, in southern Brazil, as far as Santiago de Cuba.

However, as the Commodore fleet was delivered and shaken down into service, NYRBA did everything necessary to establish the necessary credentials to obtain the coveted U.S. air mail contract—for the majority of the mail was generated from the United States, and therefore essential if the operation was to be financially viable. Attractive as the air journey was—it was given special treatment in a *National Geographic* magazine—it was also expensive, and few people could afford to pay the fare. Nevertheless, the Commodores were clearly adequate for the task, and certainly better than anything owned by Pan American; and NYRBA was, in effect, the ''sitting tenant.''

Ralph O'Neill never had a chance. Certain in the knowledge that the U.S. air mail contract was already earmarked for him, Juan Trippe and his backers launched a predatory take-over bid for NYRBA. They pleaded that Charles Lindbergh's affiliation should be counted as an asset, and had the effrontery to list the air mail contract as an asset when negotiating the terms of the merger. This was formalized on 15 September 1930. Nine days later, the U.S. Postmaster General awarded to **Pan American Airways** the east coast South American mail contract (FAM 11) at the maximum rate of $2.00 per mile. Three round trips were sufficient to pay for the purchase of a Sikorsky S-38.

Trippe offered a vice-presidency to O'Neill, but the man who, within two short years, had created a great airline, was disillusioned and embittered. He abandoned the airline business for a gold-mining venture in Bolivia. Quite apart from handing over a handsome aircraft fleet, an efficient operation, and an established chain of bases, O'Neill had done all the negotiating in South America to secure mail contracts and traffic rights. In particular, on 22 October 1929, he created a Brazilian operating subsidiary, **NYRBA do Brasil**, which on 17 October 1930 became **Panair do Brasil**. Of all Trippe's conquests, the complete absorption of NYRBA was his greatest coup, and his most ruthless.

The comfortable interior of a **Consolidated Commodore**.

A **Commodore** on the pontoon at **Dinner Key** base, Miami.

A **NYRBA Commodore** on its takeoff run.

Consolidated Commodore

22 seats • 108 mph

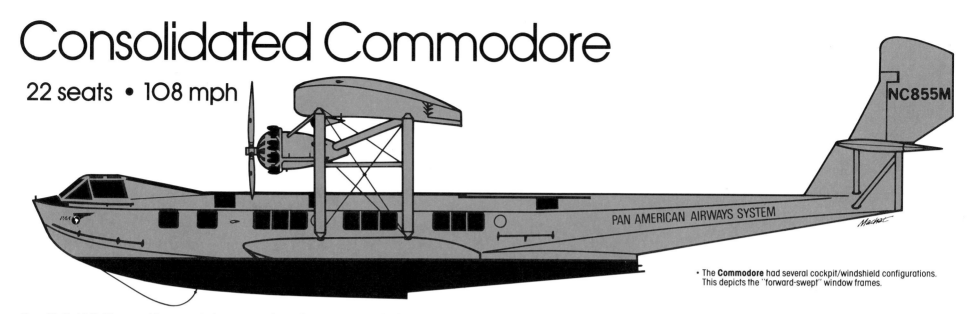

NC855M

PAN AMERICAN AIRWAYS SYSTEM

• The **Commodore** had several cockpit/windshield configurations. This depicts the "forward-swept" window frames.

Pratt & Whitney Hornet (575 hp) x 2 • 17,600 lb. max. gross take-off weight • 1,000 statute miles range

This fine flying boat was originally designed for naval patrol work but after examining all the valuable choices, Ralph O'Neill realized it was ideal for carrying passengers and mail on NYRBA's east coast route to Buenos Aires. In March 1929, he ordered six Commodores from Consolidated Aircraft, whose owner, Reuben Fleet, was a substantial NYRBA stockholder—or became so as a result of the acquisition. By the time the Commodore went into service on 10 November 1929, the order had been augmented to fourteen.

When Pan American absorbed NYRBA on 15 September 1930, the Commodore fleet (eleven of which were already in service) was an important asset. Some were transferred to the Caribbean and one of them started the Kingston-Barranquilla "cut-off" service on 2 December 1930. The 600-mile segment was probably the longest flown by any airline in the world at that time, and it shortened considerably the journey time from Miami to the Canal Zone.

Although outclassed by the Sikorsky *Clipper* flying boats during the 1930s, most of the Commodores continued in service for five to seven years, almost entirely in the Caribbean area. One or two found their way to China, to be used by C.N.A.C. Three were re-commissioned when Pan American acquired a 45% interest in Bahamas Airways on 10 December 1943, and the last two of these were finally retired on 19 September 1946, after 16 years of service.

Ralph O'Neill.

NYRBA
AIR LINES

Length 68 feet • Span 100 feet • Height 16 feet

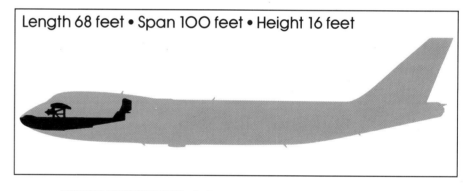

NYRBA'S COMMODORES—Delivered September 1929-November 1930
(The last three direct to Pan American)

Const. No.	Regist. No.	NYRBA Name	Panair do Brasil Reg.	Remarks	Const. No.	Regist. No.	NYRBA Name	Panair do Brasil Reg.	Remarks
1	855M	*Buenos Aires*	PP-PAJ	Argentine Reg. R-ACWZ. Ret. 1938	8	664M	*Puerto Rico*	—	Sold in 1937 to Mrs. Chamberlin
2	658M	*Rio de Janeiro*	PP-PAA	Retired 1932	9	665M	*Argentina*	PP-PAH	To China 1937
3	659M	*Havana*	PP-PAO	Caribbean until 1935	10	666M	*Miami*	PP-PAI	Argentina as R-ACWT. To Brazilian Mil. as Belém to 1941
4	660M	*Cuba*	—	Destroyed in fire, Miami, 1935	11	667M			To *Bahamas Airways* as VP-BAA 1949
5	661M	*New York/Santos*	PP-PAE	Retired 1940	12	668M			Crashed on test 24.9.43
6	662M	*Uruguay/São Paulo*	PP-PAG	To Brazilian Military as *Manaus* to 1944	13	669M			Scrapped 1948
7	663M	*Trinidad*	—	To China 1937	14	670M			Scrapped 1948

21

The SCADTA Story

The **Sociedad Colombo-Alemana de Transportes Aéreos (SCADTA)** was the airline founded in Barranquilla, Colombia, on 5 December 1919 by a group of Colombian and German businessmen. Led by an imaginative Austrian emigré, Peter Paul von Bauer, and aided by the German Condor Syndikat's energetic marketing representative, Fritz Hammer, SCADTA had opened a remarkable scheduled service on 19 September 1921. This linked Colombia's main port, Barranquilla, with a point on the Magdalena River close to the capital, Bogotá, hitherto accessible only by a combination of riverboat and packmule or horseback. The aircraft commonly employed were the sturdy Junkers metal airplanes such as the F 13 and W 34, and SCADTA had shown great enterprise in sending a delegation to the United States in 1925, with the objective of opening a trans-Caribbean service linking North and South America (see page 2).

In pursuance of normal airline expansion objectives, harmonizing at the same time with the probable commercial expansion ambitions of the German aircraft exporting industry, SCADTA ventured into international operations. By the end of 1929 it was operating to Cristóbal, in the Panama Canal Zone, and to Guayaquil in Ecuador, and its clear intention was to establish a strong presence in the northwestern corner of South America with what it termed the **Servicio Bolivariano de Transportes Aéreos.**

This did not suit Juan Trippe at all. He had already maneuvered to set up an agreement with the all-powerful W.R. Grace Corporation, to create **PANAGRA** (page 14). But SCADTA lay athwart his path, and although Colombia had signed a bilateral agreement with the U.S. on 23 February 1929, its terms were restrictive allowing PANAGRA little more than free passage along the Pacific coast. Once again, Trippe showed his machiavellian mettle.

Having followed a familiar ploy by setting up La Sociedad Anonima Colombo-Americana de Aviación as a veiled threat, he approached von Bauer, whom he knew was in financial difficulties, in spite of German support, because of the far-reaching effects of the Wall Street Crash. The two airline leaders made a gentleman's agreement, by which Pan American Airways acquired 84.4% of the SCADTA stock on 15 February 1930. Once again, Trippe got what he wanted.

SCADTA terminated its international service to the Canal Zone and Ecuador; and Pan American made its presence felt in the domestic operations of SCADTA in Colombia. These were entirely to the Colombian airline's advantage. Although the Junkers machines had done a commendable job in opening up the air transport arteries of the country, they were outdated com-

pared with the Sikorsky, Ford, and Boeing aircraft which Pan Am was able to supply. The direct link with the Pan American/PANAGRA trunkline network was also an obvious advantage, so that under the benign influence of the U.S. Chosen Instrument, SCADTA thrived and prospered.

But there were repercussions later. When the Nazi party came to power in Germany in the early 1930s, it quickly realized that the German-sponsored airlines scattered around South America, including SCADTA, could be used as a propaganda device, and even, in certain circumstances, as part of its intelligence service overseas. The United States, for its part, became edgy about the existence of an airline almost next door to the Panama Canal, and whose employees, for the most part, spoke German. For Trippe had retained the SCADTA workforce, partly because neither he nor von Bauer wanted their agreement to be known, and also because they were on Colombian, not U.S. salary scales, thus saving Pan American some expenses.

Under pressure from the U.S. State Department, with World War II already in full fling, matters came to a head in 1940. The United States wished to remove potentially dangerous German influences from South America, and especially those near the Panama Canal. Only then did the President of Colombia himself become aware of the gentleman's agreement between Trippe and von Bauer. SCADTA was nationalized, merging with another Colombian airline, SACO, to form **AVIANCA**, which survives today as Colombia's national airline and the oldest in the Western Hemisphere. On 8 June 1940, in a shattering overnight coup, all the German pilots and technicians were fired and replaced by U.S. staff who had been travelling incognito on SCADTA for several weeks.

Under the new regime, Pan American retained 64% of the stock and continued to supply good aircraft. The DC-3 became the backbone of the fleet. Peter Paul von Bauer, meanwhile, departed from Colombia within a week of the coup and died many years later in Chile.

A **SCADTA Junkers-F 13** at Barranquilla, with Magdalena riverboats in the background.

SCADTA'S Servicio Bolivariano 1929–1930

A trio of **SCADTA Junkers-F 13s** on the Magdalena River during the 1920s.

Pan Am's Covert Connections

UMCA

One of the strangest aspects of the deal which Juan Trippe made with Peter Paul von Bauer to acquire control of SCADTA (page 22) was the parallel deal with another airline enterprise in Medellín. Many years previously, Gonzalo Mejia, who had been one of the original founders of C.C.N.A., a shortlived airline which preceded SCADTA by a few months and a few flights, had dreamed up his idea of an international airline to link New York with Buenos Aires. He had subsequently worked for SCADTA, and was for some time its agent in New York City.

Mejia obtained a concession to establish an airline, **Urabá, Medellín and Central Airways (UMCA).** This was granted on 14 January 1931 and comprised not only the permission to operate from Medellín to Turbo, on the Gulf of Urabá—hence the name—but also allocated a strip of Colombian territory as UMCA's "sphere of influence." The segment was only 148 miles long, but it was the first link in what, under different circumstances, might have been an air route from Panamá to Buenos Aires, via Medellín, Bogotá, Villavicencio, Leticia, Porto Velho, and Asunción.

This bold and imaginative venture suited Juan Trippe's scheme perfectly. UMCA was incorporated in Delaware on 24 August 1931; The Aviation Corporation of the Americas (i.e. Pan American) took a 54% interest on 1 April 1932, and service began from Cristóbal and Balboa to Turbo and Medellin on 12 July. In a reversal of normal procedures, passengers only were carried at first, with the mail added on 20 June 1933.

Throughout its entire history, UMCA never owned any aircraft or employed any staff. It was simply a device to enable Pan American to connect with SCADTA at Medellin. It kept SCADTA away from Panama—a sensitive issue with the U.S. State Department; and it kept Pan American out of Colombia—also a sensitive issue with the Colombians, who had never forgotten the United States involvement in the creation of the Republic of Panamá out of Colombian territory.

Opening service with a couple of Sikorsky S-38 amphibians, UMCA provided reliable service with DC-2, DC-3, and finally Convair 240 aircraft until it was dissolved on 15 June 1961. In December 1947 Pan American had acquired complete ownership, even though it had lost its mail contract on 1 September 1940, when direct services to Colombian points directly from the U.S. got under way.

Thus ended the life of a strange little airline, whose comparative obscurity was no doubt directly related to its strategic location relating to the Panama Canal, and the special political circumstances surrounding diplomatic relations between the United States and Colombia, ever sensitive to past indignities.

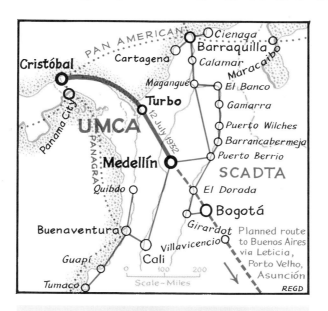

A **Sikorsky S-38** amphibian in the service of **UMCA**.

Aerovías Centrales used, among several different types, this **Fleetster** for its route from El Paso to Mexico City.

Consolidated Fleetster

This shapely utility aircraft was built by the same company that produced the fine Commodore flying boats. When Ralph O'Neill opened his service from Miami to Buenos Aires in 1920, however, **NYRBA's** Commodores, though elegant and comfortable for passengers, had difficulty in meeting the stringent demands of the Argentine mail contract which specified that the mails should reach the U.S. in seven days.

Accordingly, O'Neill stationed the faster Fleetsters at strategic points, especially at the two ends of the route. They could leave a day later, and catch up the Commodores on departure; alternatively meet the Commodores at, say, San Juan, and serve the intermediate destinations demanded by the contract.

When Pan American absorbed NYRBA on 15 September 1930, it inherited the nine Fleetsters. They were used for two or three years, until the Sikorsky Clippers came into service. One saw service with Aerovías Centrales in Mexico. Three Fleetster landplanes were later purchased for use in Alaska, and were sold soon afterwards to the Soviet trading organization, AMTORG. Whether or not these aircraft were intended to take part in an operation (similar to the Colombian UMCA) which would link North America with Asia by a Pan American-sponsored service via Alaska and northwest Siberia, is an intriguing speculation.

PAN AMERICAN'S CONSOLIDATED FLEETSTERS

Regist. No.	Delivery Date to Pan Am	Deployment	Remarks
Model 20 (Wright Cyclone engines)			
N 632M			
N 633M	15.9.30	NYRBA—Latin America	Sold March 1931
N 634M			
N 657M			
N 671M	15.9.30	NYBRA—Latin America	Disposal unknown
N 672M			
N 673M			
N 674M	15.9.30	NYRBA—Latin America	Scrapped 1934
N 675M	15.9.30	NYRBA—Latin America	Transferred to **Aerovias Centrales**, Mexico (XA-BEK)
Model 17A (Pratt & Whitney Hornet engines)			
N 703Y			
N 704Y	June 1933	Alaska	Sold to AMTORG, U.S.S.R., 1934
N 705Y	June 1933	Alaska	Written off, 1933

Mexican Maneuvering

Aerovías Centrales

Having taken absolute control of **Compañia Mexicana de Aviación (C.M.A.)**, Pan American made it abundantly clear that it would stand for no interference in its bid to control the Mexican airways. Working through government agencies, or friends of influential people in the agencies, any attempt to encroach on Juan Trippe's territory was ruthlessly suppressed. **Pickwick Airways** was the first to suffer. It had started a creditable service from Los Angeles to Mexico City on 29 March 1929 and extended this to San Francisco in July. It even planned to extend to El Salvador, but this conflicted with Pan American's wishes, and Pickwick was gone by the end of 1930.

Next one to flit briefly across the scene was **Corporación de Aeronáutica de Transportes (C.A.T.)**, founded early in 1929 by Theodore Hull, a Los Angeles banker, to connect Mexico City by the central *Aztec Trail* route to El Paso. Using a variety of aircraft and a motley crew of famous barnstormer pilots (including Wiley Post and Lowell Yerex) C.A.T. lasted only until Hull himself was killed in an air crash in November 1931. Pan American immediately founded **Aerovías Centrales, S.A.**, on 26 February 1932, two weeks after C.A.T. officially suspended operations. Ford Tri-Motors were introduced, as well as other aircraft—apparently one of almost every commercial type available at the time—and a second route to the Mexico-U.S. frontier was added, to Nogales.

Then along came the ubiquitous Walter Varney, a U.S. airline pioneer who seemed to make a habit of founding airlines and selling them. He established **Lineas Aéreas Occidentales, S.A. (L.A.O.)** to fly almost the same route as that of the late Pickwick Airways. He started flying fast Lockheed Orions and Vegas on 10 April 1934, armed with a Mexican mail contract. But this lasted only nine months, and Varney barely got his aircraft back across the border before the L.A.O. assets were impounded. Pan American took over the service the very next day.

Aerovías Centrales seemed by now to have served Pan American's purpose. In a dispute concerning Mexican insistence that all pilots should be Mexican nationals, the line closed down on 18 December 1935.

Aerovías Centrales Lockheed L-10 Electra

The **Waco**, pictured here at the *Playa Hornos* Airport at Acapulco, was **Aeronaves de Méxíco's** first aircraft.

Aeronaves de México

As Pan American controlled all the trunk routes in Mexico between the capital and the main cities, any attempts by small airlines to gain a precarious foothold during the 1930s were simply ignored or cynically brushed aside. Enterprising aviators like the Sarabia brothers, "Pancho" Buch, or Peck Woodside made little impact on a Pan Am dominance. One company, however, forced the U.S. Chosen Instrument into an accommodation, rather than a victorious confrontation.

From an idea at first promoted by Francisco T. Mancilla, a group of Mexican aviators realized that the charter work between Mexico City and the growing resort city, Acapulco, could be converted into a scheduled service. With the support of Antonio Díaz Lombardo, a rich businessman who was the uncle of one of the enterprising airmen, **Aeronaves de México** was incorporated on 7 November 1934 and a concession for the route obtained on 5 November 1935.

Watching from the wings, Pan American observed the growing traffic volume on what was beginning to look like a shuttle service to a fashionable resort, and on 12 September 1940, acquired a 40% shareholding. Following customary procedures, Pan Am immediately upgraded the fleet, introducing Boeing 247s, and using Aeronaves as a foothold, proceeded to buy up every small airline still remaining in Mexico. Pan Am defended its case before the Civil Aeronautics Board by presenting its newly-acquired associate as a complementary feeder service to the C.M.A. trunk line routes, to the advantage of everyone concerned. But of course "La Tripa" (as Mexicans disparagingly referred to the overseas monopolist) benefitted the most.

In 1946, with an injection of more capital and the addition of DC-3s for the prospering Acapulco route, Aeronaves de México began to expand rapidly. The first four-engined DC-4 was added in 1949 and then, three years later, at the instigation of President Miguel Alemán, a three-way merger between Aeronaves de Mexico, LAMSA, and Aerovías Reforma changed the whole balance of airline power in Mexico. Pan American's shareholding and influence were progressively reduced, both in Aeronaves and C.M.A. It sold its last shares in the latter airline on 13 January 1968.

Caribbean Consolidation

Cubana

A little known episode in the history of the development of airlines in the Caribbean area is the establishment, as early as October 1919, of an airline in Cuba. This was accomplished on the initiative of a local industrialist, a Señor de Mesa and his general manager, Agustin Parla. With the help of a French technical delegation, the **Compañia Aérea Cubana** started service on 30 October 1920, using Farman Goliaths, from Havana to Santiago de Cuba, via intermediate points. But the operation was shortlived and folded within a few short months.

Almost a decade later, shortly after Pan American had engulfed West Indian Aerial Express, the U.S. North American Aviation group established, on 8 October 1929, the **Compañia Nacional Cubana de Aviación Curtiss, S.A.** Although it began service on 30 October 1930 over the same route as its predecessor, the parent company got into financial difficulties. Not known for looking a gift horse in the mouth, Juan Trippe bought the company on 6 May 1932, and predictably dropped the Curtiss part of the name, to allow the abbreviation **C.N.C.A.** to stand.

As usual, Pan American demonstrated that its management of affairs was beneficial. C.N.C.A. was neatly integrated with the main system and better aircraft were introduced. The miscellaneous small Curtiss aircraft were replaced with Ford Tri-Motors and, on 29 July 1935, with Lockheed Model-10 Electras, which inaugurated the *Cuban Air Limited*, cutting the journey time from Havana to Santiago to 4 1/4 hours.

As time went on, in keeping with a general trend in its subsidiary and associate holdings, national interests gradually took over Pan American's after the end of World War II. Eventually, Cubana was to become the national airline of Cuba, chalking up some notable achievements in its own right. Today, under the Castro regime, it operates Soviet-built aircraft exclusively, and maintains both its domestic and international network, other than the route to the United States.

The Loening Air Yacht

During the 1920s, on almost any stretch of water where there was a sizable population whose status could be described as affluent, one of the amphibious craft in evidence was often the **Loening Air Yacht.** As its name suggested, it was thought to be, with a certain justification, the aerial equivalent of a luxury sailing boat. Its strange configuration, with a single centrally-placed float supporting a fuselage and biplane wings, did not make it the world's most graceful airplane, but it provided adequate reliability, and in the formative

years of air transport, efficiency, by the standards of the time, came before elegance.

Loenings were to be found along the northeastern shores, providing ferry services for wealthy vacationers, or serving cross-bay or -inlet points in San Francisco Bay and Puget Sound. They also found their way into Pan American service, and were used briefly for odd jobs

One of Pan American's **Loening Air Yachts.**

in the West Indies and for the ferry service across the River Plate on PANAGRA's route from Buenos Aires to Montevideo.

After the Great Depression, the Loening factory was taken over by the Grumman company, whose first aircraft, the Kingfisher, was a direct development of the Loening design.

PAN AMERICAN'S LOENING AIR YACHTS

Model	Const. No.	Regist. No.	Delivery Date to Pan Am	Deployment	Remarks
C-W	210	NC 8042	1928	West Indies	Crashed, San Juan, P.R., 29 October 1928
C 2-C	213	NC 9703	1929	Unknown	Sold, 29 November 1929
C 2-C	214	NC 9713	1929	Central America	Written off, San Jose, Costa Rica, 1 January 1929
C 2-C	215	NC 9717	1929	Peruvian Airways	To Peruvian, 1 July 1930; PANAGRA; written off, Montevideo, 3 April 1932

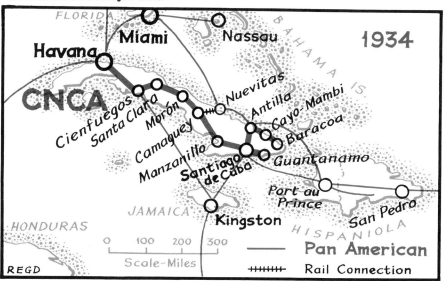

The First Atlantic Sortie

New York Airways

During the heady months of thrust and counter-thrust during the corporate Caesarian operation which gave birth to Pan American Airways, one of instruments used was a company called Southern Airlines, founded by Juan Trippe on 8 July 1927 and subsequently renamed **New York Airways.** Dormant for a while, this company came to life in 1930, starting services from North Beach airfield, Long Island, New York, to Atlantic City on 1 June of that year. The aircraft used were Ford Tri-Motors, Fokker F-10s, and Sikorsky S-38s. North Beach, of course, was to be developed later to become La Guardia Airport in 1940. The service was extended to Washington on 2 August 1930.

New York Airways did not last long. Possibly because it conflicted with the Postmaster General's viewpoint that Pan American's role as a Chosen Instrument did not extend to the operation of domestic routes, especially highly travelled ones such as New York-Washington, the entire operation was sold to **Eastern Air Transport** on 15 July 1931.

Boston-Maine Airways

Another reason may have been that Pan American itself decided to go in the opposite direction from New York, seeking greater rewards. On 25 July a Pan American Fokker F-10 made a survey flight from Boston to Bangor, Maine, via Portland. Three days later, with characteristic thoroughness, a second survey flight was made, with a Sikorsky S-41, an improved version of the S-38. The S-41 reached St. John, New Brunswick, on 29 July, and Halifax, Nova Scotia, the next day.

On 31 July **Boston-Maine Airways** opened a new mail route, under the U.S. Post Office foreign air mail contract FAM 12. The company was organized by the Maine Central and the Boston and Maine Railroads (this was before the 1934 Act which precluded railroad participation in airlines) and the flying was performed by Pan American Airways under contract.

This must have suited Juan Trippe very well. Not only did his airline gain valuable experience in unfamiliar latitudes, in unusual operating conditions, and in a direction which he eventually wished to go; but he also got paid for doing it. The Boston-Portland-Bangor segment was flown by Fokker F-10s and the Bangor-Rockland, Maine-St. Andrews, N.B–Halifax segment by Sikorsky S-41s. One of the latter was lost in Massachusetts Bay at the end of August, but was salvaged and flew in private hands for about ten years.

The service ended after only two months, on 30 September, but it could have been discerned perhaps as the proverbial cloud no bigger than a man's hand. For on 26 June 1931 Juan Trippe made public his long range intentions by sending a letter to the leading aircraft manufacturers, asking for proposals to supply "a high-speed, multi-motor flying boat having a cruising range of 2500 miles against 30-mile headwinds, and providing accommodation for a crew of four, together with at least 300 pounds of mail."

Two interesting memories survive from the shortlived Boston-Halifax service. Bangor was to become an important trans-Atlantic base during World War II and continued to be an important airfield, either for diversion or emergency use, and for charter airlines (Sir Freddie Laker flew DC-10s in from London) well into the jet age. The inaugural S-41 round trip scheduled service between Bangor and Halifax was piloted by R.O.D. Sullivan, one of the élite Pan American captains who launched the world's first trans-Atlantic airliner service in 1939.

The cockpit of a **Fokker F-10A.**

This **Fokker F-10A** took over the Florida-Cuba route from the **Fokker F-VII/3m.**

The **Sikorsky S-41,** used on the **Boston-Maine** service to Nova Scotia.

Typical scene of passengers alighting from a **Boston-Maine Fokker F-10A**

PAN AMERICAN'S SIKORSKY S-41s

Const. No.	Regist. No.	Pan Am Delivery Date	Remarks
1100X	NC 41V	26.9.30	Used at first in the Caribbean, but then transferred for use in the Boston-Maine Airways operation. Crashed in Massachusetts Bay on 27 August 1931, but salvaged. Used until 1941.
1105	NC 784Y	31.7.31	Boston-Maine Airways. Used until 1938
	NC 3V	27.8.29	Allocated to SCADTA, Colombia, as *Alfonso Lopez.* Crashed at Barranquilla, 14 February 1936

Fokker F-10A
12 seats • 118 mph

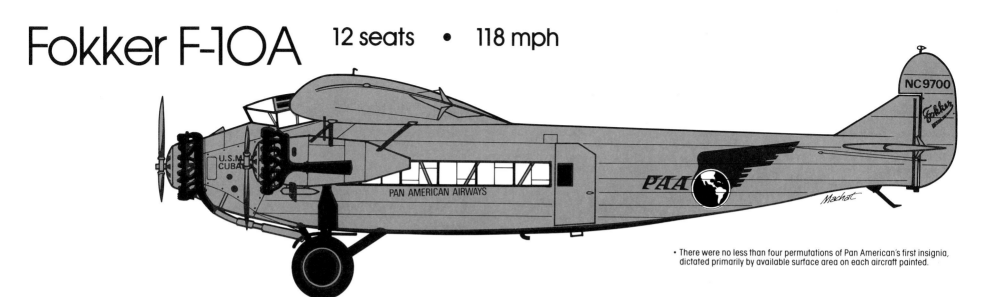

• There were no less than four permutations of Pan American's first insignia, dictated primarily by available surface area on each aircraft painted.

Pratt & Whitney Wasp (425 hp) x 3 • 13,000 lb. max. gross take-off weight • 765 statute miles range

The first Fokker F-10 was produced in April 1927 as an enlarged version of the successful F-VII series of tri-motored commercial airliners. Its 425 hp Pratt & Whitney Wasp engines, with twice the power of the Wright Whirlwinds in the F-VII, permitted a 12-passenger load instead of eight. At this time Fokker aircraft were receiving much favorable publicity from some notable achievements. F-VIIb's were used by such famous flyers as Admiral Byrd, Sir Hubert Wilkins, and Amelia Earhart, while the first crossing from California to Hawaii, by Maitland and Hegenberger, and of the Pacific Ocean, by Charles Kingsford-Smith and his crew, were also made by Fokker tri-motors of the same type.

The airlines must have been impressed also by the fact that Fokkers were close to becoming the standard commercial aircraft in Europe, and the Dutch airline particularly, echoing the national pride of the factory which built them, set up some impressive performances on its long route to the Dutch East Indies. Thus the **Fokker F-10A** was chosen by Western Air Express for its showcase experimental airline in California, sponsored by the Guggenheim Fund, and Pan American soon followed suit, ordering a dozen aircraft on 20 June 1928.

They went into service early in 1929 on the main route from Miami to San Juan, via Cuba and Santo Domingo. Some were later transferred to Mexico and two were used on the significant sortie to the north, in cooperation with Boston-Maine Airways. But in little more than a year or two after their introduction, the Fokker company as a whole suffered a severe blow, when a T.W.A. F-10A crashed in Texas on 31 March 1931. This was bad enough, but one of the victims was Knute Rockne, the Notre Dame University football coach, and the effect on the nation could not have been worse had he been the President himself. The aircraft were grounded by the Department of Commerce on 4 May, five weeks after the accident, and although permitted to fly again within two weeks, and Fokkers continued to perform well in Europe and for the U.S. Army Air Corps, the suspicion remained that the wooden construction of the wing was suspect. This view coincided with the conviction that, like motor cars, aircraft should be built of metal. The era of the wooden airplane was at an end, at least in the U.S.

All delivered during the first eight months of 1929 and at first used on the Miami-Cuba-West Indies route ➡

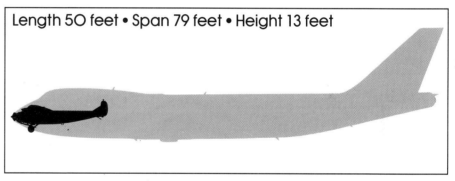

Length 50 feet • Span 79 feet • Height 13 feet

PAN AMERICAN'S FOKKER F-10As

Const. No.	Regist. No.	Pan Am Delivery Date	Remarks
1010	NC 9700	31.12.28	*Christopher Columbus.* Crashed at Santiago, Cuba, 13 June 1929
1012	NC 9701	31.12.28	Scrapped, May 1933
1014	NC 231E	31.1.29	To **Aerovias Centrales** as X-ABEA (Mexico). Crashed, Leon, 24 November 1933
1016	NC 395E	31.1.29	To **Aerovias Centrales** as X-ABEB. Served until 1933
1018	NC 396E	1.2.29	To **Aerovias Centrales** as X-ABEC. Scrapped 1932
1022	NC 454E	1.2.29	To **Aerovias Centrales** as X-ABED. Scrapped 1933
1041	NC 147H	11.7.29	Allocated to the Boston-Maine operation in the summer of 1931. Sold to Transamerican Airlines, 5 October 1931
1049	NC 810H	27.6.29	Destroyed in hurricane in Santo Domingo, November 1930
1050	NC 811H	11.7.29	To C.M.A. as X-ABCR (Mexico). Crashed at Miami, 7 August 1931
1051	NC 812H	16.8.29	(Same as 1041 NC 147H)
1052	NC 813H	26.6.29	To C.M.A. as X-ABCT. Retired in 1935
1053	NC 814H	16.8.29	To C.M.A. as X-ABCS. Crashed at Irapuato, 27 September 1934

The First Clipper Ship

Why the Flying Boat?

During the early 1930s, at the time when Juan Trippe was spinning his globe and dreaming of a Pan American world network, there was still much controversy in the aviation world as to which was the best kind of aircraft for long-distance trans-ocean flying. Should it, for example, be a lighter-than-air vehicle (i.e. the airship) or heavier-than-air craft, i.e. airplanes, and should these latter be biplanes or monoplanes?

Airships certainly had their supporters, notably in Germany, where the great Deutsche Zeppelin-Reederei perservered with its *Graf Zeppelin* and *Hindenburg* to establish the world's first trans-Atlantic passenger air services—until the disaster of 1937 destroyed all faith in airships. However, for a while, the advantages of long-range capability, measured in thousands of miles, compared with the hundreds of miles by airplanes, outweighed the disadvantages of enormous ground installations, ponderous ground handling, and a complement of crew who customarily outnumbered the passenger load.

Landplanes were not seriously considered as a trans-ocean solution until way into the mid-1930s, when the French and Germans began to operate four-engined monoplanes like the Farman 2200 and the Focke-Wulf Condor. In the United States, the landplane was not developed until Boeing bomber development opened the technical path, and the big airlines sponsored large landplane design in the late 1930s. The big problem was the establishment of suitable airports with concrete or hard runways capable of supporting the heavy machines. Such airports were very few—Detroit's Dearborn and New York's Floyd Bennett Field were exceptions to the rule in the United States. In Europe the first hard runways were built not to support large aircraft, but to combat the frost-melt in the spring which turned the grass and earth strips at Stockholm, Helsinki, Stavanger, and Amsterdam into quagmires.

Flying boats had problems of passenger convenience. Transferring from a small launch on to a Clipper Ship or an Empire Boat could be quite an adventure in choppy water. And the provision of such necessary services were expensive. But the advantages of being able to alight on a cleared waterway, whatever the size and weight of the flying boat, outweighed such considerations. There was also the matter of safety. Popular, and even specialist opinion, favored the view that a flying boat could at least alight on water in an emergency, and stood an outside chance of remaining afloat until help arrived. And the availability of large stretches of water was inestimably greater than the availability of suitable landing strips, especially in

Asia, Africa, and Latin America. As a matter of geographical coincidence, almost all the great cities of the world, especially those on the routes of Europe's colonial powers, and the United States, in its overseas territories and its Latin American sphere of influence, were either on the coast or on or near large waterways.

Juan Trippe's choice for ambitious development in the 1930s, therefore, was the flying boat. Pan American led the world in sponsoring its development, and larger landplanes did not enter extensive service until after World War II.

Consolidation of a Latin American Network

With the clandestine acquisition of the Colombian **SCADTA** by April 1931, followed by a little mopping up by the establishment of **UMCA** and **Aerovías Centrales** and the purchase of **Cubana** in 1932, Juan Trippe could sit back and contemplate the completion of his Latin American network. It had been accomplished in a remarkably short time, and most of it by acquisition rather than by normal route development. The extension from Cuba to the Greater Antilles, by taking over **West Indian Aerial Express,** had occurred in little more than a year after Pan American's first service from Key West to Miami in October 1927. The vital connections from United States border cities to the south had been consolidated by the complete absorption of Mexico's national airline **C.M.A. (Mexicana)** in January 1929. The South American west coast route was established almost simultaneously by the formation of **PANAGRA,** and on the eventful date, 15 September 1930, the cynical takeover of **NYRBA** secured the east coast route as well.

Such a heterogeneous collection of captured entities might have led to confusion. But the reverse was the case. Aided admittedly by a generous subsidy through the U.S. mail payments, Pan American's organization of its Latin American airline empire was superb. While airlines such as C.M.A. in Mexico, or PANAGRA in Lima and Santiago may have carried their

The spacious interior of the **Sikorsky S-40.**

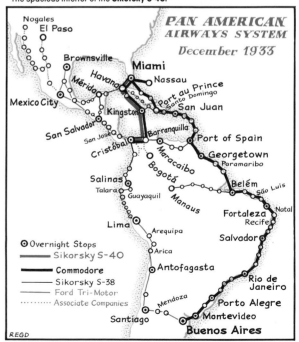

The **Sikorsky S-40** at the Dinner Key base at Miami, with the "houseboat" pontoon on the left.

Sikorsky S-40

38 seats • 115 mph

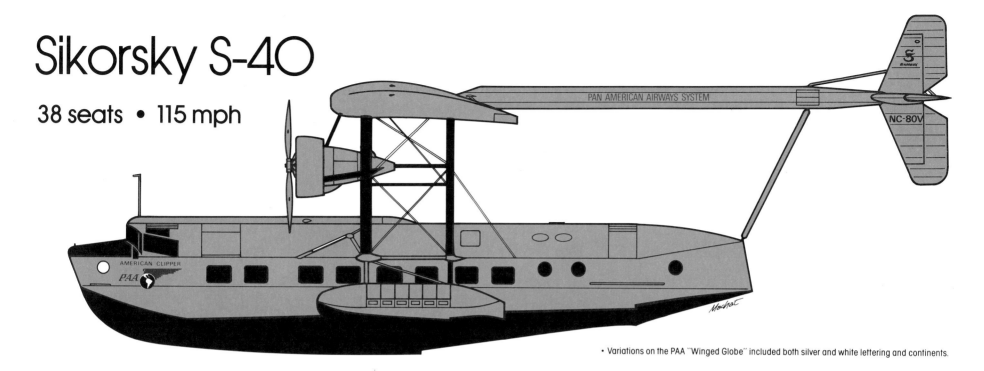

PAN AMERICAN AIRWAYS SYSTEM

NC-80V

AMERICAN CLIPPER

PAA

• Variations on the PAA "Winged Globe" included both silver and white lettering and continents.

Pratt & Whitney Hornet (575 hp) x 4 • 34,000 lb. max. gross take-off weight • 900 statute miles range

individual insignia, they were clearly part of the Pan American clan. Indeed, the actual badge carried on the aircraft, and on all installations, correspondence, and amenities, whatever the local affiliation, was Pan Am's, with slight design changes to take care of national pride and sensitivity.

Aircraft were scheduled smoothly all the way from Miami to Buenos Aires, by both the east and west coast routes, by a well integrated set of timetables, with all the feeder routes neatly dovetailed into the main system. Ralph O'Neill's NYRBA Commodore flying boats were at first the flagships of the fleet, with the Ford Tri-Motors complementing them on the overland routes. But Trippe, losing no time, restlessly moved on to bigger and better things. Turning to Igor Sikorsky, on 20 December 1929—even before the NYRBA takeover—he had ordered three S-40 flying boats. They carried a crew of six and 38 passengers—almost twice as many as the Commodore, and almost three times as many as the Ford. Easily the largest U.S. civil aircraft of the era, the first S-40, piloted by Charles Lindbergh, took off from Miami on 19 November 1931 to the Canal Zone.

The System of the Flying Clippers

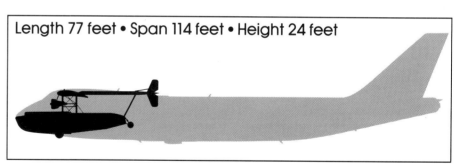

Length 77 feet • Span 114 feet • Height 24 feet

This aircraft, the *American Clipper,* was the first to carry the famous **Clipper** name, which was subsequently registered as a trademark by Pan American, to become the epitome of air travel excellence, and to represent a standard to which all competitors aspired, for the next half century.

The Sikorsky S-40

In general appearance, the S-40 seemed to be a double-sized S-38, plus a few refinements. It had the same twin booms, the same-shaped wings, floats, and tail. Only the fuselage was differently designed, effectively so. The S-40 could carry 38 passengers against the

S-38's eight. Weighing seventeen tons, it was easily the largest commercial aircraft of its time. Only three were built, all for Pan American, which operated them in Latin America until they were scrapped during World War II.

PAN AMERICAN'S FIRST CLIPPERS—THE SIKORSKY S-40s

Const. No.	Regist. No.	Pan Am Delivery Date	Clipper Name
2000X	NC 80V	10.10.31	*American Clipper*
2001	NC 81V	16.11.31	*Caribbean Clipper*
2002	NC 752V	30.8.32	*Southern Clipper*

Transoceanic Problems

While the Boston-Maine contract of 1931 may have been the portent of Things to Come, Juan Trippe's aspirations to develop a trans-Atlantic air route were frustrated from several directions, all of them from the other side of the ocean. Because of the then limitations in range of all heavier-than-air aircraft, landplane or flying boat, the route had to be via intermediate points, either by the northern countries or via island stepping stones in the Central Atlantic. The problem thus became one of territorial sovereignty, and the Europeans held all the cards.

Great Britain, through its Commonwealth connections, with Newfoundland at the time still under more direct rule from London than the Canadians liked, stood in the way for the initial segment on the Great Circle route eastwards from New York. And the British were not anxious to allow the Americans to start a service before they were ready themselves.

France, by the visionary initiative of Marcel Bouilloux-Lafont, head of Aéropostale, had secured exclusive landing rights to the Azores, the vital "halfway house" in the middle of the Atlantic, by an agreement with **Portugal,** which controlled the islands. **Denmark** still extended its political domain to the Faroe Islands, Iceland, and Greenland, and thus controlled the northern perimeter. Like Portugal, however, Denmark could not command the aviation strength to exploit its political advantage.

Germany, like the United States, did not possess any useful territory across the ocean, and was not a threat in 1930, although its technical progress in metal airframe development was to present a challenge in later years. With other leading European airline nations such as Italy, the Netherlands, Belgium, and Sweden as yet showing little commercial air interest in the Atlantic, Trippe secured his position by signing, at the end of

1930, a Tripartite Agreement with Great Britain and France, to share future mail traffic (Trippe came out of the deal with 50%) but the cumulative effect of all the European opposition led him to turn westwards to the other ocean.

Strangely enough, although the Pacific Ocean was about three times the width of the Atlantic, there were fewer operational and political problems. Pacific weather, true to the implications of the ocean's name, was normally far better than the Atlantic's. The United States controlled vital pieces of territory, so that Trippe could fly to Manila without asking permission from any foreign government. Operationally, Trippe needed an aircraft that would carry a payload from San Francisco to Hawaii. As the map shows, this was—and still is—the longest significant air route segment in the whole world. Any aircraft which could perform adequately on this critical leg could fly any commercial overseas route.

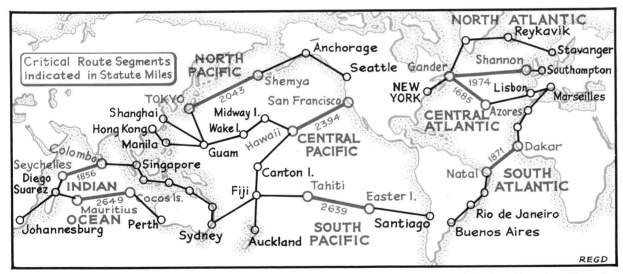

Except in the southern hemisphere, where ocean air traffic potential was insignificant, the San Francisco-Hawaii route segment was the key to world airline dominance.

The **North Haven** sets off, under the unfinished Bay Bridge at San Francisco, on its expedition to the Pacific islands in 1935.

Planning for the Pacific

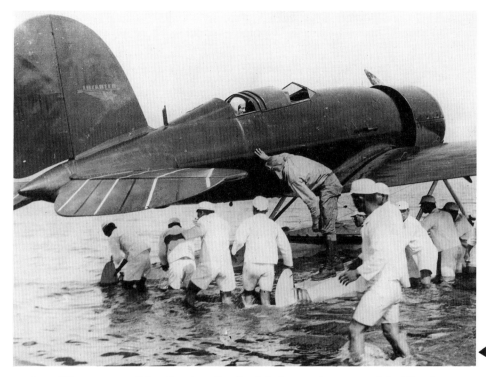

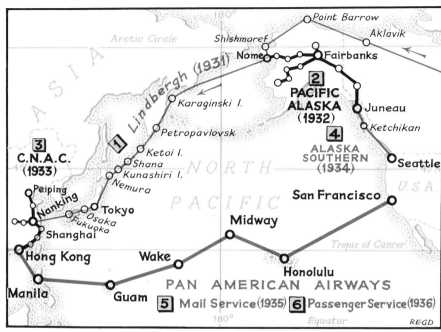

Charles Lindbergh, standing on a float of the **Lockheed Sirius,** supervises the docking procedure in Tokyo Bay. Anne Morrow Lindbergh watches from the rear cockpit. On a later flight, an Eskimo boy named the aircraft ***Tingmissartoq***—"One who flies like a Big Bird."

Juan Trippe was nothing if not methodical. In terms of commercial airline long-range planning with a visionary concept of his ultimate goal, he had no equal. Having come to the conclusion that he was beating his head against a succession of political doors in Europe, he had no sooner signed the Tripartite Agreement with Britain and France than he was planning for Pacific conquest.

Charles Lindbergh, as technical adviser and frequent inaugurator of new services, was transferred from his activities in the Caribbean to undertake a remarkable survey flight to the Orient. This was by the Great Circle route from New York to Nanking, China, via Canada, Alaska, the Soviet Union, and Japan. At the time, the summer of 1931, some prospects were held out for such a Pan American route, but the Soviet Government refused permission for further exploration, on the not unreasonable grounds that the United States still withheld diplomatic recognition.

Nevertheless, Trippe still pursued the idea, and took the necessary steps to secure the operational footholds which he would have needed, had the route materialized. Pan American purchased two airlines in Alaska and negotiated control of an airline in China (see the table on this page).

Blocked on the eastern Siberian route, however, he was forced to seek another solution, and examined the possibility of a route via Hawaii. One big problem remained, aside from the challenge of developing an aircraft capable of flying the vital San Francisco-Honolulu segment: the lack of flying boat bases between Hawaii and Manila. Pan American solved this formidable difficulty with great aplomb. It

STAGES TOWARD A TRANS-PACIFIC AIR ROUTE

27 July-19 September 1931	Charles and Anne Lindbergh's New York-China survey flight.	1
11 June 1932	Establishment of **Pacific Alaska Airways**. Purchased two local airlines.	2
31 March 1933	Negotiated a controlling interest in **China National Aviation Corporation (C.N.A.C.)**.	3
13 November 1934	Acquisition of **Alaska Southern Airways**.	4
April-July 1935	The *North Haven* Expedition.	
22 November 1935	Inauguration of trans-Pacific scheduled air mail service with the Martin M-130 *China Clipper*.	5
21 October 1936	Inauguration of trans-Pacific scheduled passenger service with the M-130 *Hawaiian Clipper*.	6

leased a depot ship, the *North Haven*, organized supplies and equipment with meticulous care, and dispatched it with 44 airline technicians and 74 construction staff. The cargo included enough material to construct two complete villages and five air bases. The most important of the latter were those at Midway and Wake Islands, two tiny specks of U.S. territory in mid-Pacific. There the engineers blasted two flying boat bases out of the coral-carpeted lagoons. The task was accomplished during about four months of the summer of 1935, and gave new meaning to the shrewd statement made by another American airline pioneer, C. M. Keys, who claimed that "ninety percent of aviation is on the ground."

Operations in Alaska

Pacific Alaska Airways

First organized as a new **Aviation Corporation of the Americas** on 29 April 1931, the name of Pan American's Alaskan subsidiary was identical to Juan Trippe's original 1928 company, and by this name suggested a certain determination about Pan American's presence in Alaska. On 11 June 1932, this was changed to **Pacific Alaska Airways,** which soon afterwards purchased the entire assets of **Alaskan Airways** and **Pacific International Airways** of Alaska. The former had been under the control of the American Airways group. Both held Star Route mail contracts, and operated Fairchild 71s and other small aircraft.

Alaska Southern Airways

On 13 November 1934 Pacific Alaska Airways bought **Alaska Southern Airways** from Nick Bez, a prominent fish canner from southeastern Alaska. He had founded the airline in 1933 with a single Loening Air Yacht, and later added two Lockheed Vegas to offer fairly regular service between Juneau and Seattle, via Ketchikan. Pan American, through its Alaskan subsidiary, lost no time in hooking this particular airline fish into its Pacific net. By the purchase, Pan American filled an important gap, without touching foreign territory, linking mainland U.S.A. to a point in the Aleutian Islands beyond the International Date Line.

The Single-engined Ford 8AT-A

Pacific Alaska Airways operated the only single-engined version of the famous Tri-Motor. This unique all-freighter type (NC 8499) first flew on 30 July 1929, and was fitted with various engines before going to Alaska in May 1934 with a 700-hp Wright Cyclone. At different times it operated with wheels, floats, or skis, according to the ever-changing demands of the Alaskan climate and terrain. After two years of service in the mid-1930s, it migrated to Colombia, and ended its days with a small airline in the eastern *llanos* of that country.

The Fairchild F100B

The Fairchild 100, known as the Pilgrim, was the largest utility type built by Fairchild. Powered by a Wright Cyclone, and able to carry up to ten people, it first flew on 14 July 1931. Pan American had three, for use in Alaska.

One of Pacific Alaska's **Fairchild Pilgrims** on skis. A Pilgrim was still flying in Alaska in 1986!

A **Consolidated Fleetster,** fitted with skis, used by Pacific Alaska during the Alaskan winters.

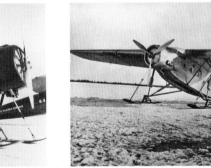

Pacific Alaska operated the only **single-engined Ford 8-AT** as a freighter.

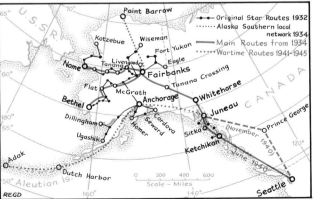

PACIFIC ALASKA'S FAIRCHILDS
In order of acquisition

Const. No.	Regist. No.	Remarks
Fairchild 71s, acquired with Alaska Airways purchase, 1 September 1930		
666	NC 153H	Used on Eielson Relief Expedition. Crashed Feb. 1934
667	NC 154H	Used on Eielson Relief Expedition. Retired 1934
663	NC 155H	First with Canadian Colonial Airways (CF-AJK) Retired 1935
642	NC 9170	First in Canada (C-9170). Crashed at Eagle, 6 Jan. 1934
644	NC 9172	First in Canada (C-9172). Crashed November 1933
611	NC 9745	First in Canada (C-9745). Retired 1936
Fairchild 71s, acquired with Pacific International purchase, 15 October 1930		
	NC 5369	Originally a Type 51. Dismantled December 1932
	NC 9765	Crashed at Livengood, 20 September 1933
647	NC 10623	First in Canada (C-9198). Retired 1936
648	NC 10624	First in Canada (C-9199). Dismantled in 1933
Additional Fairchild 71s		
657	NC 119H	First to **Aerovías Centrales**, Mexico, Nov. 1932, then Alaska
800	NC 13174	First to Central America, Dec. 1932, then to Alaska
659	NC 142H	Delivered 1934, retired 1936
Fairchild F100B Pilgrims		
6701	NC 737N	**Note:** One Pilgrim, ex-American Airlines (c/n 6605, NC 709Y) survives in flying condition at Anchorage today
6706	NC 742N	
	NC 743N	

Note: Other Fairchild 71 aircraft are listed on pages 11 **(C.M.A.)** and 15 **(PANAGRA).** One of C.M.A.'s was later transferred to Pacific Alaska.

Lockheed L-10 Electra

10 seats • 190 mph

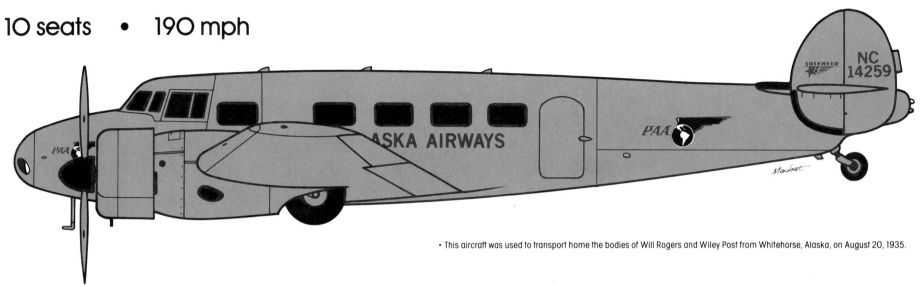

• This aircraft was used to transport home the bodies of Will Rogers and Wiley Post from Whitehorse, Alaska, on August 20, 1935.

Pratt & Whitney Wasp (450 hp) x 2 • 10,300 lb. max. gross take-off weight • 800 statute miles range

Development of the Lockheed Twins

Almost simultaneously with the development of the Douglas DC-1/DC-2 twin-engined airliners, destined to launch a new era of commercial aircraft, the Lockheed company of Burbank, California (just up the road from Santa Monica, home of Douglas) introduced its own Twin. The Model **L-10 Electra** was comparable with the Boeing 247 but was substantially smaller than the DC-2, carrying 10 passengers against the DC-2's 14; but it was faster, and this was an important marketing feature for the airlines which were beginning to flex their competitive muscles.

The L-10 made its first flight on 23 February 1934, went into service with Northwest Airlines on 11 August 1934, and by the end of the year was to be seen around the United States in areas of sparser traffic potential than would support the Douglases. Indeed, such was the caution and the economic restrictions—commercial aircraft were still expensive per seat—that some airlines elected to buy the "Baby Electra" the Model **L-12**, with fewer seats but, in compensation, more speed. Lockheed Twin operators could justly claim to be the fastest.

In September, the same launching customer, Northwest, introduced a larger and more powerful Lockheed, the Model **L-14**, which it called the *Sky Zephyr*. The military version, the **Hudson** light bomber, was sold in large numbers. The final development of the line was the Model **L-18 Lodestar**, larger still, and it too sold well to the military.

Pan American ordered a dozen Electras on 13 December 1933, and deployed them on the routes of its subsidiaries where the size matched the demand—see the table on the next page. They cost $35,000 each and additional aircraft seem to have been added to the first order. The Lodestars came later, in 1941. Following what appears to have been a custom, Pan Am had a dozen, at $85,000 each. Two were allocated to Alaska and all the rest went into service with Panair do Brasil.

Length 38 feet • Span 55 feet • Height 10 feet

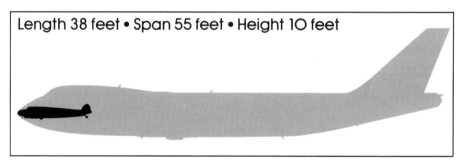

THE LOCKHEED TWINS

Type	Dimensions			Pass. Seats	Max. Payload (lb)	Engines			Max. Gross Tow (lb)	Cruise Speed (mph)	Normal Range (st. miles)
	Length	Span	Height			No.	Type	hp (each)			
L-10 Electra	38'7"	55'0"	10'1"	10	1,825	2	P & W Wasp	450	10,300	190	800
L-12 Electra Junior	36'4"	49'6"	9'9"	6	1,375	2	P & W Wasp Jr.	400	8,650	213	800
L-14 Super Electra	44'4"	65'6"	11'5"	14	4,060	2	P & W Hornet	875	17,500	215	900
L-18 Lodestar	49'10"	65'6"	11'10"	18	7,000	2	P & W Twin Wasp	1200	20,000	229	1000

See page 34 for Fleet List.

China National Aviation Corporation

Early History of C.N.A.C.

Commercial aviation made a slow start in China during the 1920s, because of the unsettled state of the country during the so-called "warlord" period, during which—from the years 1919 to about 1927—China was subdivided into a number of regions, each under the *de facto*, if not *de jure* overlordship of the local despot. Eventually, the Kuomintang Party, under Generalissimo Chiang Kai-shek, managed to gain control of most of the more developed eastern part of China and along the Yangtse River. In this area of jurisdiction, the first permanent Chinese airlines were established.

PAN AMERICAN'S LOCKHEED L-10 ELECTRA FLEET

Const. No.	Known Deployment
1004	Aerovías Centrales, then C.M.A., Mexico (XA-BEM) Cubana (NM-17)
1005	Aerovías Centrales, Mexico (XA-BEN); Cubana (NM-11); Pacific Alaska (NC 14258)
1006	Cubana; Pacific Alaska (NC 14259)
1007	Aerovías Centrales, then C.M.A., Mexico (XA-BEO)
1008	Aerovías Centrales, Mexico (XA-BEP); Panair do Brasil (PP-PAX)
1009	Cubana (NM-15); Pacific Alaska (NC 13762)
1019	Cubana (NM-12); Pacific Alaska (NC 14906)
1022	Aerovías Centrales, then C.M.A., Mexico (XA-BEQ)
1041	C.M.A., Mexico (XA-BAU)
1042	C.M.A., Mexico (XA-BCJ); Pacific Alaska (NC 14972); Panair do Brasil (PP-PAS)
1043	C.M.A. (XA-BAS)
1133	Pacific Alaska (NC 30077)
1134	Pacific Alaska (NC 30078)

PAN AMERICAN'S LOCKHEED L-18 LODESTARS
The first two were deployed with Pacific Alaska Airways
The remainder went to **Panair do Brasil**

Const. No.	U.S. Regist.	Brazilian Regist.	Const. No.	U.S. Regist.	Brazilian Regist.
2078	NC 33663	—	2113	NC 34907	PP-PBH
2079	NC 33664	—	2114	(N/A)	PP-PBI
2080	NC 33665	PP-PBB	2115	(N/A)	PP-PBQ
2081	NC 33666	PP-PBG	2116	NC 34909	PP-PBJ
2082	NC 33667	PP-PBC	2117	NC 34910	PP-PBK
2083	NC 33668	PP-PBD	2133	(N/A)	PP-PBR
2088	NC 34902	(N/A)	2215	(N/A)	PP-PBP
2099	NC 34904	PP-PBE	2216	(N/A)	PP-PBO
2112	NC 34906	PP-PBF			

CNAC operated **Loening amphibians** during the early 1930s, mainly on the Yangtse River route.

The **Stinson SM6B** served the **CNAC** route from Shanghai to Peking.

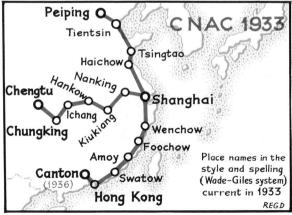

CNAC 1933

Peiping
Tientsin
Tsingtao
Haichow
Hankow   Nanking
Chengtu
Ichang   Shanghai
Chungking   Kiukiang
Wenchow
Amoy   Foochow
Canton (1936)   Swatow
Hong Kong

Place names in the style and spelling (Wade–Giles system) current in 1933

REGD

While the Germans started a line in the north, North American Aviation, a U.S. corporation, established the China Airways Federal Inc., which in turn owned 45% of the stock of **China National Airways Corporation,** founded on 8 July 1931. Operating for a while as an overseas unit of the American interests in cooperation with the local Chinese authorities, routes were established from Shanghai to Peking (Peiping, as it became known under Chiang) and to Chungking, far inland up the Yangtse. The lines were operated precariously by Stinson landplanes to Peking and Loening amphibians to Chungking.

Pan American Gains Control

As part of his master plan for the Pacific, Juan Trippe perceived that rights to operate as a U.S. airline into and within China would be difficult to negotiate. He therefore drew upon his experience in Latin America and on 7 July 1933 simply bought China Airways Federal's 45% of C.N.A.C. This gave him the opportunity to add by linking another trunk route to the system, Shanghai with Hong Kong via coastal cities. Hong Kong, of course, was the natural terminus of the final trans-Pacific segment beyond Manila, where U.S. sovereignty ended.

Once again, and following Latin American precedent, Pan Am provided good management and supplied excellent equipment, starting with the Douglas Dolphin—which was more successful than the Sikorsky S-38—and later adding a small fleet of Douglas DC-2s. Development of a promising network and airline service in China was curtailed all too soon, however, as the Japanese incident in Shanghai in 1937 provided a clear hint of future conflict, hardly conducive to commercial airline operations.

An Airline at War

With the fullscale invasion of China by Japan, whose armies advanced, by 1938, to occupy the northeast provinces of China, including the cities of Shanghai and Hankow, C.N.A.C. moved westwards and established its base in the new Kuomintang capital of Chungking. It maintained infrequent supply routes to Hong Kong, but its finest hour came in April 1942, when it began operations on the famous Burma-China "Hump," using lend-lease aircraft in cooperation with the U.S. 10th Air Force. C.N.A.C. bore the brunt of the burden of flying this incredibly difficult and dangerous route, over some of the worst mountain terrain in the world, until reinforcements arrived from the United States in April 1943.

Douglas Dolphin

8 seats • 140 mph

Development History

The Dolphin was an amphibian version of the Sinbad flying boat, with an all-metal hull and a wood-covered cantilever high wing. The two engines were mounted high above the wing, a position which was important with small flying boats—and still is today—because of the constant hazard of water ingestion from the bow wave when taking off.

Fifty-eight Dolphins were built between 1931 and 1934, in many variants. Most of them were for the U.S. Army or Navy, one of the latter being placed at the disposal of President Franklin D. Roosevelt. Curiously, one was delivered to a certain William E. Boeing, of Seattle, as a private transport.

A **CNAC Douglas Dolphin** flies over the Bund waterfront on the Wangpu River at Shanghai during the 1930s.

Pratt & Whitney Wasp (450 hp) x 2 • 9500 lb. max. gross take-off weight • 720 statute miles range

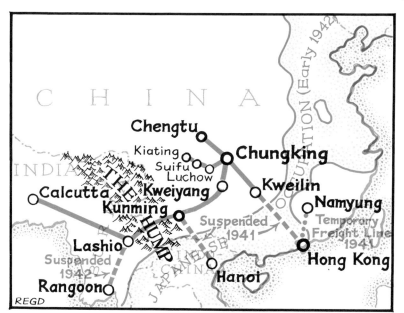

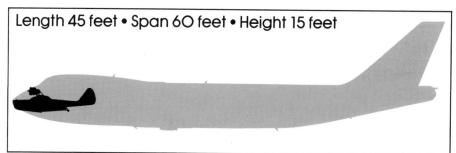

Length 45 feet • Span 60 feet • Height 15 feet

Pan Am's Dolphins

In August 1934 Pan American took delivery of two Dolphins, Serial Numbers 1348 and 1349. Registered as NC14239 and NC14240 respectively, they were allocated to C.N.A.C., where they provided excellent services for several years. Incidentally, only two other Dolphins were built for airline use, for the Wilmington-Catalina ferry service from the Los Angeles metropolitan area to the resort city of Avalon. Numbers apart, however, they were the first aircraft built and designed by Douglas specifically as commercial air transports.

Early Douglas logo

An Airliner Before Its Time

Luxury Aloft

The great Douglas DC-3 was arguably the first commercial aircraft to which the term *airliner* could be applied without fear of deception. It was derived directly from the DC-2 which went into service in 1934. Too often forgotten, however, is another airliner that also went into service at the same time, and whose effects and influence on the world of air transport were more immediate. This aircraft was the Sikorsky S-42 flying boat.

Pan American placed an order for ten aircraft on 1 October 1932. Juan Trippe wanted a luxury airliner that could fly faster and farther than the Sikorsky S-40 (the original Clipper) and which would incorporate all the technical refinements that were then revolutionizing the aircraft manufacturing industry. Trippe got exactly what he wanted.

The S-42s could carry almost twice as many passengers at least as fast and twice as far as the DC-3. Introduced on the Miami-Rio de Janeiro route on 16 August 1934 (only three months after the DC-2's inaugural) its superiority gave Pan American a clearcut preeminence over rival airlines the world over.

Pacific Duties

When Soviet intransigence over the northern Great Circle route to the Orient forced Juan Trippe to turn to the central Pacific, the S-42 (NC 823M) was selected to perform the arduous survey flights across the vast overwater inter-island segments. The Martin M-130s were not due for delivery until the end of 1935 and Trippe was impatient. Accordingly, one of the two S-42s was modified for this special assignment. Stripped of all passenger accommodation and fitted with extra fuel tanks, it had an endurance of 21½ hours and a range of almost 3000 miles.

On 16 April 1935 it flew to Honolulu, returning on the 22nd. On 12 June it surveyed the Honolulu-Midway Island segment, and on 9 August and 5 October it performed the same mission on Midway-Wake and Wake-Guam, respectively. Such a methodical approach was typical of the efficient organization that Pan American had nurtured, especially in the high standards demanded of its flying crews. On the day that the S-42 arrived back in San Francisco, 24 October 1935, the U.S. Post Office awarded Pan American the trans-Pacific air mail contract (FAM-14) at $2.00 per mile.

The S-42A

This was a modified S-42, with improved aerodynamics and a slightly longer wing span. Uprated Hornet engines permitted a higher gross weight and thus more tankage to give greater range. All the S-42A's were used in the Caribbean and South America.

The Long-Range S42B

Later, the further improved S-42B made survey flights to New Zealand in 1937 and began South Pacific service on 23 December of that year. Sadly, on 11 January 1938, on the second scheduled flight, a disastrous fire at Pago Pago caused the death of the famous Captain Musick and his crew, and the service was temporarily suspended.

The Atlantic Survey

In the Atlantic, the problems with the British were finally resolved, and a S-42B, the *Bermuda Clipper*, started service to the British islands of that name on 18 June 1937, alternating with the Short S-23 *Cavalier* of Imperial Airways. During the same year, the S-42B *Pan American Clipper III* made five round trip survey flights in preparation for the Atlantic service. The first went as far as Shediac, the next to Botwood, the next two to Southampton, by the northern route, and finally to Southampton via the Central Atlantic.

SIKORSKY S-42 TYPES

| Type | Year of First Service | Engine | | Max. Seats | Max. Range (st. miles) | Max. G Tow (lb) | Cruise Speed (mph) |
		Type	hp				
S-42	1934	Hornet S5D1G	700	32	1200	38,000	150
S-42A	1935	Hornet S1EG	750	32	1200	40,000	160
S-42B	1937	Hornet S1EG	750	24	1800	42,000	155
S-42B (Atlantic)	1937 (Survey)	Hornet S1EG	750	12 (Equiv.)	2800	45,500	145

This picture of an **S-42** at **Dinner Key**, Miami, shows passengers boarding through the top of the fuselage. Doors on the side were liable to leak.

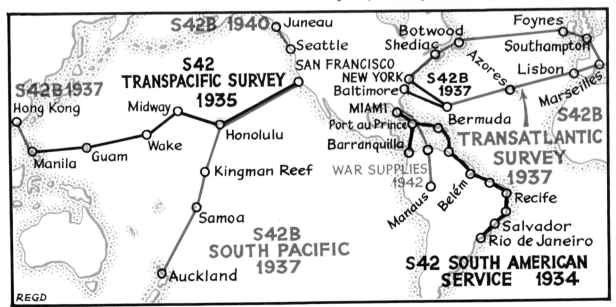

Sikorsky S-42

32 seats • 150 mph

Ed Musick, Pan American's chief pilot.

NC-822M

Pratt & Whitney Hornet (700 hp) x 4 • 38,000 lb. max. gross take-off weight • 1200 statute miles range

PAN AMERICAN AIRWAYS SYSTEM

PAN AMERICAN'S SIKORSKY S-42 FLEET

Model	Const. No.	Regist. No.	Pan Am Delivery	Remarks
S42	4200X	NC 822M	5.6.34	*Brazilian Clipper.* Used in Latin America. Renamed *Colombia Clipper* in 1937. Scrapped 15 July 1946
	4201	NC 823M	12.34	*West Indies Clipper.* Used in Latin America. Renamed *Pan American Clipper* when modified and used for Pacific survey flights. Renamed *Hong Kong Clipper* in 1937. Sank at Antilla, Cuba, 7 August 1944.
	4202	NC 824M	5.35	Unnamed. Used in Latin America. Destroyed in accident at Port of Spain, 20 December 1935.
S42A	4203	NC 15373	7.35	*Jamaica-Clipper.* Used in Latin America. Scrapped 15 July 1946.
	4204	NC 15374	12.35	*Antilles Clipper.* Details as c/n 4203.
	4205	NC 15375	2.36	*Brazilian Clipper.* Details as c/n 4203.
	4206	NC 15376	4.36	*Dominican Clipper.* Used in Latin America. Lost in accident in San Juan Harbor, 10 March 1941.
S42B	4207	NC 16734	9.36	*Pan American Clipper II.* Renamed *Samoan Clipper.* Lost at Pago Pago, with Capt. Musick and crew, 11 January 1938, after survey flight and initial South Pacific service.
	4208	NC 16735	9.36	*Bermuda Clipper.* Used on route Baltimore-Bermuda. Used briefly in Alaska in 1940 as *Alaska Clipper.* Transferred to fly the Manila-Hong Kong route as *Hong Kong Clipper II* in 1941 but destroyed by Japanese bombing on 12 July 1941.
	4209	NC 16736	37	*Pan American Clipper III.* Used on North Atlantic survey flights. Then served on Bermuda route as *Bermuda Clipper* in 1940, then to South America, where it was destroyed at Manaos, Brazil, 1000 miles up the Amazon River, on 27 July 1943.

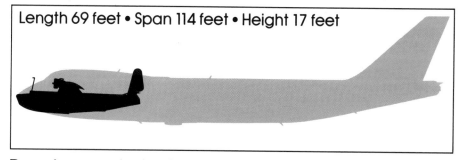

Length 69 feet • Span 114 feet • Height 17 feet

Development of a Classic Airliner

Before this aircraft was designed, its predecessors could carry full payloads on flights of only a few hundred miles. The S-42 could carry its full payload of 32 passengers over a range of 750 miles. This was more than adequate for the nonstop trans-Caribbean route to Colombia, and permitted the omission of several en route points on the long east coast route to Brazil and Argentina, where the Commodores or the S-40s had to refuel, even though traffic was sparse.

The S-42 made its first flight on 30 March 1934 and incorporated many technical refinements such as large wing flaps, extensive flush riveting, engine synchronization indicators (also on the S-40), propeller brakes, and automatic carburetors. Its wing loading was higher than that of any previous airliner and was not exceeded by any other type until 1942, eight years after it went into service. Had it been a landplane, concrete runways would have been needed at airports (then normally grass, gravel, or cinder strips) to support the wheel loads. Fully equipped, including engines, propellers, instruments, and radio, the S-42 cost $242,000, equivalent to perhaps $3,500,000 in today's currency.

Conquest of the Pacific

Pan American's inauguration of a trans-Pacific airline service from 22 to 29 November 1935 was one of the most noteworthy and historic dates in the whole history of transport. By flying the critical segment from California to Hawaii, the *China Clipper* demonstrated quite convincingly that there was, in future, no barrier to the establishment of trans-oceanic flight.

And yet there was a certain inevitability about the event. As related in the previous pages in this book, the planning which went into the preparation for the historic flight left no stone unturned, or to be exact, no potentially damaging piece of coral reef unmoved. Politically, all the bases to Manila presented no problem, as all were under United States jurisdiction. Operationally, the route had been surveyed by the faithful Sikorsky S-42 which, however, was unable to fly the critical segment without extra tankage or with a paying load. The Martin M-130 was bigger and heavier than its predecessor, and most of the extra weight was taken up by fuel. Its economical cruising speed was substantially slower than the S-42's, but this was unimportant compared with the need to guarantee the necessary range.

By a fine definition, there had been transoceanic flights on a scheduled basis before. In 1934, the Germans had started their mail service across the South Atlantic, using depot ships stationed in mid-ocean to provide refuelling for the Dornier Wals. The French had made intermittent flights with flying boats and land-planes, for mail only, but had thrown away great opportunities by squandering the foundations laid for them by the great Marcel Bouilloux-Lafont, of Aéro-postale. By comparison with these efforts, however, the flight of the *China Clipper* was epoch-making. Within a year, starting on 21 October 1936, the Martins were carrying passengers, albeit restricted to eight, or even less, on the San Francisco-Honolulu 2400-mile stretch.

The San Francisco-Manila one way fare was $799—equivalent to about $10,000 in today's money, or about twice as high as Concorde levels. But for those who could afford it, at every stopping point was a hotel, lawned and landscaped, with electricity and showers. Pan American's Martin Clippers had cut the trans-Pacific travel time from a matter of weeks to a matter of days. The world's biggest ocean was conquered. A new age had begun.

<table>
<tr><td colspan="2">The Crew of the China Clipper
22-29 November 1935</td></tr>
<tr><td>Edwin C. Musick</td><td>Captain</td></tr>
<tr><td>R.O.D. Sullivan</td><td>First Officer</td></tr>
<tr><td>Fred Noonan</td><td>Navigation Officer</td></tr>
<tr><td>George King</td><td>Second Officer</td></tr>
<tr><td>C.D. Wright</td><td>First Engineering Officer</td></tr>
<tr><td>Victor Wright</td><td>Second Engineering Officer</td></tr>
<tr><td>William Jarboe</td><td>Radio Officer</td></tr>
</table>

LOG OF THE CHINA CLIPPER—1935

Departure (D) Arrival (A)	Station	Time	Day	Date
D	San Francisco	3.46 p.m.	Friday	Nov. 29
A	Honolulu	10.19 a.m.	Saturday	Nov. 23
D	Honolulu	6.35 a.m.	Sunday	Nov. 24
A	Midway Island	2.00 p.m.	Sunday	Nov. 24
D	Midway Island	6.12 a.m.	Monday	Nov. 25
A	Wake Island	1.38 p.m.	Tuesday	Nov. 26 [1]
D	Wake Island	6.01 a.m.	Wednesday	Nov. 27
A	Guam	3.05 p.m.	Wednesday	Nov. 27
D	Guam	6.12 a.m.	Friday	Nov. 29 [2]
A	Manila	3.32 p.m.	Friday	Nov. 29

[1] One day lost by crossing international date line
[2] Remained extra day so as to arrive on schedule in Manila

8210 miles—59 hours, 48 minutes flying time

The Martin M-130 at Wake Island.

The M-130 *Hawaiian Clipper.*

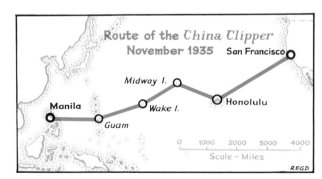

Route of the *China Clipper*
November 1935
San Francisco
Midway I.
Wake I.
Manila
Guam
Honolulu
0 1000 2000 3000 4000
Scale - Miles
REGD

Martin M-130

41 seats • 130 mph

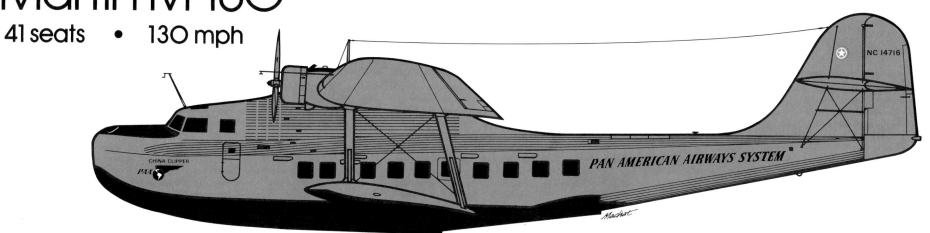

Pratt & Whitney Twin Wasp (830 hp) x 4 • 52,250 lb. max. gross take-off weight • 3,200 statute miles range

Development History

Pan American issued its specification for a long-range flying boat as early as 1931. Two bids were submitted, one for the Sikorsky S-42 and one for the Martin M-130. Juan Trippe accepted both. The Martin weighed about 26 tons, compared to the S-42's 21, and could carry up to 41 passengers, compared to the Sikorsky's 32. Nevertheless, the Martin's primary consideration was range, and it was designed primarily for this objective. As the pictures show, it was an elegant craft, capturing the aesthetic imagination and evoking the memory of the ships which gave the *Clipper* flying boats their names.

Fully equipped, the Martins cost $417,000 each, compared with the S-42's $242,000. As an interesting yardstick, the Douglas DC-2, the largest contemporary landplane airliner, cost $78,000. Contrary to the general impression given by the remarkable place in history which the M-130 justly deserves, it was not produced in large quantities. Pan American only had three.

The three Pan Am ships were used almost entirely in the Pacific. None was honorably retired. The *Hawaii Clipper* was lost without trace between Guam and Manila two years after starting the first passenger service in 1936; the *Philippine Clipper* hit a mountain in California in 1943; and the *China Clipper* sank just at the close of World War II at Port of Spain, Trinidad.

On the trans-Pacific hauls, the average passenger load was very low—sometimes only one or two people, and the crew more often than not outnumbered the customers. This was because, with the absolute necessity to carry enough fuel for the critical California-Hawaii segment, with full reserves in case of emergency, the M-130 just could not carry more than about eight passengers. For the other segments, the restrictions were not so severe, but the high fares ensured that the demand did not outstrip the capacity.

Length 91 feet • Span 130 feet • Height 25 feet

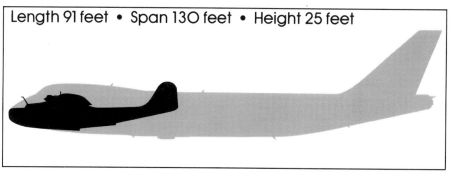

THE MARTIN CLIPPERS

Const. No.	Regist. No.	Name	Pan Am Del. Date	Remarks
556	NC 14714	*Hawaiian Clipper*	30.3.36	Inaugurated world's first transocean airplane scheduled passenger service, 21 October 1936. Name changed to *Hawaii Clipper*. Lost without trace east of Manila on 28 July 1938.
557	NC 14715	*Philippine Clipper*	14.11.35	Hit mountain at Boonville, about 100 miles north of San Francisco, 21 January 1943
558	NC 14716	*China Clipper*	9.10.35	Inaugurated world's first trans-Pacific air mail service, 22-29 November, 1935. Sank at Port of Spain, Trinidad, 8 January 1945.

Competition for Atlantic Supremacy

Pan American v. Imperial Airways

Although, for political reasons, Juan Trippe had turned to the Pacific for his first ocean conquest, Pan American's main goal was to cross the Atlantic. In 1937, a **Sikorsky S-42B**, specially modified, carried out a series of experimental survey flights. These were accomplished only when, in an extraordinary effort, Short Brothers had prepared the first of their **S.23 "Empire"** flying boats for experimental service within two years of the initial order placed by Imperial Airways in December 1934. The British had been rudely awakened by Sikorsky's genius but were, by 1937, ready to cooperate with Pan American.

The S.23 was built primarily, as its colloquial name implied, to serve the British Empire, or Commonwealth, especially to South Africa, India, and Australia. It could not carry as big a payload nor fly as far as the S-42, but on the other hand, with its "promenade deck" was very attractive to the fastidious passengers travelling the long distances to the far corners of the Empire. Its potential for eventual development was amply demonstrated by the production of almost 750 of the wartime Sunderland long range reconnaissance version and its derivatives.

Nevertheless, by 1939, the contest was not between the S-42 and the S.23. Sponsored by Juan Trippe (once again) the **Boeing Company** had produced the superb B.314, certainly the best flying boat ever to go into regular commercial service. It gave Pan American a substantial margin of technical supremacy, and almost a monopoly of airplane service across the North Atlantic. Even if the Second World War had not intervened, the British were a generation behind the Americans.

The Other Contenders

French flying boat efforts had been plagued with setbacks since the politico-industrial intrigue of 1931. Although the six-engined **Latécoère 631** had made some experimental flights across the Atlantic in 1938 and 1939 it was not ready for service at the outbreak of the war. Germany, on the other hand, made steady progress during the 1930s. It demonstrated considerable inventiveness by opening, as early as 1929, an accelerated mail service by catapulting aircraft from the ocean liners *Bremen* and *Europa*, to save up to a day at each end of the ocean crossing. Then, in 1936, the airship *Hindenburg* made ten round trips during the summer months, only to be destroyed in the Lakehurst disaster of May 1937.

Another German achievement, less publicized, was a series of experimental flights conducted between the Azores and New York, first with the **Dornier 18** flying boat in 1936, then with the elegant **Blohm and Voss Ha 139** floatplane in 1937 and 1938. Using depot ships for refuelling either in mid-ocean or at the termini, the Germans made 48 flights under the auspices of Deutsche Lufthansa during the three-year period.

End of an Era

During the same year as this curious experiment, in August 1938, a **Focke-Wulf Fw 200 Condor** four-engined landplane flew nonstop from Berlin to New York with twelve people on board and the following week flew back to Berlin, again non-stop. Though the flying boat operators at the time, including Pan American, may have been loath to admit it, this was the writing on the wall for waterborne commercial aircraft. World War II supplied the paved runways needed for the heavy landplanes; manufacturers produced the aircraft; the flying boat era was nearing its end.

Charles Lindbergh's Contribution

After his epoch-making trans-Atlantic solo flight of May 1927, Charles Lindbergh became a major influence in the painstaking preparations for the expansion of U.S. commercial air routes. Immediately following his famous flight, he had toured the United States and surveyed the Caribbean basin for Pan American in the winter of 1927-28. He then planned the transcontinental route for the airline that was to become T.W.A. During the summer of 1931 he and Anne Morrow flew to China by the Great Circle route, acting as a pathfinder for Juan Trippe. Now, in 1933, he did the same again across the northern fringes of the Atlantic Ocean.

Lindbergh again used the Lockheed Sirius, as he had done on the trans-Pacific sortie. It was specially fitted with Pan American's latest navigational equipment. Throughout the summer, as he ventured along both of the glacier-studded coastlines of Greenland and into the eastern fjordurs of Iceland, he was supported by a depot ship, the *Jelling*, after which the expedition became familiarly known in Pan Am planning circles. He returned, after six months, after inspecting all the possible terminal points in northern Europe, even as far as Moscow; then circumnavigating the British Isles; journeying back along the western coasts of Europe; and crossing the South Atlantic, with side trips to the Azores and up the Amazon for good measure.

His final reports submitted to Trippe in 1934 covered all aspects of possible airports and harbors, meteorology, and terrain. He concluded that the difficulties of air service to Europe via the northern latitudes had been greatly exaggerated, and that although the winds and weather were treacherous, their frequency and severity were not as bad as had been assumed. It had been a formidable task. The scope of Lindbergh's survey was immense, and it gave Pan American the vital operational background needed to begin serious work on planning and plotting for the North Atlantic.

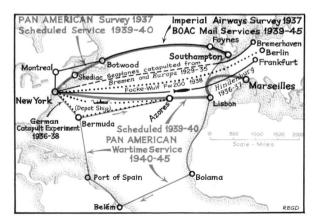

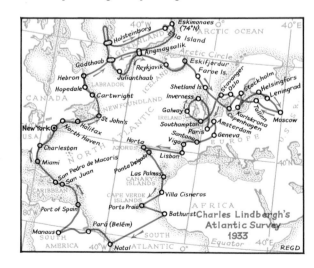

The famous German airship **LZ129** *Hindenberg* operated a regular passenger service across the North Atlantic throughout the summer of 1936. (Inset: **Dr. Hugo Eckener,** inspiration behind German airship development for two decades.)

The **Focke-Wulf Fw 200** photographed at Floyd Bennett Field in 1938, on its arrival non-stop from Berlin. This flight was the first practical demonstration that the flying boat era was nearing its end. (Inset: **Martin Wronsky,** commercial director of Deutsche Lufthansa.)

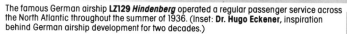

Short S.23 "Empire" flying boat shown in the waters off Port Washington, New York after a long-range survey flight of the North Atlantic in 1937. (Inset: **George Woods-Humpherey** of Imperial Airways.)

The most successful flying boat ever to enter regular service, the **Boeing 314** inaugurated the world's first sustained trans-Atlantic scheduled air route. (Inset: **Juan Trippe** who recognized the need for large, long-range flying boats.)

The Greatest Flying Boat

When Juan Trippe turned his eyes towards the Atlantic, and even while the Martin Clippers were going into service in the Pacific, Pan American engineers prepared specifications for a flying boat capable of carrying large loads on longer equivalent ranges. Not that the Atlantic segments were longer: but the severe headwinds could make the *equivalent* ranges longer.

Boeing won the design competition and signed a contract with Pan Am on 21 July 1936 for six Boeing 314s. It outstripped all rivals in size, with twice the power of the Martin M-130. The 14-cylinder double-row Wright Cyclones were the first to use 100-octane fuel. The finest flying boat to go into regular commercial service, the Boeing 314 weighed 40 tons, and the first batch cost $550,000 per aircraft.

At first, Boeing had problems with the single vertical stabilizer. It tried a twin-tail arrangement, and finally settled on the three fins which became a feature of the design. Originally due for delivery on 21 December 1937, the first B 314 was not handed over to Pan American until 27 January 1939. It was placed into service on the Pacific almost immediately. Even then, further modifications were necessary, but the 314 finally got rid of its bugs and was ready for its final test, the North Atlantic.

For the record, the Boeing 314 *Yankee Clipper* inaugurated the world's first transatlantic airplane scheduled service on 20 May 1939. Under the command of Captain A. E. LaPorte, almost a ton of mail was carried from Port Washington to Marseilles, via the Azores and Lisbon, in 29 hours. The same aircraft, commanded by

This **Boeing 314** was the last one delivered to Pan American, only three months before the Pearl Harbor attack. It worked with the U.S. Naval Air Service.

Captain Harold Gray, opened the northern mail service to Southampton on 24 June.

Captain R. O. D. Sullivan had the honor of carrying the first scheduled passengers across the North Atlantic on 28 June with the *Dixie Clipper.* Twenty-two privileged persons had the option of paying $375 one-way (about $4000 in today's money) or $675 return (say about $7000 or $8000, or twice Concorde levels). The *Yankee Clipper* opened the northern passenger route on 8 July, carrying 17 passengers at the same fare.

The whole operation had been carried out with admirable precision, the result of disciplined operational procedures, carefully refined and perfected over Pan American's years of ocean flying experience.

Other airlines could only marvel at the accomplishment, now being carried out as routine, on a mission which only a year or two previously would have been regarded as an adventure.

The outbreak of the Second World War in Europe on 3 September 1939 curtailed Pan American's opportunity to build on its success. The northern route was abandoned after only three months, on 3 October. Subsequently the Boeing 314s continued flying all over the globe, maintaining especially the Atlantic crossing by the central route, or via Brazil and West Africa. They made many important flights during the war, in support of military operations as far afield as southeast Asia. But they were overtaken by the progress made in developing long-range landplanes, and the last Boeing 314 was soon retired in 1946.

The Boeing 314's service life was all too short, considering its importance as a technical landmark in aeronautical achievement. A few months before the war, a few months after, and sporadic missions in between —a modest record, statistically. But on one occasion, in January 1942, the *Pacific Clipper* made a 31,500-mile flight around the world. The B 314 flying boat put up all kinds of records, but none could compare with the establishment of the North Atlantic service in 1939 in the epoch-making series of inaugural flights which were, perhaps, Pan American's greatest contribution to air transport in all its distinguished history.

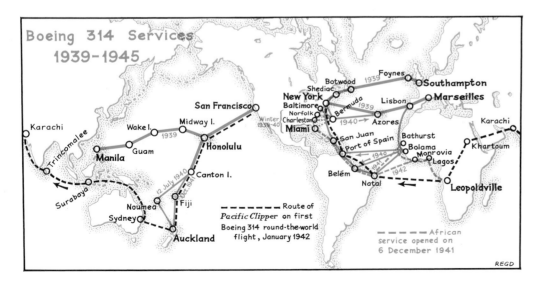

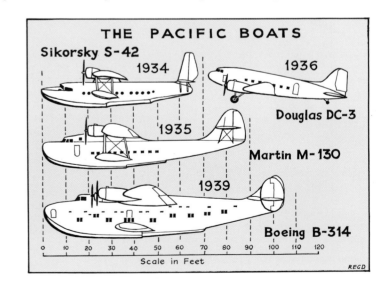

Boeing 314   74 seats • 180 mph

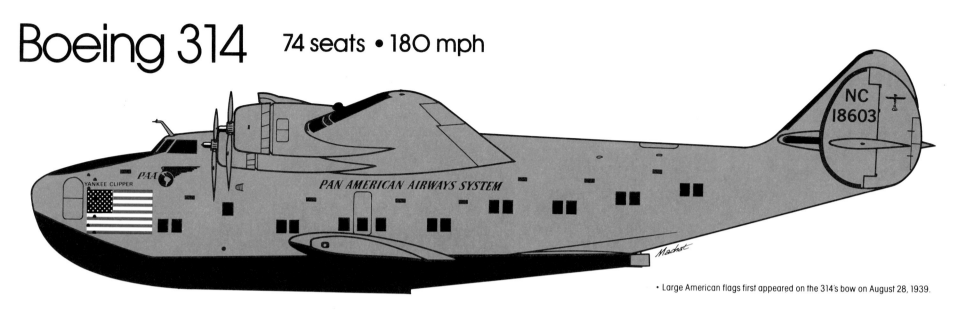

• Large American flags first appeared on the 314's bow on August 28, 1939.

Wright Double Cyclone (1500 hp) x 4 • 82,500 lb. max. gross take-off weight • 3500 statute miles range

Const. No.	Regist. No.	Name	Pan Am Del. Date	Region	Remarks
B.314					
1988	NC 18601	Honolulu Clipper	27.1.39	Pacific	Sunk at sea by U.S. Navy, 4 Nov. 1945.
1989	NC 18602	California Clipper	27.1.39	Pacific	Renamed Pacific Clipper. Purchased by War Assets Department 1946. Sold to World Airways. Scrapped 1950.
1990	NC 18603	Yankee Clipper	4.2.39	Atlantic	Inaugurated first transatlantic mail service, New York-Marseilles 20 May 1939; first air mail New York-Southampton 24 June 1939; Sank in River Tagus, Lisbon, 22 February 1943.
1991	NC 18604	Atlantic Clipper	20.3.39	Atlantic	Purchased by War Assets Department 1946, and salvaged for parts.
1992	NC 18605	Dixie Clipper	4.39	Atlantic	Inaugurated first transatlantic passenger service, New York-Marseilles, 28 June 1939. Purchased by War Assets Department 1946. Sold to World Airways. Scrapped 1950.
1993	NC 18606	American Clipper	6.39	Atlantic	Purchased by War Assets Department 1946. Sold to World Airways. Scrapped 1950.
B.314A					
2081	NC 18607	Bristol	4.41	Atlantic (U.K.)	Sold before delivery to British Purchasing Commission, 1940, and used by B.O.A.C. (G-AGBZ). Sold to World Airways, 1948.
2082	NC 18608	Berwick	5.41	(U.K.)	As above (G-AGCA). Sold to World Airways, 1948.
2083	NC 18609	Pacific Clipper	5.41	Pacific	Purchased by War Assets Department 1946. Sold to Universal Airlines. Damaged by storm and salvaged for parts only.
2084	NC 18610	Bangor	6.41	(U.K.)	See NC 18607 (G-AGCB). Sold to World Airways, 1948.
2085	NC 18611	Anzac Clipper	6.41	Pacific-Atlantic	Purchased by War Assets Department 1946. To Universal 1946, American International 1947, World 1948. Sold privately 1951, destroyed at Baltimore 1951.
2086	NC 18612	Capetown Clipper	8.41	Atlantic	Purchased by War Assets Department 1946. Am Int. 1947. Sunk at sea by U.S. Coast Guard 14 October 1947.

Length 106 feet • Span 152 feet • Height 28 feet

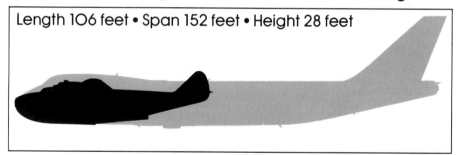

Often forgotten is the number of crew members needed for the pre-war flying boats. Captain R. O. D. Sullivan is pictured here (center) as leader of a five-man Boeing 314 flight deck team. Four pursers (standing) complete the crew. Pan American did not employ air hostesses until after World War II.

Left to right: Captains Harold Gray, J. Walker, and E. E. LaPorte.

The Modern Airliner

Land-based Clippers

Pan American did not participate in the initial introduction of either the Boeing 247 or the DC-2 into airline service, but it was not far behind in the order book of the latter aircraft, after T.W.A., General, and Eastern. Eighteen DC-2s were ordered on 9 December 1933, for $50,000 each, less than six months after the Douglas airliner's first flight. They were deployed entirely on the routes of Pan Am's associate companies, the first one entering service on **PANAGRA's** trans-Andean route from Buenos Aires to Santiago in the summer of 1934, its duties quickly being extended to replace the Ford Tri-Motors along the South American west coast as far north as Panama.

Wartime Service

As the table reveals, a number of Pan American's DC-2s were sent to its associated company, the **China National Aviation Corporation (C.N.A.C.)** which seems to have shared the privilege of early deliveries alongside PANAGRA and **Mexicana**. As many Chinese will assert, World War II started in Shanghai in 1937, when the Japanese made their first footing on a pretext of provocation, and proceeded to advance inland. C.N.A.C.'s DC-2s had only been in service for a year or so, and they performed excellent work in support of the Chinese Air Force. The incident on 24 August 1938, when *Kweilin* was forced down and strafed by Japanese fighter aircraft, killing 14 people, may have been the first occasion when a civil aircraft was the victim of a wartime attack. From 22 to 25 October of the same year, two of C.N.A.C.'s DC-2s, together with two of the veteran Commodore flying boats, transferred from the Caribbean, evacuated numbers of troops and civilians from Hankow to Chengdu and Ichang, as the Japanese forces advanced. *Kweilin* was again attacked after making a forced landing on 29 October 1940 and two or three DC-2s were destroyed on the ground in December 1941 when the Japanese attacked the airfield at Hong Kong. Meanwhile another had crashed in Hunan in February of that year, and the last one of a fleet believed to have numbered six aircraft in total, crashed at Kunming on 14 March 1942.

ADVENT OF THE MODERN AIRLINER 1933-1934

Type	First Flight	First Service	Dimensions (ft) Length	Span	Gross Weight (lb)	Seats	Cruise Speed (mph)	Number Sold
Boeing 247	8 Feb. 1933	1 June 1933	54	74	13,650	10	165	75
Douglas DC-1	1 July 1933	—	60	85	17,500	12	180	1
Douglas DC-2	11 May 1934	18 May 1934	62	85	18,200	14	170	220

(But for comparison)

Sikorsky S-42	29 March 1934	16 August 1934	69	114	38,000	32	170	10

The accompanying table, which, from the best sources available, attempts to trace the individual lives of each DC-2, tells its own story. Like depleted air force squadrons, a few DC-2s were dispatched to the remote corners of Pan Am's far-flung empire, from Montevideo to Chungking. Their fate was not far different from that of many a wartime air force unit.

PAN AMERICAN'S DC-2 FLEET
In order of delivery

Const. No.	Regist. No.	Pan Am Deliv. Date	Initial Allocation	Fleet No.	Remarks
1301	NC 14268	27.8.34	PANAGRA	P28	*Santa Ana.* First Pan AM DC-2. Deployed on trunk route on South American west coast, Panama Canal Zone to River Plate, via Lima and Santiago. Replaced Fords.
1302	NC 14269	8.9.34	CNAC	24	Crashed at Nanking on 25 December 1936
1303	NC 14270	8.9.34	PANAGRA	P29	*San Martin.* Retired 1935
1304	NC 14271	20.9.34	Mexicana		XA-BJI. To Royal Air Force, 1941
1305	NC 14272	12.9.34	PANAGRA	P30	*Santa Lucia.* Crashed on Mt. Mercedarid, Chile, in 1938.
1306	NC 14273	9.10.34	Mexicana	—	XA-BKO. Crashed in Guatemala, 1936.
1350	NC 14290	35	CNAC		(Probable allocation and identity). To Royal Air Force, 1941
1351	NC 14291	1.35	CNAC	25	To Panair do Brasil, 29 May 1941 (PP-PAY); then to PLUNA, Uruguay, as *Espirito de las Americas,* 26 December 1951. Crashed in Argentina, 2 December 1954 (CX-HEF)
1352	NC 14292	1.35	PANAGRA	P31	*Santa Silvia.* Crashed near Lima, 1942
1367	NC 14295	3.35	Mexicana	—	XA-BJG. To Royal Air Force, 1941
1368	NC 14296	3.35	Mexicana		XA-BJL. Originally delivered to TWA, and to Pan Am in 1940. Served in R.A.F. Eventually to Johnson Flying Service, at Missoula, Montana, and remained in service until mid-1970s.
1369	NC 14297	3.35	CNAC	28	*Kweilin.* Forced down and strafed by Japanese (14 killed) on 24 August 1938. Salvaged but force landed and strafed again on 29 October 1940 (9 killed)
1370	NC 14298	3.35	PANAGRA	P32	*Santa Elena.* Crashed at San Luis, Argentina, 23 August 1937
1371	NC 14950	11.35	Mexicana	—	XA-BKY. To Royal Air Force, 1941
	NC 14215	36	Alaska	—	(One of Pan Am's DC-2s believed to have been used in Alaska)
1408	NC 14978	5.37	Mexicana	—	XA-BKQ. Originally delivered to TWA in 1936
1567		5.37	CNAC	31	No U.S. registration. Delivered direct to CNAC. Crashed at Kunming, 14 March 1942 (10 killed)
1568		5.37	CNAC	32	No U.S. registration. Delivered direct to CNAC. Crashed at Kunming, 14 March 1942 (10 killed)
1586	NC 16048	25.5.37	—	—	Delivered to Pan Am for CNAC, but never delivered because of Japanese invasion. Sold elsewhere.
1249	NC 13723	22.6.37	Mexicana		XA-BJM. Originally sold to TWA in 1934. Served with Royal Air Force before passing to Mexicana after WW II
1255	NC 13729	19.6.37	PANAGRA	P35	Originally sold to TWA in 1934, and served with USAAF during WW II. Then to Mexicana as XA-BJL, possibly replacing c/n 1368
1599	NC 16049	25.5.37	Mexicana		XA-BKV
1324	NC 30076	39	PANAGRA		PP-PAZ. Originally delivered as NC 1000 to Cities Service Oil Co. in 1934. Flew in 1936 Bendix Race. Sold to PLUNA, Uruguay, as CX-AEG

Note: The above table does not include four Douglas C-39s, military versions of the DC-2, which were delivered to Mexicana in 1944 after serving with the United States Army Air Force.

Douglas DC-2

14 seats • 170 mph

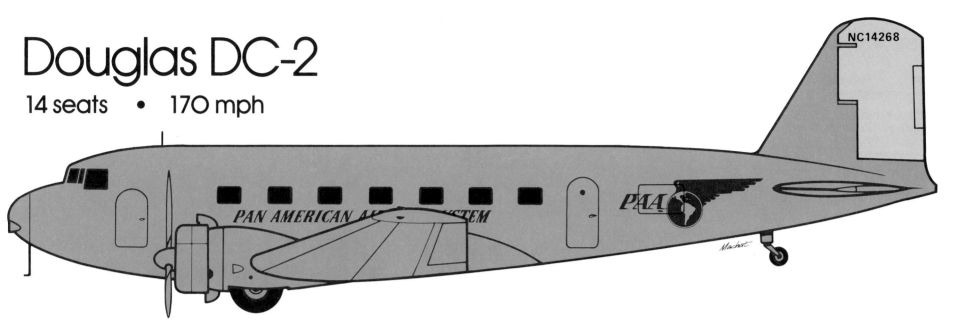

NC14268

PAN AMERICAN AIR SYSTEM

PAA

Wright Cyclone (710 hp) x 2 • 18,200 lb. max. gross take-off weight • 800 statute miles range

Hoist by Their Own Petard

The story of how the Douglas Aircraft Company, of Santa Monica, California, came to enter the commercial airliner field is one of the best known in air transport history. The **Boeing Airplane Company,** of Seattle, Washington, had, in 1933, produced an aircraft, the **Model 247,** which was so much in advance of the types of only a few years previously that it quite literally began a new era. Its justifiable claims for the title of the first modern airliner were well-based, incorporating as it did two NACA-cowled Pratt & Whitney Wasp engines, stressed skin surfaces, a monocoque fuselage, and partially retractable landing gear, among other refinements. By comparison, the 95 mph Ford Tri-Motor was completely outclassed by the 165 mph 247, and looked ponderous by comparison, as indeed it was.

The Boeing 247 first flew on 8 February 1933 and entered service with United Air Lines on 1 June, enabling the latter to steal a march on the competition. At the time, before the 1934 Air Mail Act was passed to prohibit such associations, the manufacturer, Boeing, belonged to the same industrial group as the launching customer, United. When approached by a rival airline, T.W.A., eager to keep up with the 247's pace, Boeing declared that the production of the first 60 aircraft was allocated to United, and that T.W.A. would have to wait.

Jack Frye, T.W.A.'s vice-president of operations, was not so inclined. He sent a letter to five other manufacturers with a specification of an airliner that was to be

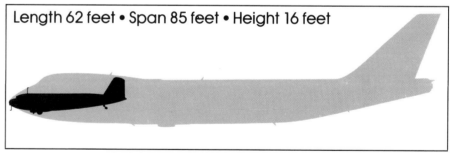

Length 62 feet • Span 85 feet • Height 16 feet

about ten percent better than the 247 in every respect—speed, range, size, and airfield performance. Douglas's proposal came close enough to pass the stringent tests imposed by Charles Lindbergh, serving as T.W.A.'s technical adviser at the time. Thus, the **DC-1,** or the **Douglas Commercial Model One,** was born.

Birth of a New Breed

There was only one DC-1. The designers quickly realized that a simple modification would permit two extra seats, so that the production version became the **DC-2.** As the accompanying table shows, the DC-2 was another step ahead of the competition, and it stopped the sales of the 247 completely to all airlines except United, and further development ceased. What the table does not show, but which was nevertheless a contributing factor in the Douglas aircraft's success, was the

superior comfort. The Douglas passenger cabin had seven seats on each side of an unencumbered aisle which the low-wing design permitted. The Boeing 247 had five seats on each side, but the aisle was interrupted by two spars, the inevitable result of the mid-wing design. Passengers had to step over one spar to reach the front seats.

Boeing had certainly led the way, but by a corporate misjudgment, had managed to let in the competition. Boeing sold 75 of its Model 247. Douglas sold 220 DC-2s and the airline world beat a pathway to the door. Furthermore, the orders came in so thick and fast that the Santa Monica plant was the first to incorporate mass production methods for building commercial aircraft; and these techniques served the company well as it developed the DC-2 into an even more successful airliner, the world-famous **DC-3.**

The Old Indestructible

Pan Am Joins the Club

Juan Trippe was in no hurry to take his place in line with the airlines which rushed to Santa Monica, California, to follow American Airlines' example in taking the wider-bodied version of the now well-proved DC-2. Douglas had already received orders from the Big Four U.S. domestic airlines and from four European airlines (not to mention one from the Soviet Union and a sub-contract from Fokker) before Pan American, with its associate PANAGRA, joined the queue.

But it soon made up for lost time. After the first one (NC 18113) was delivered on 1 October 1937, eight more were added to the fleet before the end of the year, and two more in 1939. These were powered by the popular Wright Cyclone engine, as were most of the early production DSTs (Douglas Sleeper Transports) and DC-3s, but thereafter, the Pratt & Whitney Double Wasp engines were preferred.

Post-War Acquisitions

After the war, Pan Am did something it had never done before: it bought second-hand aircraft—DC-3s, of course. No doubt its engineering staff ensured that it had the cream of the crop of war-surplus C-47s, C-53s, and other varieties of the basic breed, but the fact of the matter was that even Pan Am could not pass up the opportunity to acquire perfectly serviceable workhorse airliners for about $5000 to $8000 each.

It is sufficient to state that Pan American and its cohorts probably owned, at one time or another, about 90 DC-3s, including ex-military conversions; and that is a substantial number, by any standards.

The table shows the deployment of the aircraft when delivered. By 1942, Pan Am had taken delivery of 49.

PAN AMERICAN'S DOUGLAS DC-3 FLEET
In order of Delivery from Douglas Aircraft, Santa Monica

Const. No.	Regist. No.	Pan Am Delivery Date	Initial Allocation
1989	NC 18113	1.10.37	
1990	NC 18114	12.10.37	
1991	NC 18815	10.37	
1992	NC 18116	6.10.37	Pan Am
1993	NC 18117	8.10.37	
1994	NC 18118	12.10.37	
1995	NC 18119	1.10.37	
2011	NC 18936	19.10.37	PANAGRA
2012	NC 18937	15.11.37	
2128	NC 21717	1.7.39	Pan Am
2134	NC 21718	6.39	PANAGRA
2190	NC 14967	4.40	
2191	NC 14996	4.40	PANAGRA
2192	NC 25652	4.40	
2193	NC 25653	31.7.40	
2194	NC 25654	23.7.40	
2195	NC 25655	6.5.40	Pan AM
2196	NC 25656	5.40	
2197	NC 25657	5.40	
2228	NC 25641	5.40	
2229	NC 25642	5.40	
2230	NC 25643	5.40	Pan Am
2231	NC 25644	5.40	
2232	NC 25645	5.40	
3284	NC 28380	5.4.41	PANAGRA
3290	NC 28301	1.41	
3291	NC 28302	1.41	
3292	NC 28303	1.41	Pan Am
3293	NC 28304	1.41	
4085	NC 28305	17.1.41	
4086	NC 28306	17.1.41	
4087	NC 28307	20.1.41	Pan Am
4088	NC 28308	23.1.41	
4100	NC 33609	7.5.41	
4101	NC 33610	8.5.41	
4102	NC 33611	12.5.41	Pan Am
4103	NC 33612	14.5.41	
4104	NC 33613	15.5.41	
4105	NC 33614	23.5.41	AVIANCA

Const. No.	Regist. No.	Pan Am Delivery Date	Initial Allocation
4124	NC 33645	15.4.41	PANAGRA
4130	NC 33675	10.41	Pan Am (ex-PCA)
4179	NC 30010	2.42	Pan Am
4180	NC 30011	2.42	(thru Defense
4181	NC 30012	2.42	Supply Corp.)
4800	NC 28334	8.41	PANAGRA
4801	NC 28335	8.41	
4957	NC 34925	8.42	Pan Am
4958	NC 34947	8.42	(thru Defense
4959	NC 34948	8.42	Supply Corp.)
4960	NC 34949		
4961	NC 34950		Order not taken up
4962	NC 34951		

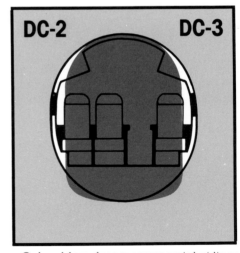

DC-2　　　**DC-3**

Only seldom does a commercial airliner undergo development by a change in the cross-section of the fuselage. Fuselages are frequently "stretched" in length and wings and empennages redesigned, but because of expensive jigging and tooling, cross-sections habitually remain constant. The transition from DC-2 to DC-3 was an exception.

PAN AMERICAN'S DC-3s (inc. C-53, C-47, etc.)
Acquired from sources other than manufacturer

The supplementary list shows the registrations of those aircraft which are in Pan American's own records, but it is not complete. Many other aircraft joined the ranks of the 29 listed.

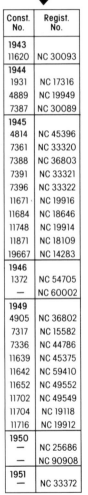

Const. No.	Regist. No.
1943	
11620	NC 30093
1944	
1931	NC 17316
4889	NC 19949
7387	NC 30089
1945	
4814	NC 45396
7361	NC 33320
7388	NC 36803
7391	NC 33321
7396	NC 33322
11671	NC 19916
11684	NC 18646
11748	NC 19914
11871	NC 18109
19667	NC 14283
1946	
1372	NC 54705
—	NC 60002
1949	
4905	NC 36802
7317	NC 15582
7336	NC 44786
11639	NC 45375
11642	NC 59410
11652	NC 49552
11702	NC 49549
11704	NC 19118
11716	NC 19912
1950	
—	NC 25686
—	NC 90908
1951	
—	NC 33372

Douglas DC-3

21 seats • 180 mph

NC18113

PAN AMERICAN AIRWAYS SYSTEM

PAA

Machat

• The **DC-3** and **Boeing 307** were the first aircraft to employ the new fuselage striping.

• Wright Cyclone (860 hp) x 2 • 24,400 lb. max. gross take-off weight • 1000 statute miles range
• Pratt & Whitney Double Wasp (1200 hp) x 2

The Development

American Airlines' sponsorship of the DC-3, at the recommendation of its chief engineer, Bill Littlewood, to his president, C. R. Smith, is one of the best known stories in the entire history of airline folklore. Originally specified as a sleeper, with 14 berths, it first went into service as a 21-seat dayplane between New York and Chicago on 25 June 1936. With its fuselage widened to accommodate three abreast seating against the DC-2's two (and this was later increased to four abreast with improved seat design) the DC-3's, success was guaranteed. As C. R. Smith was never tired of recalling, the Douglas airliner heralded the realization that, given good loads, an airline could make money without subsidy or mail payments.

By the 1940s, some 85% of the fleets of all the U.S. domestic airlines consisted of DC-3s—and much of the balance was made up of DC-2s. With this aircraft, Douglas attained a commercial airliner leadership which it did not surrender until the advent of the jet age.

The Numbers

DC-3 production statistics, at least the astonishing total of more than 13,000 of all versions, civil and military, are almost as well known as the launching story. For the record, 10,926 were built in the United States, of which, however, only 433 were originally DC-3s or DSTs. All the rest were converted from military types, mainly C-47s. 803 DC-3s of all types rolled off the production lines at Santa Monica. More than 4,000 were built at Long Beach and more than 6,000 at Oklahoma City and Chicago. Exact figures are difficult to assess with absolute precision, as a few aircraft were rebuilt, and may have been counted twice.

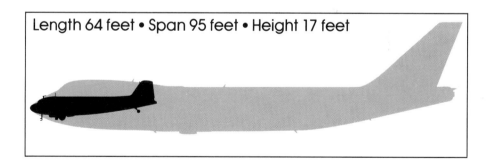

Length 64 feet • Span 95 feet • Height 17 feet

Overseas, a few were assembled by Fokker, and 487 were built in Japan, 71 by Nakajima, all for the Japanese Navy, and 416 by Showa. The number of DC-3s built under license in the Soviet Union, as Lisunov Li-2s, is uncertain. Approximately 2,500 are believed to have been built during World War II, but there are also reports that production continued after the war.

Because of the enormous wartime production, and the aircraft's own inherent qualities, the DC-3 has more nearly approached immortality than any other aircraft, military or civil. Perhaps the most amazing statistic of all is that, without counting hulks or derelicts, there are still at least 800, and possibly more, of the veteran Douglas twin flying today –none less than 42 years old. The type has never been grounded.

Flying Above the Weather

Atlantic Aspirations

Pan American finally received British landing and traffic rights on 22 February 1937, after Imperial Airways was satisfied that, if it could not compete with Pan American on equal terms, the requirements of diplomacy could be served without complete loss of dignity. Three weeks later, on 15 March, Pan Am ordered three Boeing 307s, believing that the use of landplanes would solve the problems of westbound crossings against winter headwinds on the northern route, and that the high altitude flying capability of the Stratoliner, as it was called, would also contribute to the overall performance.

The aircraft did not have the range to carry passengers economically across the ocean. In fact it could not perform adequately on a one-stop U.S. transcontinental service. But Pan Am did have plans to use it on experimental flights across the North Atlantic in 1940 carrying mail and express only, via Montreal, Moncton, Hattie's Camp, Newfoundland (later to be called Gander), and either Shannon or Dublin, to Croydon Airport, London.

These ambitious plans did not materialize. The Stratoliners saw service in the Caribbean and Mexico, (including the route to Los Angeles); to Bermuda; and, as related elsewhere on this page, as far as Brazil.

Wartime Work

However, after the outbreak of World War II, Pan American's Boeing 307s participated in all kinds of long-range missions, including regular trans-Atlantic flights for what was to become Air Transport Command, sharing the responsibilities with T.W.A., which had sponsored the aircraft and which had a fleet of five. The 307's commercial career was thus necessarily interrupted and sporadic, and with the arrival of the postwar generation of four-engined airliners such as the Constellation and the DC-4, it was overtaken by events and outclassed. Pan American sold its three Boeing 307s in 1947.

The Barreiras Cutoff

By the latter 1930s, the disadvantages of flying boat operations were becoming evident. Developments in engine power, aerodynamics, landing gear, and field performance of landplanes, in Europe as well as in the U.S.A., all combined to sound the death knell for the flying boat era, even though those elegant ships of the air fought a brave battle for survival so that their demise was by no means immediate and abrupt.

The problem with the big landplanes, however, was that the high wheel loadings demanded hard and strong runways at the airports. Often forgotten in the arguments for and against the supercession of the flying boats is that before World War II, the number of concrete or hard-surfaced airports throughout the world could almost be counted on the fingers of one hand. World War II of course changed the situation completely, with massive expenditures allocated to the construction of such airports for ferrying war materiel or heavy bombers to the various war theaters.

One area where landplanes could be of definite value was on the long-distance service to the big cities of southern South America. The Sikorsky S-42s used by Pan Am had to take a circuitous route around the northeastern shoulder of Brazil, and in the 1930s at least, the traffic to points such as Belém and Recife was insufficient to cover the extra costs of the diversion.

The **Boeing 307 Stratoliner** was the world's first pressurized airliner.

Even before the conflict, therefore, Pan American acted promptly for purely commercial reasons. It was consolidating its position in Brazil through its subsidiary Panair do Brasil which had discovered that its Lockheed Lodestars, excellent though they were for the domestic routes, had a habit of becoming bogged down on waterlogged grass or dirt strips after tropical storms. And larger aircraft were even more vulnerable.

To solve the problems of establishing a short-cut route across Brazil, Pan American built an airport at Barreiras, in the far west of the State of Bahia. Opened in September 1940, and the result of a typical Pan Am construction project involving rail, river barge, and truck transport to a remote and undeveloped area, Pan Am's original intention was to fly the Boeing 307s through to Rio de Janeiro. In fact, the new airplane was not used regularly south of Belém, and the trusty old DC-3 did the job.

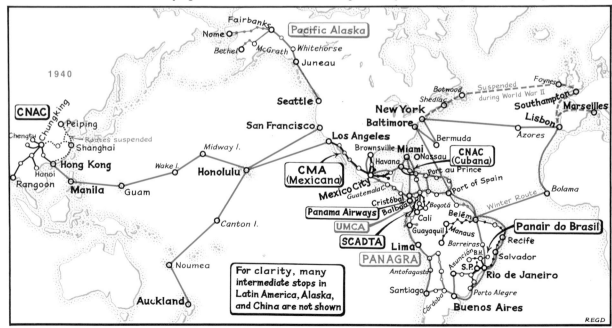

Boeing 307 Stratoliner

33 seats • 220 mph

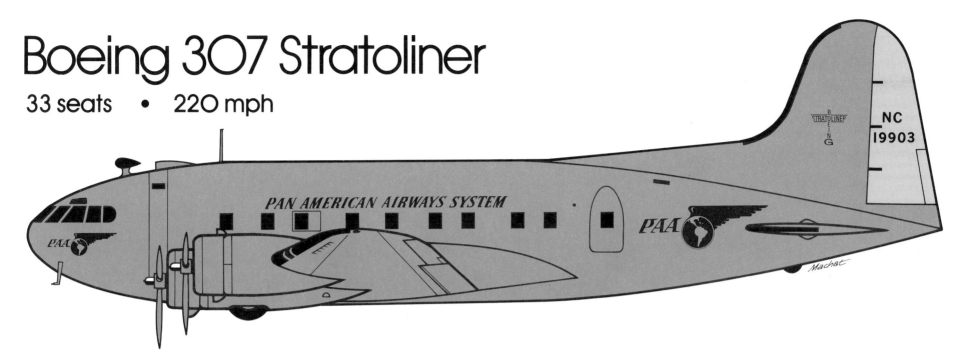

PAN AMERICAN AIRWAYS SYSTEM

PAA

NC 19903

Machat

Wright Cyclone (1200 hp) x 4 • 45,000 lb. max. gross take-off weight • 1250 statute miles range

Development History

Although Boeing had suffered a setback because of Douglas's unprecedented success with the DC-2 and DC-3 family of true airliners, it did not take long to rebound. Even as the DC-3 was starting a new era, by introducing unit operating costs low enough for an airline to make a profit, the Boeing 307 was developed to start another era, that of pressurized comfort at higher altitudes than had hitherto been contemplated.

The aircraft was the result of considerable research in high altitude flying by "Tommy" Tomlinson, of T.W.A., who was estimated to have flown more hours above 30,000 feet than all other pilots combined. Resulting from his recommendations, Boeing produced an airliner which could cruise at 14,000 feet, or, as the neatly descriptive phrase went at the time, "above the weather." The Model 307, or Stratoliner, was a straightforward conversion from the supremely successful B-17 Flying Fortress bomber, with a 33-seat commercial fuselage substituted for the bomber's. The most important technical feature was that the entire cabin was pressurized so that the use of special oxygen equipment was unnecessary. Pressure differential was 2½ lb/sq. in. Another aspect of the stringent specifications was that high octane fuel was being developed to obtain higher supercharger pressure to maintain engine power at high altitudes.

STRATOLINER BOEING

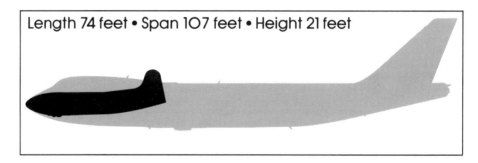

Length 74 feet • Span 107 feet • Height 21 feet

Airline Service

The Boeing 307 first flew on 31 December 1938 and T.W.A. put it into service on the transcontinental route on 8 July 1940, reducing the time to 13 hr 40 min, and cutting two hours off the DC-3's. Unfortunately, its career was short-lived as on 24 December 1941 the fleet was withdrawn from civil work and transferred to transAtlantic wartime duties. Only nine were built and Pan American was the only other customer. Each one cost $315,000 in 1937 when ordered. Most of them survived the war and performed good service for the French airline Aigle Azur, operating to French Indo-China. Here they became involved with the Vietnam War, worked with operators such as Air Laos, and paid their

dues. One example survives, and awaits the time when the National Air and Space Museum of the Smithsonian Institution can build a structure big enough for it.

PAN AMERICAN'S BOEING 307 STRATOLINER FLEET

Const. No.	Regist. No.	Clipper Name
1995	NC 19902	Rainbow
2002	NC 19910	Comet
2003	NC 19903	Flying Cloud

They Also Served

Taking Care of the Loose Ends

For Juan Trippe to plot and plan to carry the rich and famous in glamorous Clipper ships was one thing; but to provide the equipment to fly the feeder routes on which an important element of Pan American's political influence depended was quite another. In supplying aircraft for the satellite airlines of Latin America, an entirely different set of criteria controlled the selection. Versatile machines able to stagger into and out of meadows and dried-up river beds, with a few hardy passengers on board, were in striking contrast to the luxurious Sikorsky boats.

Possibly the earliest aircraft type ever to find its way into Pan American's comptroller's records was a **Lincoln Standard** biplane which still survived with **Compañía Mexicana de Aviación,** and which had probably started its service life carrying payrolls for C.M.A.'s predecessor, C.M.T.A., way back in 1920.

Then from 1929 to 1931 there were apparently a few **Fokker Super Universals.** As the rather dubious record in the accompanying table reveals, this aircraft, which was quite popular in the United States among the small fry of the airline fraternity, suffered an unhappy fate with Pan Am. The records are vague and slim, as well they might be, but no doubt the operating conditions in the three areas in which it was deployed provide grounds for special claims of hardship duty.

The last Super Universal entry involved Pan American's surrogate in central Mexico, **Aerovías Centrales.** At first, this airline appears to have received some old Fokker F-10s and Fairchild 71s from Mexicana in 1932. It was then to have received a hot ship straight from the U.S.A., no less than a 175-mph 8-seat **Northrop Delta** (U.S. registration X236Y). The allocation of a Mexican registration number (X-ABED) was premature, as the Hornet-powered Delta unfortunately blew up on its delivery flight.

Undeterred, Aerovías Centrales turned to an even hotter ship, the **Lockheed 9 Orion.** This was a low-wing Wasp-engined development of the wooden high-wing Lockheed Vega, in which famous flyers such as Amelia Earhart had performed some noteworthy flights. The Orion was the first aircraft to use flaps to reduce landing speed and to increase the angle of descent. This was no doubt a case of necessity being the mother of invention, as the Orion was the first commercial airliner (if that term can be applied to a six-seat aircraft) to be able to maintain a speed of more than 200 mph.

Last among the list of aircraft which, in one way or another, served Pan American Airways, even though, if challenged, Juan Trippe would have expressed complete ignorance of their existence, was the **Fairchild Model XA-942A,** better known, and certainly more easily remembered, as the **Type 91.** This unusual looking flying boat saw service up the Amazon River, in **Panair do Brasil's** colors. It was built by the Kreider-Reisner Aircraft Company, a Fairchild subsidiary, and made its small mark on Pan American history by extending the Amazon route to the frontiers of Bolivia and Peru. Trippe even used it as a presidential yacht.

Boarding a **Lincoln Standard** of **Mexicana** during the 1950s.

PAN AMERICAN'S FOKKER SUPER UNIVERSALS

Const. No.	Regist. No.	Pan Am Delivery	Deployment	Remarks
	NC 9786	31.5.29	Brazil	Sunk
828		10.4.31	SCADTA	Crashed Bogotá, 15.12.32
880		13.10.32	Aerovías Centrales then SCADTA	Crashed 31.10.34

A **Lockheed Orion 9** of **Aerovías Centrales.**

PAN AMERICAN'S FAIRCHILD 91 FLEET

Const. No.	Registration No. U.S.	Registration No. Brazil	Delivery Date	Remarks
9402	NC 14744	PP-PAP	23.2.36	**Panair do Brasil** Sank at Santarém, 8 May 1939. Salvaged but damaged at Belém, 1942. Taken to Rio de Janeiro and scrapped.
9403	NC 15952	PP-PAT	6.1.37	**Panair do Brasil**
	NC 14745		36	May have been sent to China

The **Fairchild F-91,** also designated the **XA-942A,** shown here at its dock at Belém, the eastern terminus of **Panair do Brasil's** route on the Amazon River.

PAN AMERICAN'S LOCKHEED ORION FLEET

Const. No.	Mexican Regist.	Remarks
169	XA-BEI	These three aircraft were delivered to **Aerovías Centrales** in 1934. Pan American records show four Orions, registered as NC 13976, NC 13977, NC 964Y, and NC 988Y; but their precise allocation is not known.
173	XA-BEJ	
174	XA-BEL	

The ill-fated **Northrop Delta,** which crashed on its delivery flight.

Sikorsky S-43
"Baby Clipper"

18 seats • 165 mph

Length 51 feet • Span 86 feet • Height 17 feet

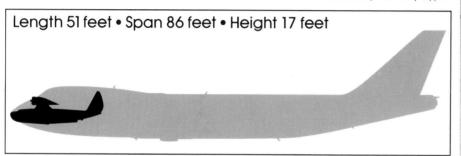

The **Sikorsky S-43** "Baby Clipper."

Pratt & Whitney Hornet (750 hp) x 2 • 20,000 lb. max. gross take-off weight • 750 statute miles range

Feederline Flying Boat

In South America, in the 1930s, the large S-42 flying boats needed a smaller aircraft to back them up, to handle the traffic to the smaller cities where average loads did not justify the large Clipper operations. The Commodores inherited from NYRBA were reliable but were rather slow. Just as the Boeing 247 and the DC-2 had swept aside the Ford Tri-Motor, mainly by an incremental speed of about 65%, so the Commodore had to give way to a flying boat roughly equal in size, but with more zip.

Once again Sikorsky came up with the answer. The **S-43** was a scaled-down S-42 with two engines instead of four and which inevitably earned the title of "Baby Clipper." A total of thirteen of these ships (which were actually amphibians) went into service with Pan American. Ordered on 10 September 1937, the first were delivered in an amazingly short time in January 1936. Seven were allocated to **Panair do Brasil** and two to **PANAGRA**. The others flew for Pan Am in the Caribbean.

A Big Baby

References to the "Baby Clipper" should be seen clearly in perspective. The S-43's all-up weight was 20,000 lb, or ten tons. This was more than the DC-2's by about 10%. The DC-3 which went into service a few months later was only 20% heavier. The Baby Clipper's 18 seats was only three short of the DC-3's and its range was not a great deal less.

Postscript to the *Jelling* Expedition

Charles Lindbergh's remarkable circumnavigation of the North Atlantic in 1933 had led to serious exploration by Pan American to fashion an air route to Europe, following the route taken by the Lone Eagle via Greenland, Iceland, and making landfall in the Eastern Hemisphere somewhere in Scandinavia. A common point in the scheme was Iceland, where Pan Am constructed, staffed, and operated an experimental radio station in 1936 and 1937.

One plan was to start a service from Copenhagen, Denmark, to Reykjavik, Iceland, by the summer of 1936, and gradually extend westwards, with the objective of full service from Denmark to the U.S. by July 1938. A cooperative agreement was made with the Danish airline **Det Danske Luftfartselskab (D.D.L.)** but in parallel with this, another was made with the Norwegian airline **Det Norske Luftfartselskap (D.N.L.)** for operations to the strategically situated airfield at Stavanger which was one of the first to have a paved runway.

D.N.L. actually ordered a Sikorsky S-43 early in 1936 for a proposed amphibian service from Stavanger to Reykjavik, via the Shetland and Faröe Islands, but the idea never materialized, as for a number of reasons, Pan American's interest in the northerly route to Europe waned. But for this change of plan, the "Baby Clipper" may not have had to take second place to its big brother in Pan Am's chronicle of transocean achievement.

PAN AMERICAN'S FLEET OF SIKORSKY S-43 "BABY CLIPPERS"

Const. No.	Registration No.		Delivery Date	Remarks
	U.S.	Brazil (P. do B.)		
4303	NC 15063	PP-PBA	January 1936	Crashed
4304	NC 15064	PP-PAW	January 1936	
4305	NC 15065	—	1936	Allocated to PANAGRA (p. 33) Santa Maria
4306	NC 15066	—	5 April 1936	Allocated to Caribbean. Destroyed at Fort de France, 3 August 1945
4307	NC 15067	PP-PAR	March 1936	Crashed or written off
4308	NC 15068	PP-PAU	March 1936	Crashed or written off
4315	NC 16926	PP-PBN	June 1936	Crashed at São Paulo, 3 January 1947
4316	NC 16927	PP-PBM	September 1936	Crashed on 28 July 1940, but rebuilt from parts of three aircraft
4317	NC 16928	—	1936	Allocated to PANAGRA. Crashed
	NC 16930	—	1936	
4322	NC 16931	PP-PBL	November 1936	
4324	NC 16933	—	December 1936	Allocated to Caribbean
4325	NC 16932	—	December 1936	

Transocean Landplane

False Start

Following joint discussions in 1936, between Douglas and Pan American and the Big Four U.S. domestic airlines, each of the five subscribed $100,000 towards the cost of developing the DC-4E, designed to carry 11,000 lb. of payload or 60 passengers over a range of more than 1,000 miles. The **DC-4E** first flew on 7 June 1938 and was the first large airliner to feature a nose wheel as well as the main landing gear. After flying some experimental services, however, United Air Lines, the main sponsor, was unable to persuade its four partners to persevere with it, and it was eventually sold to Japan. Attention was then switched to a smaller aircraft, the **DC-4.**

A Real Winner

On 26 January 1940 the group of five, with the exception of T.W.A. (Howard Hughes was beginning his close relationship with Lockheed) ordered a total of 61 DC-4s. Pan Am's contract for three was signed on 24 April of that year, and—unlike the others—specified a pressurized cabin, although none was so delivered. Juan Trippe must have been impressed, as from September 1941 to March 1942 Pan Am brought the total order up to 28. They cost $160,000 each, a bargain price.

The DC-4 made its first flight on 14 February 1942, by which time the United States was heavily involved in World War II. The Douglas long-range landplane could not have come at a better time. It went into service as the Army's **C-54** and the Navy's **R5D** and altogether, 1,163 were built. Almost 80,000 ocean crossings were made during the war, including a 250-strong armada which delivered two divisions of troops to Japan from Okinawa, following the surrender.

The Floodgates Open

As soon as hostilities ceased, the C-54s and R5Ds were released in great numbers and the big airlines could not get their hands on them quickly enough. Some had already operated them with aircraft leased from the armed forces, and the U.S. airline industry went into high gear. Pan American was no exception. As the accompanying table shows, ten had been delivered by the end of 1945, twenty during the following year, and so on to a total of no less than 92 Douglas DC-4s.

PAN AMERICAN'S DOUGLAS DC-4 FLEET

Const. No.	Regist. No.	Pan Am Delivery	Clipper Name
27289	N 88872	13.12.45	Monsoon
27314	N 88881	22.12.45	Kit Carson
27261	N 88882	17.11.45	Malay
27333	N 88883	7.12.45	Kathay
27313	N 88884	17.11.45	Lightfoot
27342	N 88885	26.11.45	Courser
27311	N 88886	14.11.45	Mandarin
27289	N 88887	13.12.45	Monsoon
27437	N 88888	17.12.45	East Indian
	N 88889	9.6.46	Black Hawk
10481	N 88890	29.5.46	Flying Arrow
10505	N 88891	3.11.45	Raven
	N 88892		
10440	N 88893	12.7.46	Syren
10496	N 88894	28.6.46	Eureka
	N 88895		
10470	N 88896	22.6.46	Eagle
	N 88897	25.7.46	Onward
	N 88898	27.6.46	Archer
10503	N 88899	10.8.46	Endeavor
10504	N 88900	17.8.46	Fearless
10506	N 88901	21.6.46	Defiance
10449	N 88902	18.7.46	Black Warrior
10445	N 88903	12.7.46	Dreadnought
18391	N 88904	19.7.46	
27237	N 88905	19.7.46	David Crockett
	N 88906		
18363	N 88907	8.9.46	Fleetwing
10465	N 88908	2.7.46	Charmer
10466	N 88909	15.6.46	Dauntless
	N 88910	15.6.46	
	N 88911	20.6.46	
27235	N 88912	8.7.46	Messenger
10400	N 88913	2.8.46	Belle of the Skies
10403	N 88914	3.7.47	Golden Eagle
	N 88915		
	N 88916	31.5.46	
	N 88917		
	N 88918		
10351	N 88919	15.3.47	Talisman
10317	N 88920	8.5.47	Talisman (2)
10334	N 88921	2.5.47	Northwind
10335	N 88922	9.3.47	Radiant
10362	N 88923	6.6.47	West Wind
10367	N 88924	15.5.47	Sunny South

Const. No.	Regist. No.	Pan Am Delivery	Clipper Name
10368	N 88925	22.11.48	Don Quixote
10381	N 88926	29.3.47	Twilight
10383	N 88927	14.3.47	Skylark
10384	N 88928	24.5.47	Union
10407	N 88929	5.4.47	Viking
10418	N 88930	21.3.47	
10391	N 88931	21.2.47	Quickstep
10323	N 88932	29.1.47	Matchless
10327	N 88933	29.5.47	Winged Racer
10366	N 88934	20.6.47	Pride of America
	N 88935	13.6.47	
10412	N 88936	8.2.47	Meteor
18337	N 88937	31.8.47	Cyclone
18385	N88938	20.7.46	Guiding Star
18397	N 88939	28.6.46	Hornet
18364	N 88940	27.7.46	Aurora
36072	N 88941		
36076	N 88942	9.10.45	Bostonian
36024	N 88943		Golden Express
35937	N 88944	2.6.48	Ocean Express
36080	N 88945	4.47	Gladiator
36069	N 88946	31.1.47	Argonaut
36066	N 88947	10.1.47	Redjacket
36043	N 88948	28.2.47	Westward Ho
	N 88949		
35933	N 88950	29.9.47	Southern Cross
35987	N 88951	22.5.47	Racer
35998	N 88952	19.3.47	Australia
35990	N 88953	11.4.47	Ocean Rover
36070	N 88954	29.11.49	Northern Light
36039	N 88955	30.4.49	Resolute
36059	N 88956	2.5.47	Polynesia
36061	N 88957	29.3.47	Oriental
36073	N 88958	2.10.45	Red Rover
36053	N 88959	13.9.45	Celestial
36060	N 88960	47	
	NC 60115	9.8.46	
10374	N 15568		
10282	N 10282		
18325	N 58018	6.6.48	Gem of the Skies
10274	N 79012	20.4.47	Reindeer
10296	N 88714	25.4.47	Golden West
18328	N 88817	31.7.46	
27338	N 90902	25.9.50	Roland
27344	NC 90905	25.9.50	Munich
27310	N 90906	25.9.50	Dusseldorf
27313	N 90913	25.9.50	White Falcon

Douglas DC-4

44 seats • 215 mph

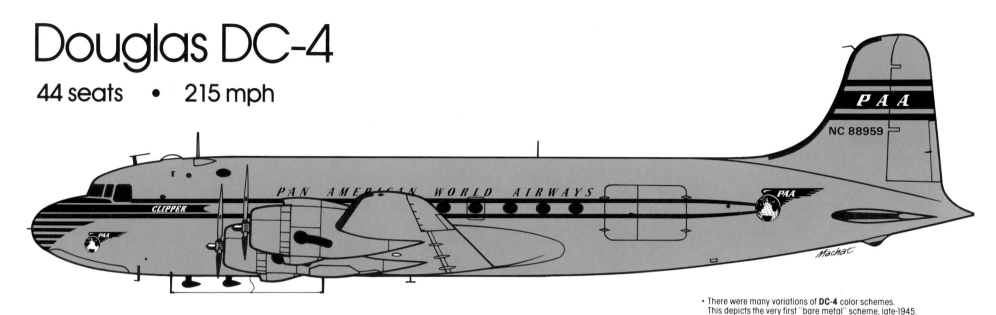

• There were many variations of **DC-4** color schemes. This depicts the very first "bare metal" scheme, late-1945.

Pratt & Whitney Twin Wasp (1,450 hp) x 4 • 73,000 lb. max. gross take-off weight • 2500 statute miles range

Length 94 feet • Span 118 feet • Height 28 feet

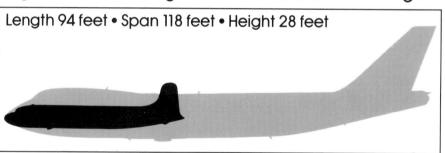

Unsung workhorse of the immediate post-war airline period, the **Douglas DC-4.**

Cinderella Status

The outbreak of war in Europe in September 1939 put an end to four-engined designs and projects such as the German Focke-Wulf Fw 200 Condor, which had flown nonstop from Berlin to New York and then back again in 1938. The British and the French had to abandon four promising designs to concentrate on more pressing requirements. Meanwhile, the Douglas DC-4 in a sense broke the transocean barrier, with its rapid development, massive production, and wide deployment by military and commercial operators alike.

Often remembered is the DC-4's lack of pressurization and its markedly slower speed, compared with its DC-6 and DC-7 developments, and of course with the Lockheed Constellation which broke the Douglas dominance by outstripping the DC-4 rather spectacularly. More often forgotten is the record of the intercontinental airlines, U.S. and foreign alike, almost all of which inaugurated their prestigious postwar trunk routes with DC-4s.

End of an Era

In an epoch-making mission, Pan American dispatched a DC-4 on 21 October 1945 on a 25,000-mile survey flight to Japan, China, southeast Asia, and India. The message was clear. To underscore the point, Pan Am replaced its Boeing 314s on the California-Honolulu route with DC-4s. The daily flight took about 10 hours, compared with the Boeing's 20, and the fare was reduced from $278 one way to $195. The era of the flying boat was at an end.

53

Efficient Elegance

Pan Am Joins the Club

Juan Trippe had been accustomed to sponsoring new generations of aircraft, and it must have been quite a shock to his system to see Hughes and T.W.A. not only taking over such leadership, but also receiving extensive international route awards from the Civil Aeronautics Board, enthusiastically supported by the President, and now challenging the Chosen Instrument, as Pan American was unofficially dubbed, on the lucrative North Atlantic route. However, Trippe knew a good thing when he saw one, and did not hesitate to purchase Constellations, at $750,000 each.

The first of the Lockheed airliners, with 54 seats in Pan Am's layout, was delivered on 5 January 1946 and christened *Mayflower*. A second arrived one week later and Pan American opened North Atlantic Constellation service on 14 January 1946. This was a measure of Pan Am's considerable organizational strength as T.W.A. itself did not start scheduled transatlantic service until 5 February. Today the World's Most Experienced Airline, as it liked to call itself, can look back with pride on such actions.

Pan American took delivery of 22 Model 049 Constellations before the end of May 1946. Two went directly to Panair do Brasil, still very much a Pan Am subsidiary, and which was the fortunate recipient of eleven more during the 1950s as they were retired from the parent company's routes. On 17 June 1947 a **Constellation Model 749,** an advanced version, one of four delivered to Pan Am, made the first round-the-world airline inaugural flight, from New York to San Francisco (Pan American was not permitted to fly transcontinentally to make the final link). Later, with the purchase of American Overseas Airlines (A.O.A.), seven more of the 049 Model were added, for a total Connie fleet of 33.

The Might-Have-Beens

The Constellation story was not Pan American's first encounter with Lockheed. On 14 November 1939 it had signed a contract for three **Model 44 Excalibur,** designed to carry 30 passengers at 262 mph in pressurized comfort over a 1,600-mile range. Delivery was to have been in the summer of 1941 but the project was cancelled.

Another impressive-looking contender was the **Republic Rainbow.** This was a commercial adaptation of the XF-12, built experimentally for the Army Air Forces, to a 1943 specification for long range, high-speed reconnaissance, at very high altitudes. The XF-12 first flew on 4 February 1946. With a design cruising altitude of 40,000 feet—the same as the jets fly at today—and a speed of 400 mph, it looked to be another winner. Pan American and American Airlines placed provisional orders, but cancellation of the military contracts forced the abandonment of the project.

Had it gone into service the **Republic Rainbow** would have out-performed all postwar piston-engined airliners by a substantial margin. But the convenient availability of hundreds of cheap war-surplus DC-4s priced them out of the market—even for Pan Am.

THE LOCKHEED CONSTELLATION FAMILY

| Model | Engines | | Dimensions (ft) | | Gross Weight (lb) | Typical Seats | Cruise Speed (mph) | Range (st. miles) | First Service | | Number Built |
	Type	h p (each)	Length	Span					Date	Airline	
L-049		2200	95	123	98,000	54	310	3000	14 Jan. 1946	Pan Am	88 (inc. military)
L-749		2500	95	123	107,000	64	300	3000	17 June 1947	Pan Am	145 (inc. military)
L-1049A	Wright R-3350 (various)	2700	114	123	120,000	88	279	2450	17 Dec. 1951	Eastern	104 (inc. C, D, E)
L-1049G		3250	114	123	137,500	99	335	4620	1 April 1955	TWA	157 (inc. H Model)
L-1649A		3400	116	150	156,000	99	350	5280	1 June 1957	TWA	44

PAN AMERICAN'S LOCKHEED CONSTELLATIONS

Const. No.	Regist. No.	Pan Am Delivery	Clipper Name	Remarks
Model 049				
2031	N 88831	5.2.46	Caribbean	Crashed, Shannon, 24.9.46
2032	N 88832	20.2.46	Flora Temple	Sold to *Panair do Brasil*
2033	N 88833	25.2.46	Bald Eagle	Sold to *Panair do Brasil*
2036	N 88836	5.1.46	Mayflower	Sold to *Cubana*
2037	N 88837	12.1.46	Challenge	Sold to *Panair do Brasil*
2038	N 88838	21.1.46	Donald McKay	Sold to *Panair do Brasil*
2045	N 88845	25.2.47	Eclipse	Crashed in Syria, 18.6.47
2046	N 88846	1.3.46	Great Republic	Crashed, Monrovia, 22.6.51
2047	N 88847	9.3.46	Hotspur	Sold to *Panair do Brasil*
2048	N 88848	15.3.46	Golden Gate	Allocated to **Pan. do Brasil**
2049	N 88849	22.3.46		Allocated to **Pan. do Brasil**
2050	N 88850	20.3.46	Intrepid	Sold to *Panair do Brasil*
2055	N 88855	22.4.46	Invincible	Sold to Delta Airlines
2056	N 88856	15.4.46	Paul Jones	Sold to *Panair do Brasil*
2057	N 88857	19.4.46	Unity	Sold to *Panair do Brasil*
2058	N 88858	25.4.46	Empress of the Skies	Crashed, Shannon, 15.4.48
2059	N 88859	27.4.46	Talisman	Sold to *Panair do Brasil*
2060	N 88860	1.5.46	Courier	Sold to *Panair do Brasil*
2061	N 88861	14.5.46	Winged Arrow	Sold to *Cubana*
2062	N 88862	14.5.46		
2066	N 88865	24.5.46	White Falcon	Sold to *Panair do Brasil*
2067	N 88868	25.5.46	Golden Fleece	Sold to Delta Airlines
Model 749				
2525	N 86527	21.6.47	Glory of the Skies	Sold to Air France, 1950
2526	N 86528	21.6.47	Sovereign of the Sky	
2527	N 86529	28.6.47	Romance of the Skies	
2528	N 86530	28.6.47	America	
Model 049 (Acquired with purchase of **American Overseas Airlines**)				
2051	N 90921	25.9.50	Jupiter Rex	Sold to B.O.A.C.
2052	N 90922	25.9.50	Mount Vernon	Sold to **Panair do Brasil**
2053	N 90923	25.9.50	Golden Rule	Sold to Delta Airlines
2054	N 90924	25.9.50	Lafayette	Sold to Master Eqpmnt. Co.
2063	N 90925	25.9.50	Courier	Sold to Delta Airlines
2064	N 90926	25.9.50	Ocean Herald	Sold to Master Eqpmnt.Co.
2065	N 90927	25.9.50	Wings of the Morning	Sold to B.O.A.C.

◀ The **L-1049 Super Constellation** series had the same wing as the Constellation, but a longer fuselage. The **L-1649A Starliner** was slightly longer, with a new wing.

Lockheed O49 Constellation

54 seats • 310 mph

Wright R-3350 (2,200 hp) x 4 • 98,000 lb. max. gross take-off weight • 3000 statute miles range

The Secret Weapon

British aviation writer Peter Brooks described the **Lockheed Constellation** as "the secret weapon of American air transport." The description was almost literally true, as it was produced, if not clandestinely, certainly behind locked doors. It was the inspired result of close cooperation between Lockheed's design staff, headed by the redoubtable Kelly Johnson, and the leadership of Howard Hughes, now actively in charge of T.W.A. Discussions were first held in 1939, T.W.A. ordered nine in 1940, and the **Model 049,** as Lockheed engineers always called it, first flew on 9 January 1943. All concerned must have known they had a winner, even if the C-54s were piling up the hours across the conflict-stricken oceans.

On 19 April 1944 Hughes and T.W.A. president Jack Frye flew the "Connie" nonstop from Burbank, Lockheed's plant location in California, to Washington, D.C. in three minutes less than seven hours, an air journey which normally took between 12 and 14 hours, including stops. The aircraft was immediately handed over to the Government for military use, and Howard Hughes no doubt made a considerable impression on the assembled bureaucratic multitude as he demonstrated it (illegally) in T.W.A.'s colors.

Length 95 feet • Span 123 feet • Height 24 feet

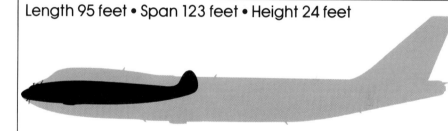

A New Class

The Lockheed 049 Constellation was in a class of its own. It was at least 70 mph faster then the Douglas DC-4; it was pressurized—at a higher equivalent altitude than the Boeing 307 had been; it was larger, with 60 seats against the DC-4's 44 at the same seat pitch; and it had the range to fly across the North Atlantic with only one stop. It sent all the Douglas design staff back to the drawing board in a hurry, to develop the unpressurized Four into something bigger and faster and higher-flying. For the path which the airlines had beaten to Santa Monica was superseded by one to Burbank, because when T.W.A. put the Constellation into service, it quickly became evident that there were two classes of airline: those with Connies and those without them.

The **Lockheed L-049 Constellation,** picture of elegance of the piston era.

Luxury Aloft

Keeping up the Competitive Pressure

Pan American Airways had, during its formative and adolescent years, enjoyed the privileged position of being officially regarded as The Chosen Instrument. It faced no direct competition on its overseas routes from the United States, whereas the domestic airlines were denied access into foreign markets. And before World War II, competition from foreign airlines simply did not exist. But the war changed all that. Several airlines were granted foreign routes, partly as a gesture of gratitude by a government which had been well served by the industry during the conflict; and Juan Trippe suddenly found himself deprived of a near-monopoly position.

At first, in 1947, he attempted to merge with the airline which posed the biggest threat: Trans World Airlines, formerly Transcontinental and Western Air (T.W.A.). But Howard Hughes had ideas of his own and rejected the proposal, and made it clear that he intended to compete with Trippe on all fronts, with the popular Constellation fleet plus a domestic route network giving him some good playing cards.

Part of Trippe's answer to the challenge was to supplement his DC-4 and Constellation fleet with Boeing 377 Stratocruisers. He had ordered a fleet of 20 on 28 November 1945, and put the first one into service on the densly-travelled San Francisco-Honolulu route on 1 April 1949. New York-Bermuda followed on 15 April, and the transatlantic route to London on 2 June as the all-first-class *President* service. This was six weeks in advance of another U.S. Stratocruiser operator, American Overseas Airlines (A.O.A.).

The American Overseas Merger

American Overseas had been created by a shipping company, American Export Lines, which, after long and complex hearings before the Civil Aeronautics Board, had obtained a permit in 1942 to form an airline, **American Export Airlines (A.E.A.)** to operate across the Atlantic; and had done so with Vought-Sikorsky VS-44s under contract to the Naval Air Transport Service. After the war, it had merged with American Airlines Inc. (Transatlantic Division) to become **American Overseas Airlines (A.O.A.),** and had actually made the first postwar commercial flight into England (to Bournemouth, as London Airport was not yet open) by any airline on 24 October 1945.

After a period of fewer than five years of unrestrained competition between three U.S. airlines on the North Atlantic, Howard Hughes and T.W.A. had to endure the indignity of seeing the other two, Pan Am and American Overseas, amalgamate; or, to be exact, to observe Pan Am purchase A.O.A. on 25 September 1950 for $17,450,000. The merger strengthened Pan Am's position immeasurably, not least in its now augmented Stratocruiser fleet, which shared with the British B.O.A.C., which also had them, the honors of providing the most comfortable service across the Atlantic, not least because the passengers had a chance to stretch their legs and take a trip to the bar.

A Pan American **Boeing 377 Stratocruiser,** epitome of airborne luxury

A **Boeing Stratocruiser** of **American Overseas Airlines,** a formidable rival of Pan American before the merger of the two companies.

The **Stratocruiser's** downstairs lounge relieved the tedium of a sixteen-hour trans-Atlantic air journey.

PAN AMERICAN'S BOEING STRATOCRUISERS

Const. No.	Regist. No.	Pan Am Delivery	Clipper Name
15923	N 1023V	19.3.49	Golden Gate
15924	N 1024V	11.6.49	Bald Eagle
15925	N 1025V	31.1.49	America
15926	N 1026V	17.2.49	Tradewind
15927	N 1027V	2.3.49	Friendship
15928	N 1028V	14.3.49	Flying Cloud
15929	N 1029V	22.4.49	Golden Eagle
15930	N 1030V	30.3.49	Southern Cross
15931	N 1031V	28.4.49	Mayflower
15932	N 1032V	21.5.49	United States
15933	N 1033V	23.6.49	Seven Seas
15934	N 1034V	3.7.49	Westward Ho
15935	N 1035V	23.7.49	Flying Eagle
15936	N 1036V	12.8.49	Washington
15937	N 1037V	8.9.49	Fleetwing
15938	N 1038V	29.9.49	Consititution
15939	N 1039V	27.8.49	Good Hope
15940	N 1040V	31.10.49	Invincible
15941	N 1041V	8.11.49	Yankee
15942	N 1042V	30.12.49	Morning Star
15922	N 1022V	24.10.50	Nightingale
(Acquired with purchase of American Overseas Airlines)			
15957	N 90941	25.9.50	America
15958	N 90942	25.9.50	Glory of the Skies
15959	N 90943	25.9.50	Sovereign of the Sky
15960	N 90944	25.9.50	Romance of the Skies
15961	N 90945	25.9.50	Monarch of the Skies
15962	N 90946	25.9.50	Queen of the Skies
15963	N 90947	25.9.50	Queen of the Pacific
15964	N 90948	25.9.50	Eclipse

Boeing 377 Stratocruiser

86 seats • 340 mph

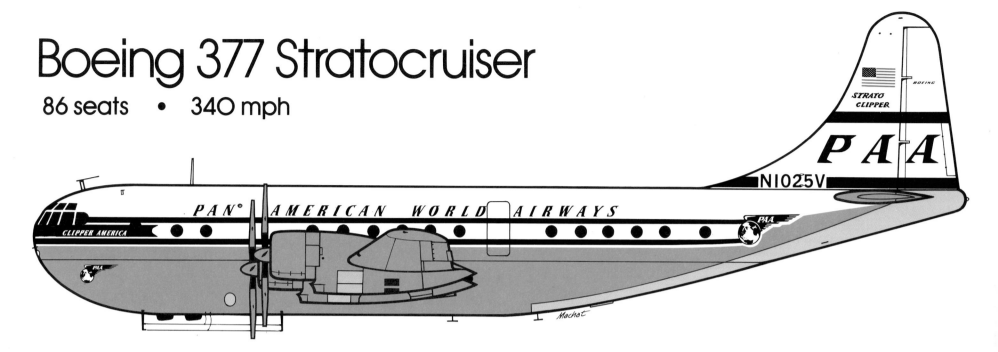

Pratt & Whitney R-4360 (3,500 hp) x 4 • 142,500 lb. max. gross take-off weight • 2750 statute miles range

Pan American **Boeing 377 Stratocruiser**

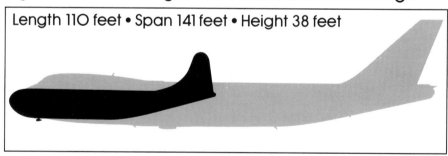

Length 110 feet • Span 141 feet • Height 38 feet

Boeing Tries Again

The engineers and designers at Seattle were entitled to feel a little unlucky in their attempts to enter the commercial airliner market. The **Model 247** of 1933 was judged to start the new era of "The Modern Airliner" but complete success was foiled by a corporate error in marketing the product. The **Model 307** Stratoliner was the world's first pressurized airliner, but World War II intervened and Boeing had to concentrate on wartime bomber production. The **Model 314** was regarded as the world's finest flying boat ever builIt, but once again World War II prevented full production, partly because the onset of long range landplanes effectively destroyed the flying boat market.

Now Boeing tried again. To support the B-29 and B-50 Superfortress bombers that it had built for the U.S. Army Air Forces, it produced almost 900 military tanker transports. Off the same production line came 55 of a commercial version, the **Model 377**, better known as the **Stratocruiser.** It looked as ponderous as the Constellation looked graceful. It seemed to bore its way through the air, defying apparent theories of clean aerodynamics. It was, in fact, as fast as the Constellation, and set up many point to point records.

The feature for which it is best remembered is the lower deck lounge, fitted out as a cocktail bar, a welcome diversion during the long transatlantic flights.

Largely because of the bar, the Stratocruiser was invariably used by the airlines for luxury or first class service. Thus, although the "Strat" had slightly higher operating costs than the Constellations or the DC-6Bs, it consistently pulled in higher revenues, usually more than restoring the economic balance.

While the Constellation is remembered with affection as the epitome of elegance of the piston-engined era, and the DC-6B for its reliability and efficiency, the Stratocruiser was the last to be retired from the world's prestige routes when, first the turboprop Britannia, and then the Comet and the Boeing 707 jets ushered in a new era that became the Jet Age.

The Second Level

Meanwhile, Back at the Hacienda...

While maximum effort was directed towards establishing a worldwide network and moreover taking a lead so that other airlines were always the followers, Pan American did not neglect its own back yard. In Central America and the Caribbean area, there was an assembly of small routes and feeder connections which needed modern postwar aircraft to succeed the trusty old Douglas DC-3. Though still thoroughly reliable, it was seen by Pan American and its clientele alike as the airline equivalent of a steam locomotive in an era of diesel and electric traction.

During the latter part of 1948, therefore, the airline purchased a fleet of 20 pressurized twin-engined **CV-240 Convair-Liners** from Consolidated Vultee Aircraft in San Diego. These 40-seaters were to be seen everywhere in the West Indian islands, many of which now had good airfields, although the experience of a Convair 240 taking off from St. Thomas and just clearing the nearby ridge was a memorable one for all those who tried it. Late in 1953, Pan Am supplemented the fleet with four of the slightly larger **Convair 340s,** but kept them only a few months, and the entire fleet was sold by the late 1950s.

Possession is Nine Points of the Law

Throughout the history of Pan American Airways expansion in Latin America, Juan Trippe had been adept—some would allege devious, or even worse—in obtaining the operating rights he needed in all the many countries athwart his line of sight. (See table, page 88). The progress was steady and inexorable, and Trippe quickly established the main trunk network in the amazingly short time of only two years, by acquisition or partnership, from September 1928 to September 1930. He then proceeded to tie up loose ends wherever these occurred, so that by 1940, when war clouds were gathering, there was hardly a corner of Latin America where the Pan Am flag did not fly. The Pan Am name became synonymous with United States commercial enterprise throughout the continent.

The Pan Am Juggernaut Rolls On

After the United States entered World War II, there was much concern that Axis interests might undermine United States influence in the region. Indeed, there were some who feared that airlines with German sponsorship, real or suspected, in Brazil, Colombia, Ecuador, and Peru, particularly, might pose a threat as a potential support resource for fifth column activity. There was

even a thought that somehow the Panama Canal might be vulnerable, and the United States adopted a policy whereby all airline activity throughout the whole of Latin America came under the control of U.S. airlines, i.e. the "Chosen Instrument" Pan American and its partner PANAGRA.

The Deutsche Lufthansa subsidiary in Peru, the Ecuadorian airline SEDTA, and the Brazilian Syndicato Condor were eliminated, as was the Italian Corporación in Argentina. PANAGRA took over the management of the Bolivian airline LAB, without, however, acquiring stock. Throughout Central America, Pan American systematically established new airlines in partnership with the governments of the chain of small countries between Mexico and Colombia.

In so doing, a bitter war was fought with the TACA empire which had been fashioned by a New Zealander, Lowell Yerex, and whose efforts to retain the services and routes so carefully built up during the 1930s were ruthlessly swept aside by Pan American's collusion with the governments. Yerex's appeals to the British Government for support fell upon deaf ears, and he was somehow portrayed as interfering with Allied interests. His elimination from the Central American scene was a case study in the way Pan American always got its own way at that time.

PAN AMERICAN'S CONVAIR 240 FLEET

Regist. No.	Const. No.	Pan Am Delivery	Disposition
N 90655	9	12.7.48	Sold to Mid Continent Airlines, 1950
N 90656	14	9.11.48	Sold to VARIG, 1957
N 90657	19	17.12.48	
N 90658	24	18.6.48	Sold to VARIG, 1954
N 90659	34	30.4.48	Sold to M.E.A., 1954
N 90660	39	25.12.48	Sold to VARIG, 1954
N 90661	44	17.11.48	
N 90662	49	23.11.48	Destroyed at Kingston, Jamaica, 1951
N 90663	55	16.11.48	Sold to Mid Continent Airlines, 1950
N 90664	59	23.6.48	
N 90665	65	1.8.48	Sold to Northeast Airlines, 1954
N 90666	67	9.10.48	
N 90667	71	20.7.48	Sold to Mid Continent Airlines, 1950
N 90668	83	9.9.48	Sold to VARIG, 1957
N 90669	84	27.9.48	Sold to Mid Continent Airlines, 1952
N 90670	90	1.9.48	Sold to Northeast Airlines, 1954
N 90671	91	6.9.48	Sold to VARIG, 1954 and 1957
N 90672	98	20.10.48	
N 90673	99	22.10.48	
N 90674	103	2.11.48	

PAN AMERICAN'S CONVAIR 340 FLEET

Regist. No.	Const. No.	Pan Am Delivery	Disposition
N 11136	136	18.12.53	Sold to National Airlines, 1954
N 11137	137	22.12.53	
N 11150	150	11.2.53	
N 11151	151	18.2.54	

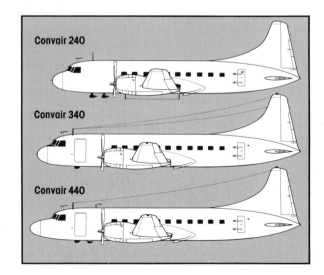

Convair 240

Convair 340

Convair 440

The **Convair 240,** which served Pan Am in Latin America.

Convair 240

40 seats • 240 mph

• DC-3, DC-4, Constellation, Convair 240, C-46 and Stratocruiser all appeared in both the late 1940's "bare-metal," and the white top or "white crown" scheme, introduced in 1951.

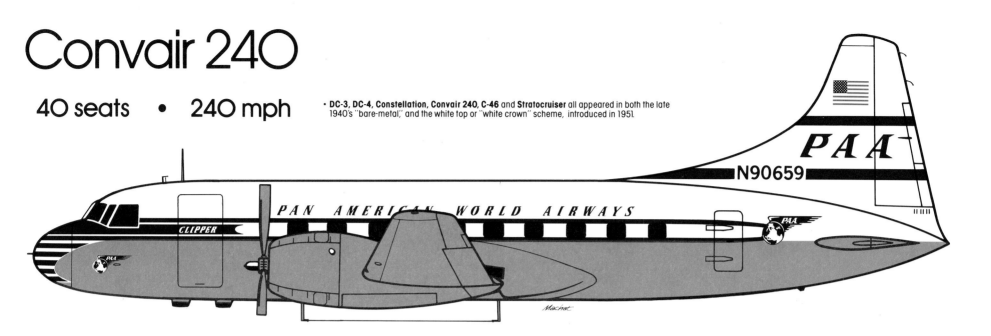

Pratt & Whitney R-2800 (2000 hp) x 2 • 41,790 lb. max. gross take-off weight • 1000 statute miles range

Development

After World War II the major airlines of the United States realized that they had to have a modern airliner to serve the secondary, or feeder routes which supplemented the trunk systems. The Consolidated-Vultee and Martin companies, both wartime manufacturers of flying boats, competed for the market. **Martin** was actually in the lead at first, its **Model 2-0-2** going into service in November 1947. But it was unpressurized, and there was also a structural deficiency which led to its withdrawal from service. United withdrew its support for a later variant, the **Model 3-0-3**, and even though T.W.A. and Eastern started service with the vastly improved (and pressurized) **Model 4-0-4** in October 1951, most of the airlines turned to Consolidated-Vultee, or Convair, as it became known, for its fine series of twin-engined airliners.

The **Convair 240** first flew on 3 July 1947, by which time American Airlines had reduced its unprecedented order, placed in 1945, from 100 to 75. Altogether 553 Convair-Liners were sold, and they were popular in Europe, as well as in the U.S.

An Interesting Family

Differences in the various Convair models were not too easy to detect, as the table shows. The **Model 340** was more popular than the basic **Model 240**, yet the **Model 440**, known as the Metropolitan, was more popular in Europe than at home. Later on, stimulated by the threat of the British Viscount, launched in the U.S.A. by enterprising airlines such as Capital and Continental, Convair produced successful conversions to turbine power of all models of the Convair-Liner.

Of these, the most popular was the Allison-powered **Model 580**, whose performance was superior to the Rolls-Royce-engined **Models 600** and **640**. In 1960, Allegheny Airlines put into service the **Model 540**, with British Napier Elands, and initiated a no-reservation commuter route; but Napier abruptly cancelled the project thus terminating a promising line of development.

Length 75 feet • Span 92 feet • Height 27 feet

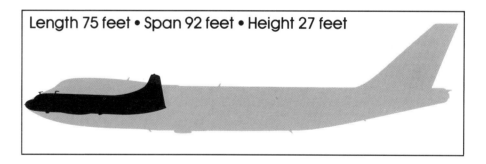

THE CONVAIR-LINER FAMILY

Series	Engines		Dimensions (feet)			Remarks
	Type	hp	Length	Span	Seats	
240	P & W R2800-CA18	2000	75	92	40	—
340	P & W R2800-CB16	2400	79	106	44	—
440	P & W R2800-CB17	2800	79	106	52	Known as the Metropolitan
540	Napier Eland	3500	79	106	44	Turboprop conversion of CV340
580	Allison 501	3750	82	105	52	Turboprop conversion of CV340/440
600	Rolls-Royce Dart 10	3025	75	92	52	Turboprop conversion of CV240
640	Rolls-Royce Dart 10	3025	82	105	56	Turboprop conversion of CV340/440

Horsepower at maximum rating; turboprops at equivalent horsepower (e.g. 3500 hp = 3230 hp + 700 lb static thrust)

Lest We Forget...

Better Late than Never

Not too often did Pan American wait a full six years after a new type entered service before putting it to work itself. But such was the case with the ubiquitous Curtiss C-46, known by some airlines as the Commando. Not counting the operations of C.N.A.C. (see below) Pan American did not acquire a fleet of its own until 1948, and then only second-hand, an uncharacteristic exception to the U.S. flag carrier's normal procedure.

However, this was an eminently sensible purchase, as the C-46 served as an all-cargo aircraft in the Caribbean and Central America, often venturing further south to Brazil and to other countries. By so doing, it released front-line aircraft from such onerous duties, and it was much in demand in areas where a flying truck was an economic asset. Most of Pan Am's C-46s were sold back to the Army in 1953, after performing unfashionable but none-the-less vital chores in support of its upper class contemporaries.

PAN AMERICAN'S CURTISS C-46 COMMANDOS

Regist. No.	Const. No.	Pan Am Delivery	Regist. No.	Const. No.	Pan Am Delivery
N 74170	22477	8.6.48	N 74175	22588	1.9.48
N 74171	22472	28.8.48	N 74176	22592	3.9.48
N 74172	22541	28.8.48	N 74177	22596	7.9.48
N 74173	22487	31.8.48	N 74178	22597	11.9.48
N 74174	22581	31.8.48	N 74179	22598	15.9.48

N 74170 and N 74176 were destroyed in accidents at Mérida, Mexico, and São Paulo, Brazil, respectively, 1950-1951. N 74177 was named *Golden Chance II*.

Pan American workhorse in the postwar years, this **C-46** is seen loading freight.

This **CNAC C-46** almost certainly saw rugged wartime service over the formidable mountains between China and India, known as "The Hump."

This **LACSA C-46** served the Costa Rican national airline while still in association with Pan American, as indicated by the lettering and insignia.

The Hump

The C-46 had its share of criticism during its service career, inevitably being compared with the DC-3. Its single-engined performance was less than adequate, and nowhere was this deficiency more acutely felt than by the wartime pilots who flew the "Hump" in 1944 and 1945. This was the section of the eastern Himalayas, whose cliff-like cordilleras formed a great barrier to communications with the Allied forces who were trying to stop the Japanese from occupying China.

A large number of C-46s were ferried out to China via the South Atlantic and southern Asia, and these bore the brunt of the airlift of supplies of men and materials to the war zone centered around Chungking, where the besieged Chinese were defending themselves against direct Japanese attack. They were aided by contingents of the U.S. Army Air Forces, together with the Chinese airline, **China National Aviation Corporation (C.N.A.C.)**, still a Pan American associated company.

Backwards and forwards between airfields in northeast India and Chinese bases in the southwest, especially Kunming, the C-46s did wonderful work. One was out of action for only four days during a whole month, and that was for the essential 100-hour maintenance check. During the other 27 days the single aircraft averaged two round trips per day across the dreaded and deathly terrain, where no emergency landing was possible. The C-46's fine wartime service record is one of the best kept, if unintentional secrets of World War II.

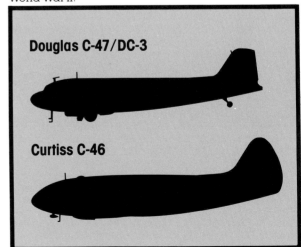

Douglas C-47/DC-3

Curtiss C-46

Curtiss C-46 Commando

40 seats • 170 mph

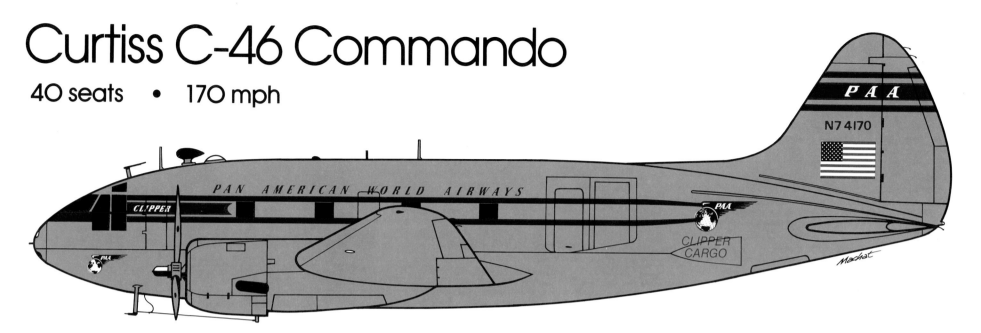

Pratt & Whitney R-2800 (2000 hp) x 2 • 48,000 lb. max. gross take-off weight • 1200 statute miles range

Development

The Curtiss-Wright C-46 made its first flight on 26 March 1940. Curiously, the CW-20 prototype, known by the U.S. Army Air Corps as the C-55, was delivered to the British airline, B.O.A.C., which badly needed a good cargo carrier. **Eastern Air Lines** played a big part in developing this large aircraft which had its fair share of teething troubles. Eastern's Miami base identified more than 300 faults, and most of its recommendations were accepted by Curtiss-Wright. Eventually, the C-46 went into service in February 1943 for Eastern's Military Transport Division on a wartime supply route from Miami to Natal, then extended this across the South Atlantic on 1 June 1944. The route to West Africa was via Ascension Island, where an air base had been hewn out of the rock, and the C-46s carried extra fuel tanks for the two almost-1500-mile transoceanic segments.

The C-46 was always compared unfavorably with the DC-3, mainly because the latter was more adept at getting itself out of trouble. Yet in spite of allegations that take-off performance was not exactly dramatic, C-46s were almost standard equipment on freight runs into and out of La Paz, Bolivia, where the 13,400-foot altitude airport is still a challenge for almost any aircraft.

A Beast of Burden

One reason why stubborn airlines in Latin America, operating vital services into jungle and savannah regions on a shoestring, hung on the C-46s with as much affection as the DC-3s, was that it carried twice the payload. Because of its clean lines, its apparent size was deceptive. In fact, it was twice as heavy as the DC-3. It was bigger than the Convair-Liner, but of course was not as fast. Indeed, it was not very much smaller than the four-engined DC-4 and could carry almost as much payload, although not as far.

Used mainly as an all-cargo aircraft, some C-46s were pressed into service as passenger "airliners" and pioneered many a low-cost route for cavalier entrepreneurs who successfully undercut Pan Am and PANAGRA in Latin America. The

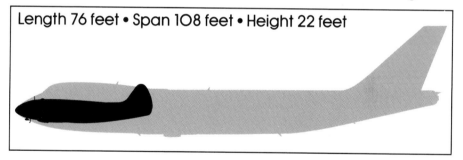

Length 76 feet • Span 108 feet • Height 22 feet

number of seats varied and many a seating layout echoed wartime parachutist transport style, with benches down each side of the cabin, and sometimes down the middle. In this way, there seemed to be almost no limit to the number of undemanding passengers who could be squeezed in. The 10,000 lb. payload theoretically allowed for 50 with full baggage; but for Mexican airlines transporting illegal immigrants whose baggage was minimal, as many as 80 could sometimes be observed disembarking, almost magically, from a C-46's fuselage.

THE CURTISS C-46 IN PERSPECTIVE

Aircraft	Dimensions			All-up Weight (lb)	Payload (lb)	Typical Seats	Normal Range
	Length	Span	Height				
DC-3	64'5"	95'0"	16'11"	24,400	3840	21	1000
C-46	76'4"	108'0"	21'9"	48,000	10,000	50	1200
Convair 240	74'8"	91'9"	26'11"	41,790	9,350	40	1800

The Thoroughbred Airliner

In company with the world's leading airlines, Pan American had resumed full peacetime service after World War II with the reliable **Douglas DC-4**, already route-proven by the U.S. Army Air Forces as the **C-54** (or the Naval R5D). But Juan Trippe had turned promptly to the Lockheed Constellation as this aircraft demonstrated its clear superiority of performance, not to mention its pressurized comfort, over its Douglas rival. Even though the Boeing Stratocruiser supplemented the "Connie" on the prestige routes, however, Pan Am went back to Douglas as the Old Firm responded to Lockheed's challenge, and produced an airliner which could match the Constellation.

Pan American ordered 45 **Douglas DC-6B's** during the month of September 1950. All were delivered between February 1952 and June 1954. The first one to enter service was the *Clipper Liberty Bell* which, on 1 May 1952, inaugurated the all-tourist *Rainbow* service on the prestigious New York-London route. This one was fitted with 82 seats, although a more typical all-tourist

arrangement was 88. The DC-6B's capacity varied from 44 first-class to 109 economy class, and it was a truly versatile aircraft. (Pan Am also had five of the DC-6A all-cargo version.)

But it was upstaged. Its contribution to widening the scope of air travel, with its good economics permitting Pan Am to offer the newly-agreed tourist class fares, was all but forgotten in the blaze of publicity that accompanied the opening of the world's first jet airliner service, by the British Comet, on B.O.A.C's route from London to Johannesburg, the day after the *Liberty Bell's* debut.

The two events were perhaps symbolic. As the Comet ushered in the new jet age, the Douglas airliner represented the pinnacle of achievement of the great long-range piston-engined types. Most of Pan American's DC-6B's served until well into the 1960s, and the last fifteen were finally sold on 17 September 1968. They were to make them bigger and faster and with more range than the 6B, but they never made them better.

PAN AMERICAN'S DOUGLAS DC-6B FLEET

Const. No.	Regist. No.	Pan Am Delivery	Clipper Name
43518	N6518C	29.5.52	Freedom
43519	N6519C	27.2.52	Liberty Bell
43520	N6520C	12.3.52	Priscilla Alden
43521	N6521C	31.3.52	Goodwill
43522	N6522C	5.4.52	Plymouth Rock
43523	N6523C	12.4.52	Betsy Ross
43524	N6524C	19.4.52	Pocohontas
43525	N6525C	24.4.52	Resolute
43526	N6526C	29.5.52	Evening Star
43527	N6527C	23.6.52	Stargazer
43528	N6528C	3.7.52	Midnight Sun
43529	N6529C	20.8.52	Fidelity
43530	N6530C	21.8.52	Pathfinder
43531	N6531C	23.8.52	Viking
43532	N6532C	31.8.52	Aurora
43533	N6533C	5.9.52	Flying Arrow
43534	N6534C	12.9.52	Carib
43535	N6535C	19.10.52	Mercury
43838	N6538C	20.2.54	Northwind
44061	N4061K	7.7.53	Dawn
44102	N6102H	9.7.53	Golden Age
44103	N6103C	18.7.53	Virginia
44104	N6104C	8.8.53	Defender
44105	N6105C	15.8.53	Sam Houston
44106	N6106C	24.9.53	Andrew Jackson
44107	N6107C	30.9.53	Balboa
44108	N6108C	4.10.53	Inca
44109	N6109C	21.12.53	Mohawk
44110	N6110C	1.12.53	Natchez
44111	N6111C	6.12.53	Peerless
44112	N6112C	14.12.53	Reindeer
44113	N6113C	21.12.53	Golden West
44114	N6114C	6.3.54	Northern Light
44115	N6115C	11.3.54	Lark
44116	N6116C	25.3.54	Arctic
44117	N6117C	3.4.54	De Soto
44118	N5118V	6.4.54	John Alden
44119	N5119V	13.4.54	Miles Standish
44120	N5120V	26.4.54	Mermaid
44121	N5121V	26.4.54	Splendid
44424	N5024K	6.5.54	White Falcon
44425	N5025K	18.5.54	Windward
44426	N5026K	28.5.54	Panama
44427	N5027K	7.6.54	Ponce de Leon
44428	N5028K	15.6.54	Fair Wind

The **Douglas DC-6B**.

Douglas DC-6B

88 seats • 315 mph

Pratt & Whitney Double Wasp R-2800 (2500 hp) x 4 • 107,000 lb. max. gross take-off weight • 3000 statute miles range

All-Economy Class in the **DC-6B**—
twilight of the piston-engined era.

Length 106 feet • Span 118 feet • Height 29 feet

Development of the DC-6B

Responding to the challenge of Lockheed to out-class its four-engined DC-4, already route-proven with the U.S. Air Forces during the latter part of World War II as the C-54 and the R5D, Douglas stretched the DC-4's fuselage by seven feet, and pressurized it. The launching airline was United, which put the new **DC-6** into service on 27 April 1947. After being grounded for four

months in the winter of 1947-48 because of inflight fire problems, this aircraft was further improved when Slick Airways, an all-cargo operator, ordered the **DC-6A**, a freighter version, and even longer. This type was then produced in a passenger version, the **DC-6B**, five feet longer than the DC-6 (and twelve feet longer than the DC-4). United put it into service on 11 April 1951.

The aircraft was considered to be marginally more economical to operate than the Constellation, and from an engineering viewpoint was easier to put through the system of inspection, maintenance, and overhaul checks, for both airframes and engines. Although later developments of the Douglas line were to outperform the 6B, this was the aircraft that wise old

airline folk would refer to as a thoroughbred. A total of 288 DC-6B's were built for the airlines, plus 175 DC-6s. Including military versions, 704 of the DC-6/DC-6A/DC-6B type were produced by Douglas.

PAN AMERICAN'S DC-6A FLEET

Const. No.	Regist. No.	Pan Am Delivery	Clipper Name
44258	N6258C	30.4.54	*Gladiator*
44259	N6259C	18.5.54	*Jupiter*
44260	N6260C	21.6.54	*Westwind*
45520	N7822C	6.8.58	*Undaunted*
43297	N90908	5.6.58	*Ocean Express*

Non-Stop Trans-Atlantic At Last

The Competition Intensifies

The U.S. coast-to-coast competition between Douglas and Lockheed was repeated on the North Atlantic. Aiming for the non-stop prize, Pan American matched its best equipment against T.W.A.'s Super Constellations, constantly being improved by Kelly Johnson and Lockheed at Burbank. At first **Pan Am** fitted some of its Stratocruisers with extra tanks, and then introduced the **DC-7B**, a slightly improved version of the DC-7, on 13 June 1955. **T.W.A.'s L.1049G**, the Super-G, began service on 1 November 1955, and Pan Am answered back with the **DC-7C**, the **Seven Seas**, on 1 June 1956.

Juan Trippe stuck with the Seven Seas to see Pan American through to the Jet Age. On the North Atlantic, which by now had become the prestige air route of the world, he had to watch patiently as the British airline, **B.O.A.C.**, stole some traffic away with the **Britannia** (see opposite page). T.W.A. also lost some ground, and came close to ordering the British aircraft, and might have done so, had Howard Hughes learned more about it sooner. But the die was cast in preparation for the Jet Era and Juan Trippe had been a major instrument in the casting process.

The Polar Route

With the growing importance of California as a leading economic center with an affluent and mobile population, direct service from Europe to the West Coast became justified. The Scandinavian airline **S.A.S.** was the pioneer, opening service with DC-6Bs on 15-16 November 1954, using airfields in Greenland and Canada as en route stops. The time saved was considerable: as the flight took about 20 hours instead of about 30 via New York. **Canadian Pacific Airlines** joined S.A.S. on 3-4 June 1955, but **Pan American** waited for the availability of enough DC-7Cs so that it could open service on the Great Circle Route on 11 September 1957 with fewer stops. **T.W.A.** followed suit with L.1649A Starliners on 2 October of that year.

The last of the Douglas line of long range piston-engined airliners, the **DC-7C**.

Prelude to the Jet Age

For such an advanced aircraft, the DC-7C had a short service life. Pan American's first DC-7B had been delivered in May 1955, but it only had seven of this series, and had ordered 26 DC-7Cs, including the freighter version, on 14 July 1954. The first one was delivered on 23 April 1956, only two and a half years before Pan American itself was into the Jet Age. They cost $2,250,000 each but within ten years most were disposed of to aircraft traders or the occasional non-scheduled airline; and some were even sold as scrap, an ignominious end to a fine example of commerical airliner technical development.

PAN AMERICAN'S DOUGLAS DC-7 FLEET

Const. No.	Regist. No.	Clipper Name
DC-7B		
44864	N 771PA	Evening Star
44865	N 777PA	Jupiter Rex
44866	N 772PA	Friendship
44867	N 773PA	Endeavour
44868	N 774PA	Winged Racer
44869	N 775PA	Nautilus
44870	N 776PA	Nonpareil
DC-7C		
44874	N 732PA	Black Hawk
44880	N 738PA	Empress of the Skies
44882	N 740PA	Northern Light
44885	N 743PA	Ocean Rover
44886	N 744PA	Pacific Trader
44887	N 745PA	Midnight Sun
45091	N 747PA	Ganges
45092	N 748PA	Georgia
45093	N 749PA	Defender
45094	N 750PA	Matchless
45095	N 751PA	Morning Light
45097	N 753PA	Rainbow
45130	N 756PA	Courser
DC-7CF		
44873	N 731PA	Bald Eagle
44875	N 733PA	Bluejacket
44876	N 734PA	Seven Seas
44877	N 735PA	Caroline
44878	N 736PA	Charger
44879	N 737PA	Climax
44881	N 739PA	Flora Temple
44883	N 741PA	Great Republic
44884	N 742PA	Fidelity
45090	N 746PA	Eclipse
45096	N 752PA	Rambler
45121	N 754PA	Derby
45123	N 755PA	East Indian

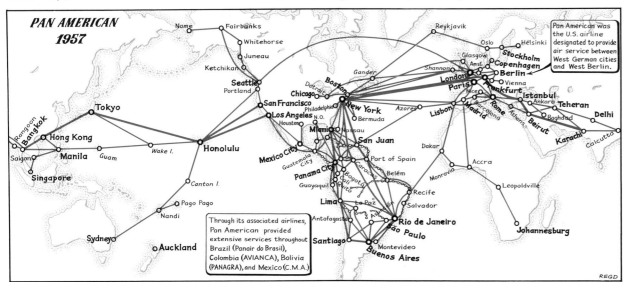

PAN AMERICAN 1957

Pan American was the U.S. airline designated to provide air service between West German cities and West Berlin.

Through its associated airlines, Pan American provided extensive services throughout Brazil (Panair do Brasil), Colombia (AVIANCA), Bolivia (PANAGRA), and Mexico (C.M.A.).

Douglas DC-7C – The "Seven Seas"

84 seats • 355 mph

• Note unusual word spacing of Pan American title. Also, compare antennae configuration to that of DC-4, Pg. 53.

Wright R-3350 (3400 hp) x 4 • 143,000 lb. max. gross take-off weight • 4000 statute miles range

The Spur of Competition

Lockheed had stolen a march on Douglas by producing the Constellation, sleek, fast, and pressurized, to threaten the Santa Monica manufacturer's grip of the commercial market. Douglas was forced to act quickly with an improved version of the DC-4, the **DC-6 series.** Then, T.W.A. introduced the first U.S. transcontinental nonstop service in October 1953 with the **L.1049C** version of the Super Connie. One month later, American Airlines responded with the Douglas **DC-7,** matching the nonstop capability.

The Seven Seas

Douglas then produced a development of the DC-7, the **DC-7B,** with a slightly higher gross weight, permitting either more payload or longer range. Pan American was the first to place this into service, but was followed by only three other U.S. domestic operators before Douglas developed the breed even further. Hitherto, all the four-engined Douglases had flown on the same wing—only the fuselage was stretched. Now, in 1956, an extra wing section was added, increasing the wing area by 12 percent, thus enabling weights, payloads, and tankage all to be increased. The wing also allowed the engines to be placed five feet further away from the fuselage, which was a definite advantage, as the Wright turbo-compound R-3350s tended to have high noise and vibration levels. This **DC-7C** was neatly called **The Seven Seas.** Douglas sold just over 300 of all three DC-7 types, less than the DC-6B production and sales alone. It was the end of the line.

Swan Song of an Airline Generation

Lockheed and T.W.A. played one more competitive card with the **L.1649A Starliner** which had marginally more range than the DC-7C. Its debut was on 1 June 1957, and the British **Bristol Britannia,** agonizingly delayed by a series of misfortunes, entered service on the London-New York route non-stop in both directions, on 19

Length 112 feet • Span 128 feet • Height 32 feet

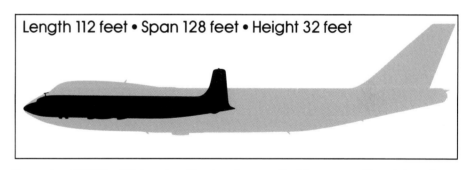

December 1957. The Whispering Giant, as it was called, because of its quiet engines, was the harbinger of Things to Come; for the engines were Bristol Proteus turboprops.

THE DOUGLAS FOUR-ENGINED PROPELLER AIRLINERS

| Series | Engines | | Dimensions (ft) | | | Remarks | Year of First Service |
	Type	hp	Length	Span	Seats		
DC-4	Pratt & Whitney Twin Wasp	1450	94	117	44	Unpressurized	1946
DC-6	Pratt & Whitney R-2800	2100	101	117	56	First pressurized Douglas	1947
DC-6A	Pratt & Whitney R-2800	2500	100	117	—	Freighter	1951
DC-6B	Pratt & Whitney R-2800	2500	106	117	66	Most popular type of the Series	1951
DC-7	Wright R-3350	3250	109	117	70	Non-stop transcontinental U.S.	1953
DC-7B	Wright R-3350	3250	109	117	70	Marginally non-stop transatlantic	1955
DC-7C	Wright R-3350	3400	112	127	84	Non-stop transatlantic	1956

The Jet Age Begins

An Airline Shakes the World

On 13 October 1955, Pan American Airways ordered 45 new jet airliners. Each had twice the capacity of all but the largest of the piston-engined generation, had the potential of trans-Atlantic nonstop range, and was twice as fast. In economic terms this multiplied to about four or five times the productivity of the DC-7Cs or the Super Constellations, and furthermore the reliability of the engines and airframes held out the prospect of far higher levels of annual utilization. The collective economic advantage, measured in seat-mile costs, represented such a dramatic improvement that Boeing hardly had to market the product. The world of airlines beat the proverbial pathway to Boeing's assembly plant doors in Seattle.

Hedging the Bet

Often forgotten is that the order was for **25 Douglas DC-8s and 20 Boeing 707s.** This suggested that Pan American was prepared to support the company which had supplied it with so many reliable aircraft during the postwar years, but was also warning it that its product had to be good and that tradition and sentiment would not guarantee a continued market. In the event, Boeing proved that its determination not to let this chance slip was matched by its actions. It assembled a production and marketing team that outproduced and out-sold the experienced Douglas. More important, Pan American switched to Boeing as its main supplier. And at this time, when Pan American sneezed, the rest of the aviation world felt a severe draught and most of it caught cold or worse.

Day of Infamy for the British

The effect of Pan American's order on the British commercial aircraft industry was shattering. The technical lead which, given a slightly better throw of the dice, could have established the Comet as a permanent, rather than a temporary world-beater, was irrevocably lost. De Havilland was too heavily committed to the Comet line to undertake a completely new design. Vickers worked on a large jet project, the V-1000, but this was abandoned, and many years were to pass before the fine rear-engined VC-10 made its appearance. Before the Boeing 707, Great Britain stood an outside chance of securing perhaps a 25% share of the world's commercial market; now its chances were reduced to the extent that it had to struggle to stay in the market at all, and it did not help itself by a series of appalling blunders from which it never recovered. Pan American's press release read like an obituary in the boardrooms of the British aircraft industry.

The aircraft that started the jet age in 1952, the British **Comet** flew for 20 months in scheduled service before encountering structural problems unforeseen because of lack of continuous high altitude experience.

One of Pan American's early **Boeing 707s,** delivered in 1958.

Juan Trippe, completely in charge.

The 707's Place in History

The lower seat-mile costs mentioned above constituted the biggest advantage, in most emphatic terms, of the Big Jets (as they became known at the time) over previous types. This factor, and this alone, caused the technical revolution which launched the Jet Age. The dramatic increase in speed from the 300 mph of the piston-engined airliners to the 600 mph of the jet giants was only a contributory element in the economic equation. People did not flock to the jets only because (as is so often claimed by the advocates of supersonic and hypersonic airliners) of their speed, but because of the economy fares that the lower operating costs made possible.

The Boeing 707 clearly ranks as one of the half dozen most significant airliners of all time. Closer analysis would probably grant it even higher status. While aircraft such as the Ford Tri-Motor, the Boeing 247, and the Comet had their hours and years of glory, only four commercial airliners have so influenced their contemporary scenes as to launch entire eras of air transport; the **Junkers-F 13**, the **Douglas DC-3**, the **Boeing 707**, and the **Boeing 747.** These aircraft were so good as to survive in a harsh competitive environment for at least two decades and still be a force to be reckoned with. The 707 was in good company.

These photographs, taken by the artists' parents show the inauguration of commercial transatlantic jetliner service by **BOAC's Comet IV** and **Pan Am's 707** (in from a test run only) at New York's Idlewild Airport on Oct. 4, 1958.

Boeing 707-120

143 seats • 600 mph

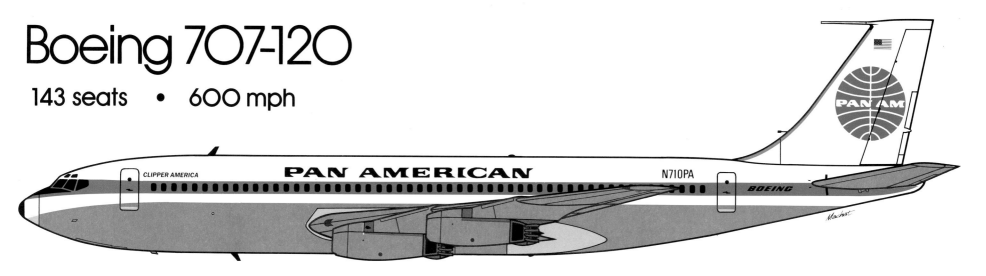

CLIPPER AMERICA

PAN AMERICAN   N710PA   BOEING

Name later changed to "**Jet Clipper Caroline**."

Pratt & Whitney JT3C-6 (13,500 lb thrust) x 4 • 124 tons max. gross take-off weight • 3000 statute miles range

The Dash Eighty

After the British Comet had demonstrated in 1952 that the advent of commercial jet operation was much closer in the aircraft development cycle than aviation engineers, designers, and economists alike had dared to imagine, the United States industry harnessed its vast resources to enter the race.

Boeing drew on its experience of having previously produced piston-engined tankers for the B-29 bomber fleet. The jet-powered **Type 367-80**, or the **Dash Eighty**, first flew on 15 July 1954, five years after the Comet's first flight. This was a little more than two years after the British aircraft's entry into service, and ominously only three months after the second Comet disaster which dashed de Havilland's hopes. Designed as a tanker for the B-47 and B-52 jet bombers, the Air Force ordered a production batch in March 1955.

The Boeing 707

The Dash Eighty's fuselage had to be widened, to match the Douglas DC-8's six-abreast seating. The redesigned Boeing's wings, by comparison with the DC-8, had a slightly greater angle of sweep, 35° against the DC-8's 30° but otherwise the two rival aircraft were remarkably similar, with the Boeing's smaller windows a key recognition feature. The resultant **Boeing 707**, the **100 Series**, equipped with Pratt & Whitney JT3C-6 engines, made its first flight on 20 December 1957, and such was the momentum of the production effort that the first aircraft was delivered to Pan American on 15 August 1958.

Incidentally...

The Soviet Union inaugurated the first *sustained* commercial jet airliner service. The **Tupolev Tu-104** went into service on medium-stage U.S.S.R. domestic routes in 1956, the design bureau in Moscow having taken a giant step when it moved straight from outdated aircraft such as the Ilyushin IL-14 to a twin-engined jet.

But the Tu-104 was never more than a medium-haul airliner, and could not cross the oceans. Indeed, many more years were to pass before the rear-engined **Ilyushin IL-62**, remarkably similar to the British **Vickers VC-10**, was to make its debut on the

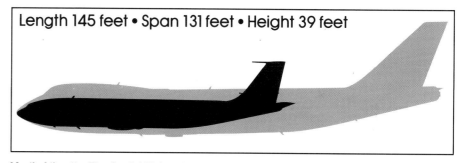

Length 145 feet • Span 131 feet • Height 39 feet

North Atlantic. The Soviet Union, for its own reasons, never placed enough emphasis on the development of main line jets. It fell behind by at least a whole aircraft generation; and it is still behind by at least that measure. The Boeing 707 was a landmark and swept aside all the claims of the British and the Soviets alike for pride of place in the Jet Age.

PAN AMERICAN'S BOEING 707-121 FLEET

Const. No.	Regist. No.	Pan Am Delivery	Clipper Name	Remarks
17586	N 708PA	30.11.58	Constitution	Crashed at Montserrat Island, 30 Nov. 1958
17587	N 707PA	19.12.58	Maria	
17588	N 709PA	15.8.58	Tradewind	Crashed at Elkton, Maryland, 8 Dec. 1963
17589	N 710PA	29.9.58	Caroline	
17590	N 711PA	16.10.58	Mayflower	Inaugurated trans-Atlantic jet service
17591	N 712PA	31.10.58	Washington	
17903	N 778PA	5.12.62	Skylark	Type 707-139
17904	N 779PA	5.12.62	Southern Cross	Type 707-139. Crash landed at New York, 7 April 1964

Change of Allegiance

End of a Partnership

Since the advent in 1933 of the first commercial aircraft that, without stretching too far the terms of the trades description regulations, could be called an airliner, leadership of the manufacturing industry has fallen into distinct eras. Until 1946, when Lockheed forced Santa Monica to share the spoils, Douglas dominated, almost to monopoly status. The 1950s witnessed a threat from the British to make a breakthrough by advanced technology, and during a "wait and see" period, Lockheed elected to build the L.188 Electra. Convair failed to break into the market for long-range pure jets, leaving Douglas and Boeing with the field to themselves from the late 1950s onwards. Although Pan Am gave Douglas the edge in its epoch-making order of 13 October 1955, Boeing subsequently drew steadily ahead, and the traditional understanding between Pan American and Douglas came to an end.

Locked Out

In fact, Pan American changed its original order for the Big Jets so that it took delivery of only nineteen of the 25 DC-8s ordered. It went on to buy about 130 Boeing 707s of all types; and such was the relationship struck up between Pan Am and Boeing that the airline ultimately bought 300 Boeing jet airliners. The effect on Douglas, if not catastrophic, certainly swayed the balance of the market shares during this period. Pan American made the difference between outstanding success and only just getting by.

This was in spite of Douglas producing, in the mid-1960s, what was clearly a superior aircraft in the "Stretched Eight" whose outstanding economic performance would have been of great benefit to Pan American on its heavily travelled routes. It would also have provided an aircraft which could have made the transition in size from the 707/DC-8 generation to the 747 wide-bodied era, thus protecting the operator from severe problems of matching frequency with capacity on routes of varying density.

The reason, or combination of reasons, why Pan American deserted Douglas will probably never be known. Pan American never bought another Douglas aircraft again, and this may have been the beginning of a trend that ultimately led to Pan American's decline, the proverbial cloud no bigger than a man's hand. For when it made its next move, with the Boeing 747, the massive size increment did not match the modest worldwide 1970s traffic growth, which had slowed down considerably from the heady years of the 1960s.

Flirtation with Domestic Routes

On 10 December 1958, **National Airlines**, competing bitterly with Eastern Air Lines on the "gravy run" between New York and Miami, leased Boeing 707s from Pan American, thereby becoming the first U.S. domestic operator of turbojets. The device enabled National to prepare for its own jets, DC-8s, which entered National service on 18 February 1960.

Pan American preceded the lease agreement with a proposed exchange of stock, 25% of National's for 6% of Pan Am's. During post-deregulation days, this would have been an eminently sensible and mutually profitable arrangement. Such an interlocking relationship was then regarded, however, by the Civil Aeronautics Board as sheer heresy, and it ordered a divestment of stock. Had Pan American been able to pull off this deal, Juan Trippe and his advisers may have had a chance to make a true comparison between the Boeing 707 and the DC-8.

JET AGE CHRONOLOGY OF PIONEER SERVICES

Airline	Aircraft	Date	Route	Remarks
B.O.A.C.	Comet 1	2 May 1952	London-Johannesburg	Two crashes in Mediterranean, 10 Jan and 8 Apr 1954, led to grounding and redesign of aircraft
Aeroflot	Tupolev Tu-104	15 September 1956	Moscow-Irkutsk	First commercial jet to enter sustained scheduled service
B.O.A.C.	Comet 4	4 October 1958	London-New York	First trans-Atlantic jet service
Pan American	Boeing 707-121	26 October 1958	New York-Paris	First trans-Atlantic jet service by U.S. airline, and first on a daily schedule

PAN AMERICAN'S DC-8-32 FLEET

Const. No.	Regist. No.	Pan Am Delivery	Clipper Name	Remarks
45253	N 802PA	15.2.61	Cathay	Sold to Delta, 25.8.69
45254	N 801PA	8.4.61	Queen of the Pacific	Sold to Delta, 17.9.69
45255	N 800PA	2.6.61	Flying Cloud	Sold to Panair do Brasil, 29.9.62
45256	N 803PA	7.2.60	Mandarin	First delivery. Sold to Delta, 30.12.68
45257	N 804PA	17.3.60	Midnight Sun	Sold to United Air Lines, 15.11.68
45258	N 805PA	20.3.60	Nightingale	Sold to United Air Lines, 20.9.68
45259	N 806PA	7.5.60	Northern Light	Sold to United Air Lines, 27.9.68
45260	N 807PA	3.6.60	Polynesia	Sold to United Air Lines, 5.10.67
45261	N 808PA	10.6.60	Gauntlet	Sold to United Air Lines, 27.10.67
45262	N 809PA	22.6.60	Great Republic	Sold to United Air Lines, 18.10.68
45263	N 810PA	17.7.60	Intrepid	Sold to United Air Lines, 3.11.67
45264	N 811PA	23.8.60	Pacific Trader	Sold to United Air Lines, 11.10.68
45265	N 812PA	10.9.60	Blue Jacket	Disposed of on 13.5.71
45266	N 813PA	13.10.60	Bostonian	Sold to Air Cargo, 10.6.69
45267	N 814PA	18.10.60	Caroline	Sold to Delta, 31.12.68
45268	N 815PA	7.11.60	Charger	Sold to Air Cargo, 11.6.69
45269	N 816PA	10.11.60	East Indian	Sold to Delta, 30.12.68
45270	N 817PA	15.12.60	Derby	Sold to Delta, 31.12.68
45271	N 818PA	22.12.60	Rambler	Sold to Pan. do Brasil, 23.11.63; ret. to Pan Am 9.9.65, sold to Delta 1968

Pan American launched the **Douglas DC-8** with the first order, but subsequently turned to Boeing for all future jets.

Douglas DC-8-32

127 seats • 590 mph

Pratt & Whitney JT4A-11 (17,500 lb thrust) x 4 • 157 tons max. gross take-off weight • 3500 statute miles range

Back to the Drawing Board

Whether or not Douglas was superstitious, the date 13 October 1955 was certainly an unlucky day at Long Beach. Overnight all plans to build a turboprop airliner were dropped as the Pan Am order brought the startling realization that the folks in Seattle had stolen a march.

Douglas lost precious time in developing its new breed. The Boeing 707 actually went into service with Pan American an agonizing sixteen months before the first DC-8 was delivered; and but for faithful customers like United, K.L.M., and other European airlines, as well as Japan Air Lines, Douglas would never have come close to covering the costs of the DC-8 production. As it was, even though some 450 aircraft were sold, the company estimated that it lost money on the entire project.

Superb Development

The losses would have been much greater, had Douglas not been past masters at developing commercial airliners, The original **DC-8** was longer than the Boeing 707 by about six feet and was only shorter than the longest version of the 707 by about two and a half feet. Douglas was able to stretch its basic DC-8 fuselage by no less than 37 feet. Boeing, in contrast, now paid a penalty for the higher wing-sweep angle and a design which would have resulted in the tail scraping the ground as the aircraft rotated on take-off.

Douglas proceeded to develop a sub-family of larger airliners which were quite remarkable. The **DC-8-61** first flew on 14 March 1966 and could carry an unprecedented 252 passengers in an all-economy layout. Shortly after United's first service on 24 February 1967, Braniff introduced the **DC-8-62**. This version was only six feet longer than the original DC-8 but had a new wing, and with greater fuel capacity had an enormous range. The Scandinavian S.A.S. and its associate Thai International, for example, regularly flew it non-stop on routes such as Copenhagen- Bangkok.

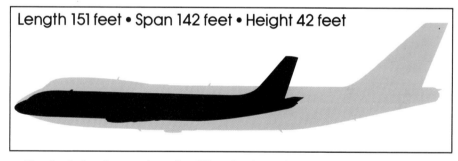

Length 151 feet • Span 142 feet • Height 42 feet

The final development, and a fitting finale to the era of the Big Jets was the **DC-8-63**, combining all the best qualities of the Douglas thoroughbred design and coming close to being the most economical long-range airliner ever built.

THE DOUGLAS DC-8 FAMILY

Series	Engines (P & W)*		Dimensions (ft)		Allup Weight (short tons)	Max. Seats	Range (st. miles)	Year of First Service
	Type	Thrust each (lb)	Length	Span				
DC-8-10	JT3C-6	13,500	151	142	137	179	3800	1959
DC-8-20	JT4A-3	15,000	151	142	140	179	4000	1960
DC-8-30	JT4A-11	17,500	151	142	157	179	4500	1960
DC-8-40	Conway	18,000	151	142	163	179	4800	1960
DC-8-50	JT3D-3B	18,000	151	142	163	179	4800	1961
DC-8-61	JT3D-3B	18,000	187	142	164	252	4500	1967
DC-8-62	JT3D-7	19,000	157	148	175	189	5500	1967
DC-8-63	JT3D-7	19,000	187	148	177	252	5000	1968

*Except the Rolls-Royce Conway powered DC-8-40.

The Era of Domination

Statistics Don't Always Lie

The table of data on this and the following page tells its own story. Such was Pan American's dominance of the international airline arena during the 1960s—a decade when the volume of air transport quadrupled, that it acquired 120 of the **Boeing 707-300** Series. Twenty-six of these were of the basic version, with Pratt & Whitney JT4A-9 straight jet engines—the so-called "Ole Smokies" as they became known rather unkindly in later years, along with the original JT3C-6 engines of the 100 Series. Then came the JT3D-3 turbofan, or bypass—engines which resulted in the "B" versions and the further developments which resulted in the Advanced models. The turbofans gave the aircraft greater range, capacity, and profitability than before, and above all cut about half a mile off the almost two miles takeoff distance required for the Boeing 707.

This total of 120 does not include the eight 707-100 series (pages 66-67) or the nine 720Bs (pages 72-73). Thus Pan American had no less than 137 of the 707 family, such was the pace of airline growth during the successful Sixties. The last two digits of the series number -321, incidentally, refers to the customer identification allocated by Boeing and Pan American's was -21. Pan American bought six from T.W.A. (or more correctly the Hughes Tool Company, which always bought aircraft and leased them to Hughes's airline.) The series number of these was thus -331, denoting that airline.

All the Boeing 707s served Pan American well and were intensively used for an average of about 15 years, until they were gradually retired when the Boeing 747s replaced them.

On Top of the World

During this heady period, Pan American seemed to be able to do no wrong. By the middle of 1962 it had completed 100,000 Atlantic flights, a figure not even approached by any other airline at that time, although the pendulum was to swing later on. On 7 March 1963 it moved into the new building which towered over Grand Central Station, New York, with the *Pan Am* abbreviation in huge letters on the top, and visible for several miles up or down Park Avenue, almost symbolically telling the world the aviation industry had taken over from surface travel.

Subtle changes were being made to the network. Interests in Latin American associates, including substantial organizations such as the two Mexican airlines and Panair do Brasil, were sold in the early 1960s. With possible ambitions to acquire a connecting domestic network—by buying National Airlines (see page 68)—and even to merge with T.W.A., the Atlantic and Pacific Divisions amalgamated to form the Overseas Division at the end of 1959, and the Latin American Division was closed down in 1964.

This was the year when Harold Gray, once a pilot in the 1930s with a Mexican airline, later Pan American's Chief Pilot and one of the first to fly the Atlantic in the Boeing flying boats, succeeded Juan Trippe as President. This was the beginning of the end of an era during which Pan American had been run almost single-handedly by an amiable despot. Trippe had built the airline from nothing to world dominance in twenty years, and had maintained that dominance with confidence and complete authority until he handed over. He finally retired on 7 May 1968, a true giant of the airline world.

One of the great airliners of all time, the **Boeing 707-320** (Series -321 in Pan American service).

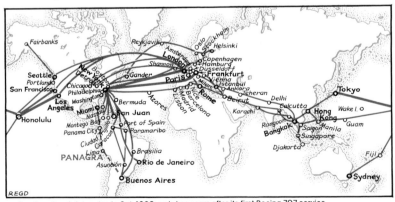

Pan American's jet routes in Oct. 1960, *only two years* after its first Boeing 707 service.

Const. No.	Regist. No.	Clipper Name
Boeing 707-321 (*First Del. 19 July 1959*)		
17592	N 714PA	Golden Eagle
17593	N 715PA	*Liberty Bell
17594	N 716PA	Flying Eagle
17595	N 717PA	Fleetwing
17596	N 718PA	Invincible
17597	N 719PA	Windward
17598	N 720PA	Fairwind
17599	N 721PA	Splendid
17600	N 722PA	Lark
17601	N 723PA	Viking
17602	N 724PA	Mercury
17603	N 725PA	Aurora
17604	N 726PA	Westward Ho
17605	N 727PA	Mohawk
17606	N 728PA	Peerless
17607	N 729PA	Isabella
17608	N 730PA	Bald Eagle
18083	N 757PA	Pathfinder
18084	N 758PA	Resolute
18085	N 759PA	Freedom
Boeing 707-331 (*First Del. 5 Nov. 1959*)		
17674	N 701PA	*Donald McKay
17677	N 702PA	Hotspur
17680	N 703PA	Dashaway
17683	N 704PA	Defiance
17686	N 705PA	Wing of the Morning
17689	N 706PA	Courier
Boeing 707-321B (*First Del. 12 Apr. 1962*)		
18335	N 760PA	Evening Star
18336	N 761PA	Friendship
18337	N 762PA	*Endeavor
18338	N 763PA	Yankee
18339	N 764PA	Nautilus
Boeing 707-321C (*First Del. 2 May 1963*)		
18579	N 765PA	Gladiator
18580	N 766PA	*Jupiter
18591	N 767PA	Challenger
Boeing 707-321CF (*First Del. 27 Feb. 1964*)		
18714	N 790PA	*Courser
18715	N 791PA	Fidelity
18716	N 792PA	Good Hope
18717	N 793PA	Messenger
18718	N 794PA	Undaunted
18765	N 795PA	Jupiter Rex
18766	N 796PA	Mermaid
18767	N 797PA	Northwind
18790	N 798PA	Caribbean
18824	N 799PA	Racer

Boeing 707-321C
135 seats • 600 mph

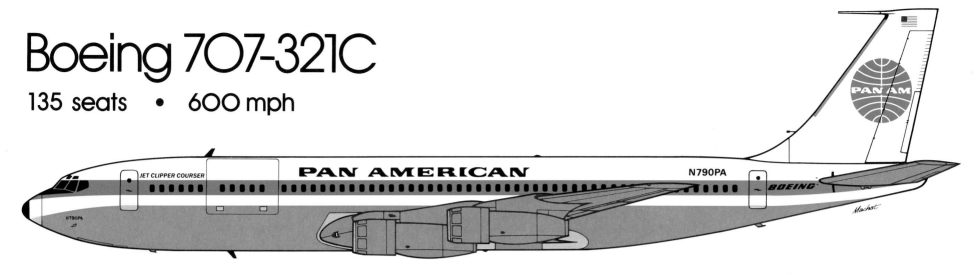

• Ventral fins appeared below the tails on certain models of **707-320** series. Pan Am freighters did not have them.

Pratt & Whitney JT3D (18,000 lb thrust) x 4 • 168 tons max. gross take-off weight • 4000 statute miles range

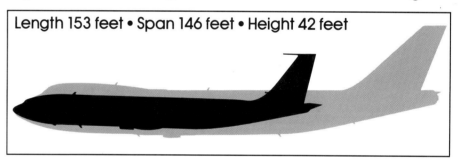

Length 153 feet • Span 146 feet • Height 42 feet

Const. No.	Regist. No.	Clipper Name
Boeing 707-321B Advanced (*First Del. 6 Feb. 1965)		
18832	N 401PA	*Dauntless
18833	N 402PA	Black Hawk
18834	N 403PA	Goodwill
18835	N 404PA	Seven Seas
18836	N 405PA	Stargazer
18837	N 406PA	Kingfisher
18838	N 407PA	Celestial
18839	N 408PA	Morning Star
18840	N 409PA	Eclipse
18841	N 410PA	Argonaut
18842	N 412PA	Empress of the Skies
18956	N 414PA	Ann McKim
18957	N 415PA	Monsoon
18958	N 416PA	Paul Jones
18959	N 417PA	Winged Racer
18960	N 418PA	Yankee Ranger
19264	N 419PA	Gem of the Skies
19265	N 420PA	Monarch of the Skies
19266	N 421PA	Charmer
19275	N 422PA	Mount Vernon
19276	N 423PA	Glory of the Skies
19277	N 424PA	Golden West
19278	N 425PA	Virginia
19361	N 426PA	National Eagle
19362	N 427PA	Crystal Palace
19363	N 428PA	Star of Hope

Const. No.	Regist. No.	Clipper Name
19364	N 433PA	Glad Tidings
19365	N 434PA	Queen of the Sky
19366	N 435PA	Celestial Empire
19374	N 453PA	Universe
19376	N 454PA	Radiant
19378	N 455PA	Waverly
19693	N 491PA	Chariot of Fame
19694	N 492PA	Eagle Wing
19695	N 493PA	Priscilla Alden
19696	N 494PA	Malay
19697	N 495PA	Nor'wester
19698	N 496PA	Northern Eagle
19699	N 497PA	Victory
20019	N 880PA	Emerald Isle
20020	N 881PA	Reindeer
20021	N 882PA	Queen of the Pacific
20022	N 883PA	Kathay
20023	N 884PA	Nightingale
20024	N 885PA	Northern Light
20025	N 886PA	Sea Lark
20026	N 887PA	Flora Temple
20027	N 890PA	Gauntlet
20028	N 891PA	Gem of the Ocean
20029	N 892PA	Star King
20030	N 893PA	Whirlwind
20031	N 894PA	Polynesian
20032	N 895PA	Herald of the Morning
20033	N 896PA	Norseman
20034	N 897PA	Ocean Express

Const. No.	Regist. No.	Clipper Name
Boeing 707-321C Advanced (*First Del. 14 Dec. 1966)		
19267	N 445PA	Archer
19268	N 446PA	Climax
20016	N 870PA	Dreadnought
20017	N 871PA	Sirius
20018	N 872PA	Swordfish
Boeing 707-321CF Advanced (*First Del. 1 May 1967)		
19269	N 447PA	*Onward
19270	N 448PA	Pacific Raider
19271	N 449PA	Red Rover
19272	N 450PA	Borinquen

Const. No.	Regist. No.	Clipper Name
19273	N 451PA	Union
19274	N 452PA	Golden Fleece
19367	N 457PA	Phoenix
19368	N 458PA	Titian
19369	N 459PA	Western Continent
19370	N 460PA	Starlight
19371	N 461PA	Rising Sun
19372	N 462PA	Eagle
19373	N 463PA	Queen of the East
19375	N 473PA	Pride of America
19377	N 474PA	Morning Glory
19379	N 475PA	Sea Serpent

Variations on a Theme

Marketing Style

Although Boeing had unmistakably "seen Douglas off in a big way"—as one impartial British commentator put it—it still had its work cut out to overcome the marketing strength of Douglas which, with its world-wide network of agents, representatives, and travelling salesmen, possessed a solid base from which to conduct its DC-8 campaign. Boeing countered this by producing what it called a family of airliners, emphasizing the commonality of parts between the various models. Although this did not begin to look like a family until the Boeing 727 was launched in 1963, the idea was nevertheless effective, even though all the 707s seemed to look the same.

Boeing made much of its willingness to build a 707 that would meet a customer's precise requirements, whereas Douglas was inclined to be more rigid, offering a choice of DC-8 series but reluctant to deviate from the basic specifications of each series. The Boeing 707s for Braniff and the Australian airline QANTAS were sized and specified precisely to the requirements of each and no others were built.

A Smaller 707

As the best example of its flexibility, Boeing produced the Model 720, with a fuselage sixteen feet shorter and a wing span fifteen feet shorter than the 707's. First ordered by United Air Lines, it marked that airline's return to the Boeing camp after its extensive DC-8 program, and went into service on the one-stop Chicago-Los Angeles route on 5 July 1960. Other orders followed but the Boeing 720 did not sell in great numbers. Nevertheless, it served Boeing's purpose in being able to offer an airliner which was smaller than the 707/DC-8 standard and was suitable for medium-stage routes of lower traffic density.

Curiously, when, as the 720B, the variant was fitted with the Pratt & Whitney JT3D fan engines, and because of its lighter weight, it had for a short time the longest range, exceeding 4,000 miles, of any commercial airliner. Pan American had a few 720Bs but did not use them extensively. Nine were delivered from 1963 to 1965, mainly for use in the Caribbean and Latin America, but all were disposed of by 1974.

Every Little Bit Helps

While the Boeing 720 did not sell in such numbers as the Boeing 707-300 series, its contribution to the 707 program as a whole was significant. It actually outsold the original -100 Series (154 v. 146) and was thus almost a fifth of the total sales of 848. In the unrelenting fight for commercial markets among the few manufacturers, it was a major factor in the virtual elimination of the Convair 880, also marketed as a mainline jet smaller than all the others. United's 720 order was a big nail in Convair's coffin.

Arguably, the Boeing 720/720B, combined with Pan American's 128 other Boeings, made the difference in relative market shares, particularly when compared with the Douglas DC-8. Had Boeing not obtained a share of what could have been almost exclusively Convair's medium-haul market, and had Douglas snatched the lion's share of the Pan American requirement, Boeing's and Douglas's sales might have been about equal, at perhaps 600 each. In the event, the Boeing 707s outsold all the DC-8s by a ratio of 3:2.

The basic **Boeing 707-100**, first of a great line of classic airliners.

The **Boeing 707-320** (Series -321 in Pan American service).

The flight deck instrumentation of the new jets was a marked advance

PAN AMERICAN'S BOEING 720B FLEET
(*First Delivery 13 February 1963)

Const. No.	Regist. No.	Clipper Name
18033	N 780PA	Carib
18036	B 781PA	Flying Arrow
18037	N 782PA	Desoto
18057	N 783PA	Bonita
18059	N 784PA	Panama
18060	N 785PA	Balboa
18248	N 786PA	Winged Arrow
18250	N 787PA	Guiding Star
18251	N 788PA	Nonpareil

The **Boeing 720B** was, unusually, a shortened version of an already successful airliner formula, designed to match a special need.

Boeing 720B

127 seats • 600 mph

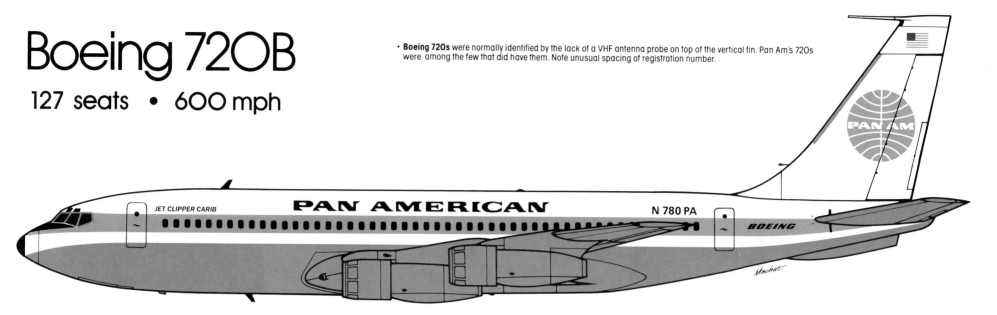

• **Boeing 720s** were normally identified by the lack of a VHF antenna probe on top of the vertical fin. Pan Am's 720s were among the few that did have them. Note unusual spacing of registration number.

PAN AMERICAN

JET CLIPPER CARIB

N 780 PA

BOEING

Machat

Pratt & Whitney JT3C-7 (12,500 lb thrust) x 4 • 115 tons max. gross take-off weight • 4000 statute miles range

Boeing 720B

Boeing 707-120

Boeing 707-320B

Length 137 feet • Span 131 feet • Height 38 feet

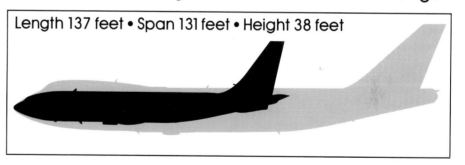

THE BOEING 707 FAMILY

Series	Engines (P & W)		Dimensions (ft)		Allup Weight (short tons)	Max. Seats	Range (st. miles)	Year of First Service
	Type	Thrust each (lb)	Length	Span				
[1]Boeing 707-100	JT3C-6	13,500	145	131	124	181	3,000	1958
Boeing 707-200	JT4A-3	15,800	145	131	129	181	4,500	1960
Boeing 707-300	JT4A-3	15,800	153	142	156	189	4,500	1959
[2]Boeing 707-300B	JT3D-3	18,000	153	146	168	202	5,000	1963
Boeing 720	JT3C-7	12,500	137	131	115	167	3,000	1960
Boeing 720B	JT3D-3	18,000	137	131	117	167	5,000	1961

[1]A special version was built for QANTAS, the -138, 10 feet shorter than standard, and with longer range capability.
[2]Several airlines ordered B-707s with Rolls-Royce Conway engines, with little difference in overall performance.

The Most Successful Airliner

Another Large Fleet

Pan American was not primarily a short- or even medium-haul airline, but it did have pockets of such networks in its system, notably in the Caribbean and in Europe. Consequently, in its own good time, Pan Am ordered 25 Boeing **727-121s** (21 was Boeing's numerical code for Pan Am) on 1 February 1965, at $4,110,000 each, to serve these routes. They were later supplemented by a large influx of 727s of both the **-100** and the **-200** series when it purchased **National Airlines** in 1980. Altogether, Pan Am had 97, an impressive number for a second-line aircraft.

The I.G.S.

One part of Europe where the Boeing 727s saw intensive service was on the **Internal German Service (I.G.S.)** This is a special kind of commercial airline operation which does not fall into any of the Five Freedoms of the Air categories, as defined by the International Civil Aviation Organization (ICAO). Because of the special political status of the city of Berlin, an anachronistic survival of World War II, the German national airline, Lufthansa, is not allowed to fly there; and the airline service is provided by Pan Am and British Airways, under the auspices of the Allied Control Commission.

Boeing 727s were also based in Europe to provide feeder services in that continent by a change of gauge from the wide-bodies arriving at the main European gateway airports such as London, Paris, or Frankfurt.

Clippers Galore

The Boeing 727s, and the 737s that later supplemented them on the I.G.S., bore some unlikely Clipper names. In the past many of Pan Am's aircraft had changed their names, often to be associated with the areas or cities served, as the aircraft were deployed around the worldwide network. Now, many a Clipper Ship bore many a Teutonic name as well as those of the cities served, such as Stuttgart or Hamburg.

In the lists of aircraft on this and other pages, the Clipper names selected are those preferred in the Pan American permanent records. Frequently the same Boeing 727 had, at different times, as many as five different names, and the etymology and the reasoning behind the selection would make an excellent subject for a book in its own right.

The de Havilland (later Hawker Siddeley) Type 121 **Trident** was the first trijet airliner. It surrendered its lead to Boeing by serious marketing misjudgments.

Pan American had 27 of the earlier Series 100 **Boeing 727s** and later acquired 19 more from National Airlines.

The most successful airliner of all time, Boeing sold no less than 1,260 of the **Boeing 727-200**, as well as 572 of the -100 series. Pan Am had 51.

Const. No.	Regist. No.	Clipper Name
PAN AMERICAN'S BOEING 727 FLEET (The dates indicate year of first delivery of each sub-series)		
Boeing 727-121 (1965)		
18992	N 314PA	Sam Houston
18993	N 315PA	White Falcon
18994	N 316PA	Buena Vista
18995	N 317PA	De Soto
18996	N 318PA	Inca
18997	N 319PA	Spreeathen
18998	N 320PA	John Alden
18999	N 321PA	Matchless
19005	N 323PA	Langer Lulatsch
19006	N 324PA	Pocohontas
19007	N 325PA	Luftikus
19035	N 326PA	Raven
19036	N 327PA	Meteor
19037	N 328PA	Natchez
19038	N 329PA	Lightfoot
19257	N 355PA	Archer
19258	N 356PA	Argonaut
19259	N 357PA	Berolina
19260	N 358PA	Flotte Motte
19261	N 359PA	Sause Wind
19262	N 360PA	Golden Rule
Boeing 727-121QC (1966)		
19134	N 339PA	Schrager Otto
19135	N 340PA	Dusendroschke
19136	N 341PA	Shooting Star
19137	N 342PA	Golden Age
Boeing 727-121C (1967) Sold to Air Vietnam, Jan. 1968		
19818	N 388PA	Ganges
19819	N 389PA	Golden Light
Boeing 727-135 (ex-National) (1980)		
18811	N 4610	Pathfinder
18812	N 4611	Empress
18813	N 4612	Pacific Raider
18814	N 4613	Prima Donna
18815	N 4614	Reporter
18816	N 4615	Ring Leader
18817	N 4616	Young Mechanic
18845	N 4617	Young Brander
18846	N 4618	Wizard
18847	N 4619	Roman

Boeing 727-100

94 seats • 580 mph

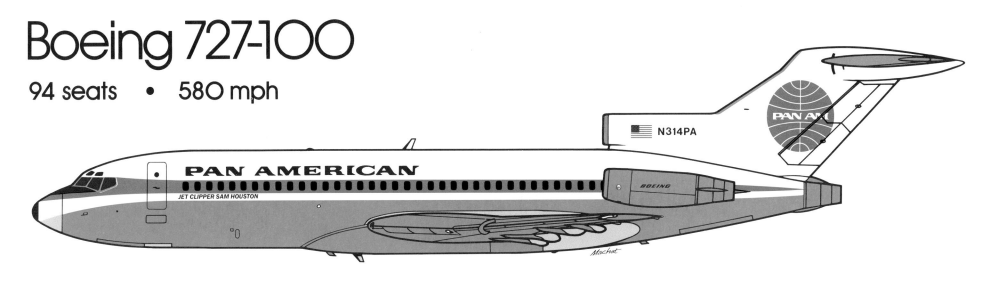

N314PA

PAN AMERICAN

JET CLIPPER SAM HOUSTON

Machat

Pratt & Whitney JT8D (14,000 lb thrust) x 3 • 71 tons max. gross take-off weight • 1700 statute miles range

Boeing Wins some Battles–and also the War

On a previous occasion, the Boeing company had been able to use its massive production strength to overcome a challenge from across the Atlantic, when the British very nearly stole a substantial portion of the airliner market by its initiative in developing the world's first jet airliner, the D.H. 106 Comet. Unforeseen problems associated with structural design denied the British their chance, and arguably luck was not on their side. Boeing cashed in on the unexpected opportunity and launched the 707.

Now, in the late 1950s, history repeated itself, except on this occasion luck had nothing to do with the British failure. The same company that built the Comet, de Havilland, offered Boeing a world market, on a plate. Luck was not a factor in the appalling decisions made during the development of its Type 121, the **Trident,** the world's first trijet airliner, fitted with engines at the rear, like the Caravelle. Not only did D.H. shorten the original fuselage, which had been correctly sized for the market in western Europe and the United States; it also invited Boeing to inspect it, under the naïve impression that some kind of cooperative production could be arranged. Boeing could not have done a better job, had they employed a team of fifth columnists to infiltrate the de Havilland organization. The Boeing 727-100 was remarkably similar to the first Trident, the one that never flew.

Off to the Races

Even with an aircraft that had lost the advantage it once had, not only in being right for the market, but also being about 20 months ahead of Boeing when it started, de Havilland put up a brave fight against the **Boeing 727**—for this was the aircraft that Boeing announced three weeks after arriving back from its inspection trip to the Hatfield factory in England in 1960. Boeing won important sales battles in Japan and Australia, and with the U.S. home market comfortably in its pocket, it launched the most successful commercial airliner program in history.

The **Boeing 727-100** first flew on 9 February 1963, thirteen months to the day after the Trident. But it went into service well before the Trident on 1 February 1964, with

Length 132 feet • Span 108 feet • Height 34 feet

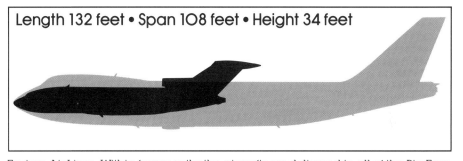

Eastern Air Lines. Within four months the aircraft was delivered to all of the Big Four U.S. domestic airlines, and by the time Pan American started to receive its consignment, 727s were rolling off the production line at Seattle like Chevrolets in Detroit.

Const. No.	Regist. No.	Clipper Name
Boeing 727-135 (ex-National) (1980)cont.		
19165	N 4620	*Sportsman*
19166	N 4621	*Stowaway*
19167	N 4622	*Templar*
Boeing 727-151 (ex-National, ex-Northwest) (1980)		
18804	N 5607	*Wild Ranger*
18805	N 5608	*Yankee Ranger*
18806	N 5609	*Norseman*
18942	N 3605	*Viking*
18943	N 3606	*Wild Hunter*
19124	N 604NA	*Troubadour*

PAN AM

Permutations On The Pedigree

Boeing 727-204 (Ord. by Ozark, deliv. to Pan Am)(1979)		
21849	N 361PA	*Berlin*
21850	N 362PA	*Frankfurt*

Boeing 727-214 (ex-PSA) (1984)		
20678	N 373PA	*High Flyer*
20679	N 374PA	*Flying Arrow*
20680	N 375PA	*Flying Cloud*

Boeing 727-221 (1981)		
22535	N 363PA	*Racer*
22536	N 364PA	*Whistler*
22537	N 365PA	*Peerless*
22538	N 366PA	*Expounder*
22539	N 367PA	*Matchless*
22540	N 368PA	*Goodwill*
22541	N 369PA	*Hotspur*
22542	N 370PA	*Splendid*

Boeing 727-235 (ex-National) (1980)		
19450	N 4730	*Fidelity*
19451	N 4731	*Alert*
19452	N 4732	*Challenger*
19453	N4733	*Charger*
19454	N 4734	*Charmer*
19455	N 4735	*Daring*
19456	N 4736	*Dashaway*
19457	N 4737	*Defiance*
19458	N 4738	*Electric*
19459	N 4739	*Electric Spark*
19460	N 4740	*Endeavor*
19461	N 4741	*Defender*
19462	N 4742	*Friendship Force*
19463	N 4743	*Good Hope*
19465	N 4745	*Invincible*
19466	N 4746	*Intrepid*
19467	N 4747	*Lookout*

Const. No.	Regist. No.	Clipper Name
Boeing 727-235 (ex-National) (1980) cont.		
19468	N 4748	*Progressive*
19469	N 4749	*Quick Step*
19470	N 4750	*Rapid*
19471	N 4751	*Competitor*
19472	N 4752	*Surprise*
19473	N 4753	*Undaunted*
19474	N 4754	*Resolute*
Boeing 727-295 (ex-Delta, ex-Northeast) (1983)		
20248	N 371PA	*Friendship*
20249	N 372PA	*Onward*
Boeing 727-227 (ex-People Express) (1986)		
20772	N 551PE	*Argonaut*
20773	N 552PE	*Red Jacket*
20774	N 553PE	*Empress*
20775	N 554PE	*Mohawk*
20837	N 555PE	*Pathfinder*
20838	N 556PE	*Rambler*
20839	N 557PE	*Sportsman*
20840	N 558PE	*Yankee*
Boeing 727-230 (ex-Lufthansa) (1986)		
20430	N 876UM	*Yankee Ranger*
20525	N 877UM	*Glad Tidings*
20431	N 878UM	*Fleetwing*
20526	N 879UM	*Northwind*

BOEING

The most popular family in the sky.

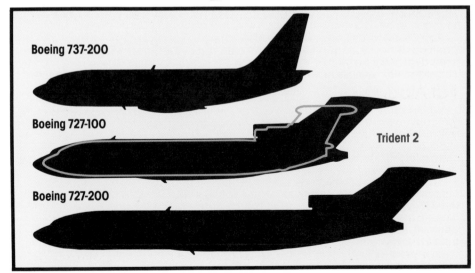

The Ideal Stretch

When Boeing stretched the length of the 727's fuselage to almost exactly the same length as that of the Boeing 707-320's, it must have known that its biggest problem would be to keep the market supplied. Burgeoning traffic increases had created an almost insatiable demand for short- and medium-range airliners, and the 163-seat **727-200** was ideal. The first one flew on 27 July 1967. It had only half the gross weight of the 707, as it did not need the fuel for long range. Nevertheless, it could fly 2,000 miles with full payload, and, at a pinch, this was almost transcontinental range. What airline could ask for more?

Boeing built 1,832 of both series of 727s, 1,260 of which were of the -200 series. This represented a turnover in the $10 billion dollar range, a great deal more than the annual budget of at least half of the members of the United Nations, most of which, however, managed to raise the funds to buy a Boeing or two.

Boeing 737-200

115 seats • 570 mph

Pratt & Whitney JT8D (14,500 lb thrust) x 2 • 52 tons max. gross take-off weight • 2135 statute miles range

Twin-Jet Development

If the competition for the trijet market had been stiff, that for the twinjets was intense, and there were three contenders, not two. Once again the British had made the early running, with the British Aircraft Corporation's BAC One-Eleven, which went into service with Braniff on 25 April 1965. Like the Caravelle, the Trident and the Boeing 727, the One-Eleven's engines were mounted on the rear of the fuselage. But by the time of its first service, Douglas had produced a similar aircraft, the DC-9, which, in its first version, the DC-9-10, had first flown on 25 February of the same year.

The Douglas company outsold B.A.C. very quickly because, true to Douglas tradition, it developed the basic type almost as soon as the first blueprints were signed off. Indeed, the DC-9-30, the most popular of the line, was into service on 1 February 1967, with Delta, before Boeing got into the twin-jet act.

Fat Albert

Going against the apparent tide of design trends, Boeing decided to mount the 737 engines on the wing. This was partly because it had taken the decision to make yet another permutation of the possibilities of the successful 727 fuselage and by shortening it, had compromised engine location. However, although the stubby shape led to ribald remarks from the aesthetically-minded, and the low-slung engines drew serious reservations from the technical critics, Boeing perservered.

The 737-100 first flew on 9 April 1967 and went into service with the German airline Lufthansa, and was not a marketing success. But Boeing soon followed this up with the 737-200, which, although slow in the early years, became a big winner. United was the first operator, starting service on 28 April 1968, and slowly but surely, Boeing began to steal the markets away from Douglas and B.A.C., which by now was a poor third in the running. Once again, Boeing was ready to comply with special customer wishes, producing its now well-known gravel kit to enable the 737, even with its low-slung engines, to be able to use strips that the rear-engined rivals could not.

Length 100 feet • Span 93 feet • Height 37 feet

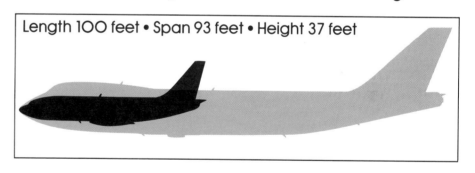

PAN AMERICAN'S BOEING 737 FLEET

Const. No.	Regist. No.	Clipper Name	Const. No.	Regist. No.	Clipper Name
20205	N 383PA	Steglitz	19059	N 69AF	Charlottenburg
21719	N 385PA	Berlin	20670	N 380PA	Neukolln
20440	N 4902W	Wilmersdorf	20588	N 381PA	Wedding
19921	N 382PA	Kreuzberg	22276	N 387PA	Tiergarten
19553	N 63AF	Schoneberg	22277	N 388PA	Reinickendorf
19549	N 64AF	Spandau	22516	N 389PA	Frankfurt
19554	N 67AF	Tempelhof	21739	N 70723	Luftikus
	N 68AF	Zehlendorf	21740	N 70724	Spreeathern

All are in the B-737-200 series.

The Ultimate Airliner

Pan Am Does It Again!

On several previous occasions, Pan American had set the pace of airliner sponsorship to the extent that it had been the launching customer for many a famous line of aircraft, from the Sikorskys, Martins, and Boeings of the flying boat era to the Big Jets. In 1955 Juan Trippe had shaken the airline world by ordering 25 Douglas DC-8s and 20 Boeing 707s, to usher in the jet age for the United States airline industry. He then repeated the process, even more dramatically.

With the rate of increase of airline traffic keeping to an average of about 15% per year over several decades, larger aircraft were obviously necessary to keep up with the growth. Trippe had always been far bolder than his contemporaries in going for larger aircraft; indeed he seemed to have followed a policy of ordering types which were typically twice the size of the previous generation.

In the late 1960s, following a period of unprecedented growth, especially in transatlantic traffic, other considerations arose. In the past, airlines had been able to cope with the additional demand by other means, besides simply adding more or larger aircraft to the fleet. Faster aircraft—as in the case of the quantum leap from piston-engined aircraft to jets—took care of growth, because far more hours and miles could be flown in a given time, thus earning more revenue. Also, streamlined operating procedures enabled aircraft to fly more hours per day, thus extracting more productivity for the same investment. Finally, with better reservations procedures, load factors—the percentage of seats filled—steadily improved. The average productivity of a DC-6B was based on an average cruising speed of about 300 mph, an annual utilization of about 2500 hours, and a load factor of perhaps 52%. The Boeing 707's was based on 550 mph, 4000 hours utilization, and about 60%.

By 1970, when Pan American introduced the Boeing 747, it had reached, in company with other leading airlines, the limits of reasonable levels of speed, utilization, and load factor. The only way to increase capacity, apart from adding frequencies—another method of coping with increased demand, but which was practically impossible, because of airport and airway congestion—was to increase the aircraft size.

This time, Trippe went for broke. The new Pan American airliner generation was more than twice as big as the Boeing 707's which were currently the flagships; and almost twice as big as the biggest airliner then in service, the "stretched" Douglas DC-8-63. Predictably, the new airliner was immediately dubbed the Jumbo Jet, a name deplored by many, but destined to stick to the type, whether the purists liked it or not.

A Pan American **Boeing 747** takes off from John F. Kennedy Airport, New York.

PAN AMERICAN'S BOEING 747 FLEET

Const. No.	Regist. No.	Pan Am Delivery	Clipper Name
Series 121			
19637	N731PA	11.7.70	Ocean Express
19638	N732PA	13.7.70	Ocean Telegraph
19639	N747PA	3.10.70	Juan T. Trippe
19640	N733PA	12.12.69	Pride of the Sea
19641	N734PA	19.12.69	Champion of the Seas
19642	N735PA	9.1.70	Spark of the Ocean
19643	N736PA	20.1.70	Victor
19644	N737PA	21.1.70	Ocean Herald
19645	N738PA	5.2.70	Belle of the Sea
19646	N739PA	15.2.70	Maid of the Seas
19647	N740PA	24.2.70	Ocean Pearl
19648	N741PA	28.2.70	Sparking Wave
19649	N742PA	2.3.70	Neptune's Car
19650	N743PA	28.3.70	Black Sea
19651	N744PA	21.3.70	Ocean Spray
19652	N748PA	31.3.70	Crest of the Wave
19653	N749PA	10.4.70	Dashing Wave
19654	N750PA	26.4.70	Neptune's Favorite
19655	N751PA	24.4.70	Gem of the Sea
19656	N752PA	2.5.70	Fortune
19657	N753PA	30.4.70	Queen of the Seas
19658	N754PA	26.5.70	Ocean Rover
19659	N755PA	31.5.70	Sovereign of the Seas
19660	N770PA	31.5.70	Queen of the Pacific
20347	N652PA	25.4.71	Mermaid
20348	N653PA	8.4.71	Pride of the Ocean
20350	N655PA	28.5.71	Sea Serpent
20351	N656PA	18.6.71	Empress of the Seas
20362	N657PA	19.6.71	Seven Seas
20354	N659PA	20.12.73	Romance of the Seas
Series 121F (Freighter)			
19661	N771PA	4.8.70	Messenger
20349	N654PA	27.4.71	Pacific Trader
20353	N658PA	2.7.76	Fortune
Series 123 (ex-American Airlines)			
20109	N9670	30.5.84	Empress of the Skies
20326	N9674	22.12.83	Beacon Light
Series 123F (formerly leased to American) (Freighter)			
20100	N903PA	8.1.78	Express
20391	N901PA	28.6.77	Messenger
Series 132 (formerly leased to Delta Air Lines)			
19896	N902PA	9.5.78	Seaman's Bride
19898	N725PA	9.5.84	Mandarin

Boeing 747-100

370 seats • 589 mph

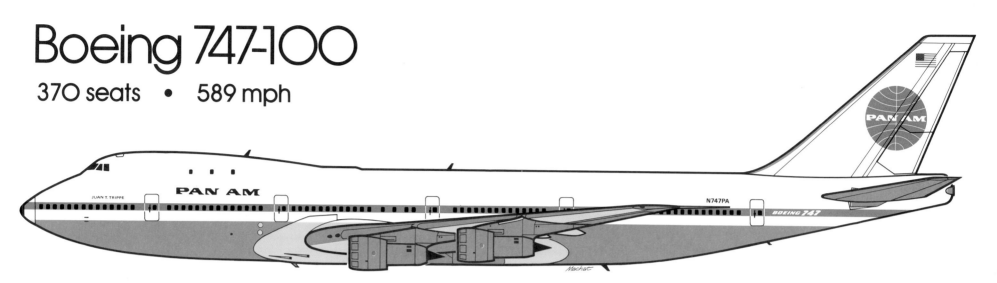

Pratt & Whitney JT9D (43,500 lb.) x 4 • 710,000 lb. max. gross take-off weight • 5500 statute miles range

A Pan Am crew rejoices at the **Boeing 747** inaugural, Heathrow, 1970.

Length 231 feet • Span 196 feet • Height 63 feet

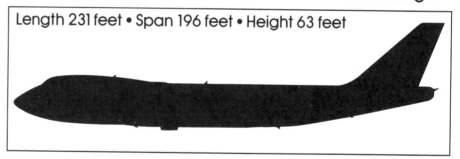

Development History

On 13 April 1966, Pan American Airways, in conjunction with the Boeing Aircraft Company, launched a new generation of airliners, by placing an order for twenty-five Boeing 747s. In mixed class seating, each could carry between 360 and 380 passengers. In all-tourist or all-economy configuration, it would later carry about 450, while special versions built for Japanese domestic services and inclusive tour operators would carry 500. By the standards of the period, and even today, twenty years later, the size of the airliner is—at the risk of over-working the term—somewhat awe-inspiring. Each 747 cost $21,000,000. Incidentally, the 1986 price averaged $110,000,000.

Boeing built a complete new factory, at Everett, north of Seattle, and construction of the 350-ton giant proceeded at a shattering pace, breaking all previous records for production, even by Boeing standards. Pan American had originally intended to start scheduled service across the North Atlantic before Christmas of 1969, following the successful maiden flight on 19 February 1969. But some irritating engine problems postponed this notable landmark date until 21 January 1970. Even then, an overheating engine delayed the take-off from John F. Kennedy Airport, New York, until 1.52 a.m. on 22 January. But the aircraft reached London the same day. A new era had begun, and during the next 16 years, almost 800 of the giant aircraft were to roll off the Everett production line—and still are.

Const. No.	Regist. No.	Pan Am Delivery	Clipper Name
PAN AMERICAN'S BOEING 747 FLEET (Continued)			
Series 200C (Freighter)			
20651	N535PA	20.10.74	Mercury
Series 212B (ex-Singapore Airlines)			
20712	N728PA	24.2.83	Water Witch
20713	N729PA	24.2.83	Wild Wave
20888	N730PA	24.2.83	Gem of the Ocean
21048	N726PA	25.6.84	Belle of the Sky
21162	N727PA	8.6.84	Cathay
21316	N724PA	28.11.84	Fairwind
21439	N723PA	26.4.85	Fleetwind
Series 221F (Freighter)			
21743	N904PA	25.7.79	Industry
21744	N905PA	28.8.79	Courier

The Ultimate Range

As shown by the accompanying aircraft inventory lists, Pan American was to augment its original order to a total of 60 of the Boeing 747 type. Most were of the basic -100 series, and some of the improved -200 series, almost indistinguishable from the first off the line, but with uprated engines to provide for a higher gross weight and thus greater lifting capability, both in passengers and cargo, and in range. For practicable purposes, however, no more passengers could be squeezed in, although some airlines ordered versions with the "stretched upper deck."

The World's Most Experienced Airline did, however, order a special version, with one main objective, the ability to fly with a full payload between New York and Tokyo, non-stop. Convinced that the traffic demand warranted such specialization, Pan Am persuaded Boeing—always ready to explore imaginative market possibilities—to produce a shortened 747, with the suffix SP, for Special Performance. This remarkable airliner could perform the mission demanded of it, and was able to carry 233 passengers, in mixed class, over the range of 6754 statute miles in about thirteen or fourteen hours. Pan American opened the New York-Tokyo service on 25 April 1976.

The Boeing 747SP's ability to cross the North American continent, plus the Pacific Ocean nonstop, was impressive. But it was not the outstanding success which the manufacturer had expected. The problem was that there were not enough markets comparable with New York-Tokyo, the world's two largest metropolitan areas. Later, Pan Am introduced other transpacific routes and other airlines were to use the SP. A passenger could, for example, fly from Hong Kong to San Francisco or Sydney to Los Angeles non-stop. But traffic demand for routes of such extreme range was normally insufficient to support a large production line. Just for once, the airline world did not beat a pathway to Boeing's door; and Boeing was itself partly to blame, because as time went on, technical improvements in the basic Boeing 747 permitted the standard-sized series to fly the same ranges as the SP, with the extra seats and cargo capacity as a bonus.

PAN AMERICAN'S BOEING 747SP FLEET

Const. No.	Regist. No.	Pan Am Delivery	Clipper Name
21022	N530PA	30.4.76	Mayflower
21023	N531PA	17.5.76	Freedom
21024	N532PA	29.3.76	Constitution
21025	N533PA	5.3.76	Young America
21026	N534PA	28.5.76	Great Republic
21441	N536PA	6.5.77	Lindbergh
21547	N537PA	9.6.78	Washington
21548	N538PA	12.7.78	Plymouth Rock
21648	N539PA	20.4.79	Liberty Bell
21649	N540PA	11.5.79	China Clipper
21992	N529PA	23.9.83	America

This is the flight deck of the world's largest airliner. Its three-man crew is responsible for passenger loads of up to 500 in high density seating versions.

The width of the spacious cabin of the **Boeing 747** is unlikely to be exceeded in the foreseeable future.

The upper deck of the **Boeing 747** is an added attraction, usually for the exclusive use of first class or business class passengers.

ADDENDUM (Boeing 747)

Const. No.	Regist. No.	Clipper Name
19753	N 4703U	Nautilus
19754	N 4704U	Belle of the Sea
19755	N 4710U	Sea Lark
19756	N 4711U	Witch of the Wave
19757	N 4712U	Tradewind

BOEING 747 TYPES

Except for the B-747SP, the dimensions of all types are the same.

Type	Year of First Service	P & W JT9D thrust (lb)	Mixed Class Seating	Max. Range (st. miles)	Max. GTOW (lb)
B-747-100	1970	43,500	350	5,000	710,000
B-747SP	1976	50,000	233	7,000	660,000
B-747-200	1971	50,000	350	6,000	800,000
B-747-300	1983	54,000	380	6,500	775,000

Boeing 747 SP

233 seats • 594 mph

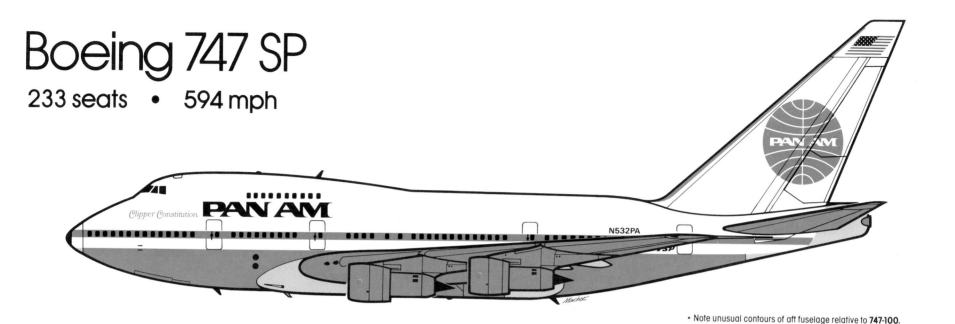

• Note unusual contours of aft fuselage relative to **747-100**.

Pratt & Whitney JT9D (50,000 lb.) x 4 • 660,000 lb. max. gross take-off weight • 7000 statute miles range

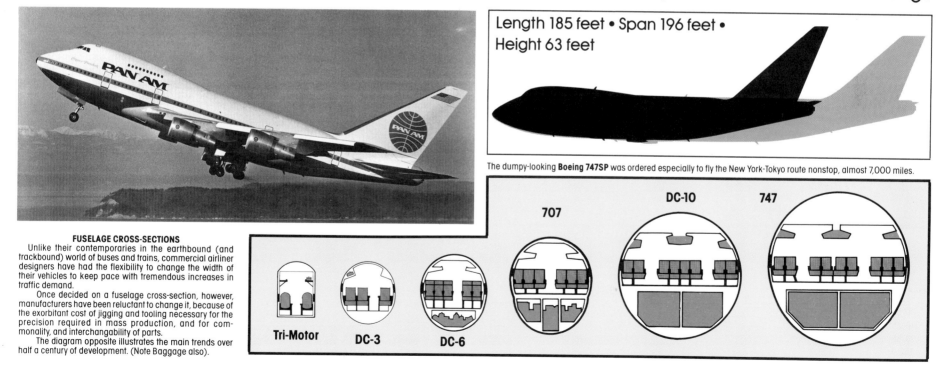

Length 185 feet • Span 196 feet • Height 63 feet

The dumpy-looking **Boeing 747SP** was ordered especially to fly the New York-Tokyo route nonstop, almost 7,000 miles.

FUSELAGE CROSS-SECTIONS

Unlike their contemporaries in the earthbound (and trackbound) world of buses and trains, commercial airliner designers have had the flexibility to change the width of their vehicles to keep pace with tremendous increases in traffic demand.

Once decided on a fuselage cross-section, however, manufacturers have been reluctant to change it, because of the exorbitant cost of jigging and tooling necessary for the precision required in mass production, and for commonality, and interchangability of parts.

The diagram opposite illustrates the main trends over half a century of development. (Note Baggage also).

Tri-Motor   DC-3   DC-6   707   DC-10   747

Domestic Routes at Last

A Longstanding Ambition

Ever since the 1930s Juan Trippe had coveted domestic routes. He was irritated to have to carry passengers and mail across the world's oceans, only to have to hand them over to domestic carriers en route to final destinations at inland cities. The thought that perhaps the domestic airlines might feel the same way about his *de facto* monopoly of international U.S. air traffic either did not occur to him; or, more likely, he preferred to ignore it because it did not suit his purpose. Juan Trippe wanted to have his cake and eat it too.

Ambition Fulfilled

At long last, Trippe lived to see the day when Pan Am was able to operate domestic routes. Two months before the passing of the Airline Deregulation Act, it applied to merge with **National Airlines.** Then followed a battle for control with Eastern Air Lines and Texas International, and the value of National stock went up in a seller's market. After 16 months of litigation, the Civil Aeronautics Board finally approved the merger, and Pan Am took over on 7 January 1980, paying a high price for the doubtful privilege.

Questionable Judgment

Juan Trippe died just over a year later, on 3 April 1981, having retired from the airline he had created more than 50 years previously. He might just have disapproved of this most recent transaction, which was Pan Am's last expansionary move before a severe curtailment of all its many activities was put into motion. For in many ways, the merger made little sense.

First, the age-old need to link the international gateways was no longer valid. Whereas in former decades Pan Am had been at a disadvantage, against T.W.A., for example, which could carry people from London to California via New York because of its joint international-domestic system; and New Yorkers had had to take a domestic flight to Miami to catch a Pan Am connection to Rio or Buenos Aires. These were no longer a problem, as direct flights had been the rule since the long-range Boeings and the Douglas DC-8s flew nonstop anyway.

Second, the aircraft fleets were not wholly compatible. Only the Boeing 727s of both airlines could be integrated for maintenance and operational convenience. Whereas Pan American had been a dedicated

Boeing customer since the beginning of the jet age, National had equally been faithful to Douglas. And so, with the merger, Pan Am acquired eleven DC-10-10 and five DC-10-30 wide-bodied trijets. Not only were these incompatible with the 12 Lockheed L-1011 TriStars which had been ordered; this latter order had been placed only four months before the first proposal to merge with National, and presumably by the same people. The TriStar, furthermore, had to be modified to attain the range requirements, and its Rolls-Royce engines were as new to Pan Am as were the General Electric engines of the DC-10s.

By its acquisition of National Airlines in 1980, Pan American went back to Douglas, after a decade of complete disassociation with that company's products.

PAN AMERICAN'S DC-10 FLEET

Const. No.	Regist. No.	Clipper Name
McDonnell Douglas DC-10-10 (ex-National) (GE.CF6-6 engines)		
46700	N 60NA	*Meteor*
46701	N 61NA	*Evening Star*
46702	N 62NA	*Morning Star*
46703	N 63NA	*Eclipse*
46706	N 64NA	*Shooting Star*
46707	N 65NA	*Silver Star*
46708	N 66NA	*Sirius*
46709	N 67NA	*Star of Hope*
46710	N 68NA	*Star Gazer*
46942	N 69NA	*Star Light*
46943	N 70NA	*Star King*
McDonnell Douglas DC-10-30 (ex-National) (GE CF6-50 engines)		
46711	N 80NA	*Star of the Union*
46712	N 81NA	*Atmosphere*
46713	N 82NA	*Aurora*
46714	N 83NA	*Celestial Empire*
46715	N 84NA	*Glory of the Skies*

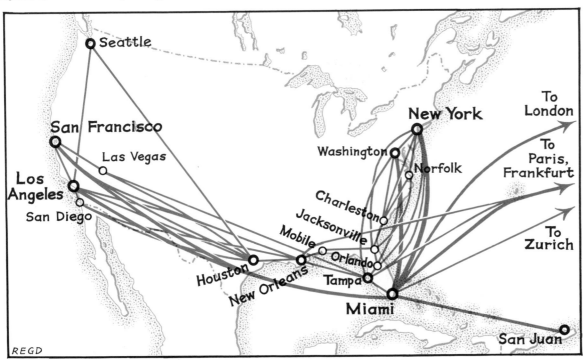

Seattle
San Francisco
Las Vegas
Los Angeles
San Diego
Houston
New Orleans
Mobile
Orlando
Tampa
Miami
San Juan
New York
Washington
Norfolk
Charleston
Jacksonville

To London
To Paris, Frankfurt
To Zurich

REGD

McDonnell Douglas DC-10-10

270 seats • 590 mph

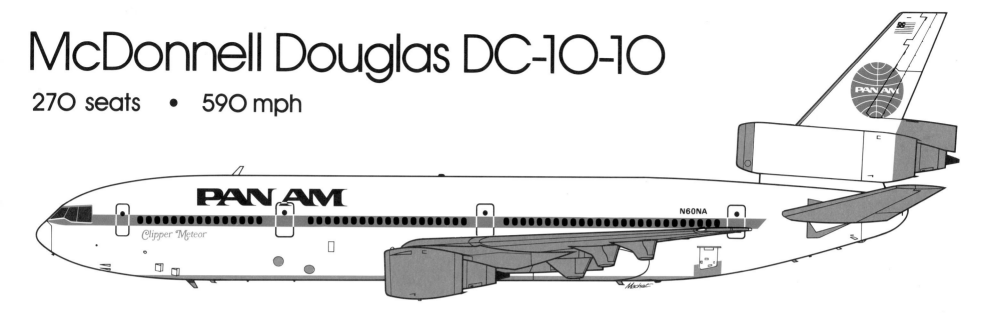

General Electric CF6-6 (40,000 lb thrust) x 3 • 215 tons max. gross take-off weight • 2760 statute miles range

The Widebodied Trijet Solution

Even while Boeing and Pan American were planning to launch the wide-bodied era with the Boeing 747, the Europeans were studying the problems of coping with the dense airline traffic on the world's busiest air routes, invariably short-haul city pairs. Meanwhile, in the United States, both Douglas and Lockheed, traditional rivals of a previous airliner era, studied the problem with a different set of criteria from the Europeans.

The two companies tried to split the difference between the size of the Boeing 747 and that of the supplanted Boeing 707/DC-8 family. It was a simple equation. Halfway between 380 and 160 was 270 in mixed class seating layouts. U.S. transcontinental range was essential. To attain this objective, three engines were necessary. Douglas and Lockheed both placed one on each wing, and one in the rear.

The **DC-10-10** first flew on 24 October 1970, three weeks ahead of the Tristar, and went into service with American Airlines on 5 August 1971. National was the third airline to put the aircraft, described by American as of "unprecedented dependability," on its routes. This airline had, on 14 October 1969, already ordered some long-range **DC-10-30**s, as it had managed to enter the transocean market by suc-

Length 181 feet • Span 155 feet • Height 58 feet

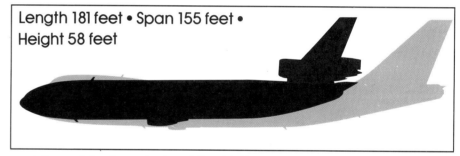

cessfully applying for routes from Miami to Europe—another erosion of Pan American's case for acquisition.

The DC-10-30 basically delivered three quarters of the payload of a 747 on three quarters of the power—and therefore three quarters of the fuel consumption. Its range was only a few hundred miles short of the 747's and close analysis of worldwide traffic patterns showed that such marginal routes demanding the extra mileage were few.

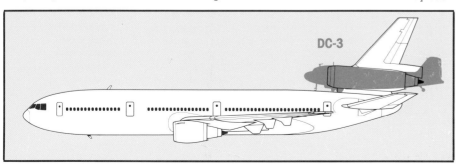

THE McDONNELL DOUGLAS DC-10 FAMILY

Series	Engines		Dimensions (ft)		Allup Weight (short tons)	Max. Seats	Range (st. miles)	Year of First Service
	Type	Thrust each (lb)	Length	Span				
DC-10-10	GE CF6-6	41,000	181	155	227	345	2760	1971
DC-10-40	P & W JT9D	49,000	182	165	279	345	4500	1972
DC-10-30	GE CF6-50	51,000	182	165	286	345	4500	1972
DC-10-30ER	GE CF6-50C2B	54,000	182	165	290	345	7000	1983

Trijet Quandary

Need for a Mid-Sized Trijet

Although during the 1970s the Boeing 747 did well, there were many routes on Pan Am's network which could not sustain year-round loads, and so the airline sought a smaller aircraft to fill the gap.

Bearing in mind that, in August 1978, Pan American took the initial steps to fulfill a 40-year-old ambition to acquire a domestic route network by buying National Airlines, which had 16 perfectly good McDonnell Douglas DC-10s, the decision to order, only four months earlier, 12 **Lockheed L-1011 TriStars**, seemed strange. In fact Lockheed had to compromise the design (see opposite page) to provide Pan Am with an aircraft for the "long thin routes."

Electing to concentrate on a standardized fleet of Boeing 747s for all its long-haul operations, and impressed with the claims of the European Airbus program, however, Pan Am sold all wide-bodied trijets, including the TriStars, within five years of their acquisition. Most of the DC-10s were sold by June 1984 and the TriStars by February 1986. The first L-1011-500 had gone into service only on 1 May 1980.

Tightening the Belt

The finances of the World's Most Experienced Airline deterioriated sharply early in 1980. One immediate reaction was to sell the lease of the **Pan American Building** on 5 January 1981 to Metropolitan Life for $400 million, the largest real estate transaction for a single building in recorded history. Pan Am had also sold its 50% share of the **Falcon Jet Corporation** and in 1981 also it sold the **Intercontinental Hotels Corporation (I.H.C.),** one of the biggest innkeepers in the world, to Grand Metropolitan of London for $500 million.

On 1 September 1981, C. Edward Acker had succeeded William T. Seawell as Chairman. He tried employee ownership plans and public stock offerings, but the drain in the cash flow continued. In a desperate move, and to the astonishment of the entire airline world, a joint announcement on 22 April 1985 revealed the transfer of 23% of Pan American's network—all the Pacific routes, no less—to United Air Lines for $750 million. The sale included the whole fleet of Boeing 747SPs, half the TriStars, and a DC-10.

This extraordinary measure was taken after an excruciating analysis of all other possible options. While the Pacific routes were profitable, were the fastest growing, and served a world region of inexorable growth in prosperity, it did not make so much money as the Atlantic routes; and Acker had to follow the hard facts rather than sentiment or an Oriental future that might never come.

To make matters worse, the political events of 1985 saw terrorism raise its ugly head in Europe, with the public shying away from that destination for its annual vacations. But there were reverberations at the Pan American headquarters in Park Avenue, allegedly caused by Juan Trippe turning in his grave.

The **Lockheed TriStar** was Pan Am's choice as a second string to the Boeing 747.

Pan American Airways network early in 1987, after sale of Pacific routes.

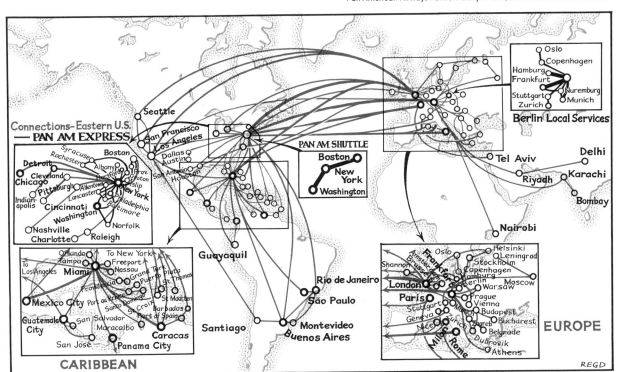

PAN AMERICAN'S LOCKHEED TRISTAR FLEET
(L-1011-385/Rolls-Royce RB211 engines)

Const. No.	Regist. No.	Clipper Name
1176	N 501PA	Eagle
1177	N 503PA	Flying Eagle
1181	N 504PA	National Eagle
1184	N 505PA	Eagle Wing
1185	N 507PA	Northern Eagle
1186	N 508PA	Bald Eagle
1188	N 509PA	Golden Eagle
1194	N 510PA	George T. Baker
1195	N 511PA	Black Hawk
1197	N 512PA	War Hawk
1208	N 513PA	Wild Duck
1210	N 514PA	White Falcon

Lockheed L-1011-500 TriStar
280 seats • 590 mph

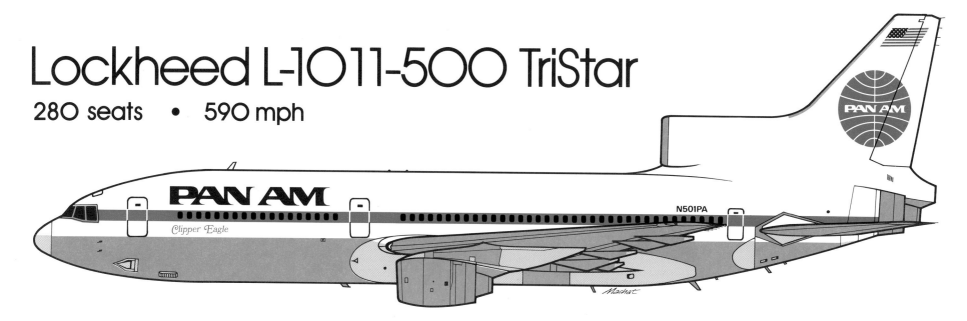

Rolls-Royce RB211 (50,000 lb thrust) x 3 • 248 tons max. gross take-off weight • 6000 statute miles range
Traditional Rivalry Renewed

The competition was good while it lasted. Lockheed appeared to have the edge when, in 1967, it first announced its trijet wide-bodied airliner, to return to the commercial business again after it had terminated its turboprop L-188 Electra, program and concentrated on military and space production, notably with the giant C-5A transport. While Douglas followed the rather unexpected customer preference for General Electric as the main engine supplier over the traditional Pratt & Whitney, Lockheed teamed up with Rolls Royce.

With its great production experience, Douglas narrowly won the race for first flight honors. The DC-10 made its maiden flight on 24 October 1970, the **L-1011 TriStar** on 16 November of the same year. But Douglas pulled ahead, with the DC-10 entering airline service on 5 August 1971, the Tristar on 26 April 1972. Subsequently, both companies experienced setbacks. Lockheed lost ground when Rolls Royce went bankrupt and severely disrupted the TriStar program. Lockheed was saved by the U.S. Senate's approval of the Emergency Loan Guarantee Act (by a margin of one vote) on 2 August 1971. The program survived but Lockheed's competitive stature was badly compromised.

Later, the dice fell against its rival. On 25 May 1979, an American Airlines DC-10-10 crashed spectacularly in full view of a critical audience at the busiest airport in the world, Chicago's O'Hare. Douglas's reputation was in jeopardy for many months, and although it was later exonerated from the vicious charges directed against it, the DC-10 lost many orders to Boeing as a result; and in Pan American's case, may have been one of the factors influencing its choice of the TriStar.

Compromising a Design

Whether by accident or calculated design, Douglas had been able to build a long-range DC-10. While the lighter weight of the TriStar compared with the DC-10 (about ten tons difference) may have given it a slightly superior economic performance, this was more than offset by a critical disadvantage. The DC-10 could be developed by a substantial increase in allup weight—more than 60 tons. Most of this could be used to advantage by adding enough extra tankage to make the DC-10-30 or the DC-10-40 competitive not only with the TriStar but also with the 747, and 747SP.

Length 164 feet • Span 155 feet • Height 55 feet

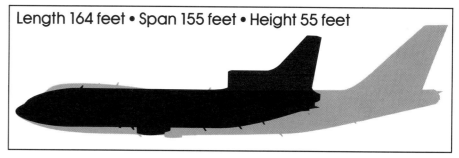

In contrast, the TriStar's range could be increased only by a trade-off, and after much heart-searching this was done. The additional range necessary to turn the Lockheed trijet into a transocean airliner was achieved only by reducing the size so as to lighten the all-up weight, at the same time adding extra tankage in place of payload. Thus the economics of the aircraft were compromised. Lockheed could take some satisfaction of knowing that its launching customer was Pan American, but somehow, the old magic was gone. No longer did the rest of the world follow the Juan Trippe standard. In the event, few airlines followed Pan Am's example, and the so-called long-range TriStar was sold to a mere handful of specialized airlines.

THE LOCKHEED L-1011 TRISTAR FAMILY

Series	Engines		Dimensions (ft)		Allup Weight (short tons)	Max. Seats	Range (st. miles)	Year of First Service
	Type	Thrust each (lb)	Length	Span				
L-1011-1	RB211-22	40,600	178	155	215	345	3000	1972
L-1011-200	RB211-524	48,000	178	155	238	345	4000	1975
L-1011-500	RB211-524B	50,000	164	155	258	305	5500	1979

The Wind of Change

Sixty Glorious Years

For several decades under Juan Trippe's leadership, Pan American represented the United States in the international airline arena, and did everything expected of it and more. During the 1930s it established a technical supremacy which was the envy of the world. Visionary planning, organizational élan, solid infrastructure, and an élite corps of airmen carried the U.S. flag to the four corners of the globe.

During these formative years, in some cities in both hemispheres, the Pan Am local office probably had more influence than did the local U.S. consulate. During World War II, by maintaining essential communications, and by building strategic airfields, Pan American confirmed its role as an American institution, transcending that of a mere airline.

After the war, Flights PA1 and PA2 became known to almost every frequent air traveller from New York to San Francisco, via Europe, the Middle East, and Asia. In 1958, Pan Am ushered in the Jet Age; and in 1970 repeated the performance by starting the era of the Jumbo Jets. For half a century, Pan Am led and the rest of the airline world followed.

A Creature of Habit

The pressures of airline deregulation have been crippling to an airline nurtured in a regulated environment, but Pan American's latent strength has allowed it to dispose of assets—to maintain essential cash flow—the loss of which would have annihilated a lesser organization. It has nevertheless maintained its operational momentum and is coming to terms with an industry which has itself undergone a metamorphosis.

Chairman Ed Acker has moved effectively to reduce the number of aircraft types and to extract the maximum productivity from the re-aligned fleet. The last Boeing 707 was retired on 26 January 1981, and since then the Boeing 747SPs, DC-10s, and TriStars have all gone. The 727s are still hard at work, with 737s ideally deployed on the Internal German Service. Now the efficient Airbuses are swelling the ranks, A300B4s since 23 December 1984, and A310s since 28 May 1985. These versatile aircraft are to be seen everywhere, from Berlin to Barbados, and (now that the authorities have lost their fears about twin-engined over-ocean flying) on the connecting routes in between.

As it explored new territory in the past, Pan American still seeks fresh fields. On 1 June 1986 it added a short-haul feeder market in the densely populated northeast by acquiring the leading commuter airline, **Ransome**, to form **Pan Am Express**. Exactly four months

The versatile **A300B4** came into service at the end of 1984 and is establishing itself as a replacement for the Boeing 727-200.

The **A310**, smaller cousin of the A300, has quickly become the favorite of the air shuttle passengers on the Internal German Service to Berlin.

The 40-seat **Dash Seven,** dwarfed by its wide-bodied neighbors on the ramp, is ideal for the feeder routes into New York from smaller cities in the vicinity.

later, it opened the **Pan Am Shuttle** in the heavily travelled Northeast Corridor, the first such service on the Boston-New York-Washington route since Eastern started its famous predecessor on 30 April 1961.

Ghosts of the Past

There was a neat touch about the Pan American Shuttle. Its New York terminus was not the congested La Guardia terminal building. It was the renovated and rejuvenated **Marine Air Terminal,** whence the Boeing 314 Clipper flying boats once departed on their pathfinding schedules to Europe.

To gaze at the murals in this historic building is to evoke memories of the true greatness that has been Pan American during its sixty glorious years. The ghosts of the past must walk there still; and during difficult times when the staff of Pan American is demonstrating traditional qualities of resilience and determination, they may lend a spectral hand to ensure that an American institution continues in its accustomed role as the world's leading international airline.

PAN AMERICAN'S AIRBUS FLEET

Const. No.	Regist. No.	Clipper Name
A300 B4 (G.E. CF6-50C2 engines)		
195	N 202PA	America
227	N 203PA	New York
198	N 204PA	Washington
247	N 205PA	Miami
234	N 206PA	Tampa
236	N 207PA	Los Angeles
304	N 208PA	San Francisco
305	N 209PA	Boston
238	N 210PA	Dallas
235	N 211PA	Houston
208	N 212PA	Detroit
210	N 213PA	Chicago
A310-200 (P & W JT9D engines)		
288	N 801PA	Berlin
333	N 802PA	Frankfurt
343	N 803PA	Munich
345	N 804PA	Hamburg
A310-222 (P & W JT9D engines)		
339	N 805PA	Miles Standish
342	N 806PA	Betsy Ross
346	N 807PA	Kit Carson

Airbus A300B4
254 seats • 560 mph

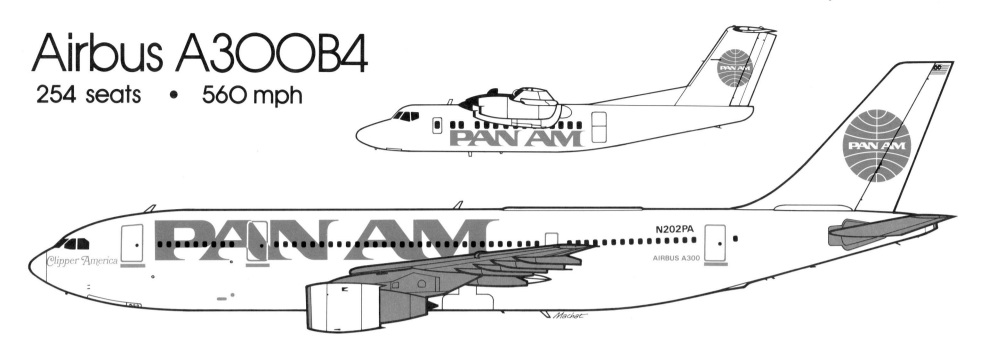

Clipper America

PAN AM

N202PA

AIRBUS A300

Machat

General Electric CF6-50c (51,000 lb thrust) x 2 • 165 tons max. gross take-off weight • 2800 statute miles range

A European Consortium

The idea of a wide-bodied aircraft designed especially for short-haul air routes germinated during the 1960s in Great Britain and France. First thoughts at the de Havilland plant at Hatfield, England, appear to have occurred at about the same time as those for a Breguet-Nord project in Paris. Joint discussions resulted in a cooperative study for the **HBN-100**. Breguet-Nord then merged with Sud Aviation (which was working on its *Galion*) to become Aérospatiale. The joint project became known as the **A300**, with design leadership centered at Toulouse.

Great Britain and France were at first equal partners, and this was soon modified by the late 1960s to 40% France (Sud), 40% Great Britain (Hawker Siddeley), and 20% Germany (Deutsche Airbus of Munich). The British Government then withdrew its support because the French would not agree to use Rolls-Royce engines. Fortunately for Britain, Hawker Siddeley remained as an important sub-contractor, building the wings, worth about 17% of the total project.

Since then, the British share, held by British Aerospace, has recovered to 20% with additional participation by CASA Spain (4%), with Fokker, (Netherlands), and Belairbus (Belgium) as associates, to make the A300 a genuinely European effort. The General Electric or Pratt & Whitney engines, pods, and pylons are built in the United States so there is a substantial American content.

Tortoise and Hare

Although the Airbus sales teams were convinced of the large potential market, simply because the majority of the world's air passengers fly on short-haul journeys, initial sales were sluggish.

Slowly, however, the superior economics of the A300's twin engines against those of either of the trijets, applied to major short-haul markets, began to win customers. During the latter 1970s, sporadic A300 bridgeheads were established all over the world.

Length 176 feet • Span 141 feet • Height 52 feet

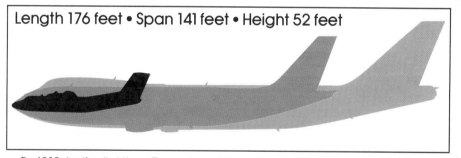

By 1980, for the first time, Europe's world percentage of commercial airliner markets went into double figures. Today, with the smaller A310 in service and the larger A320 on the production lines, the Airbus has established a firm foundation to carry the European airliner manufacturing effort successfully into the 21st Century.

PAN AMERICAN'S AIRBUS FAMILY

Series	Engines (2)		Dimensions (ft)		Typical Seats	All up Weight (tons)	Range (st. miles)
	Type	Thrust (lb)	Length	Span			
A300B4	GE CF6-50C	51,000	176	141	252	165	2800
A310	P & W JT9D	50,000	153	144	214	145	3250
A320	CFM 56-5	23,500	123	111	144	72	2300

FLAGSHIP OF PAN AM EXPRESS

Series	Engines (2)		Dimensions (ft)		Typical Seats	All up Weight (tons)	Range (st. miles)
DHC-7	P & W PT6	1,120	80	93	50	22	1200

Heritage of an International Giant

PAN AMERICAN WORLD AIRWAYS

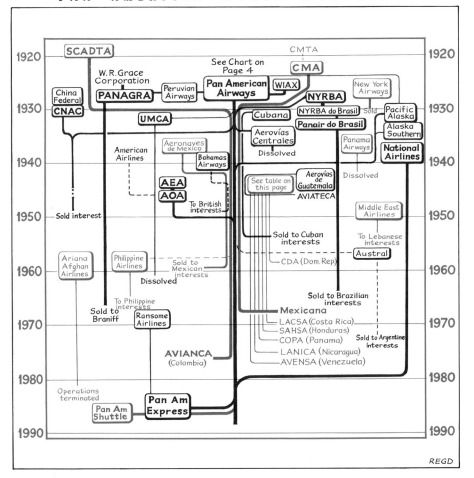

PAN AMERICAN SUBSIDIARIES AND ASSOCIATES IN LATIN AMERICA
(in order of initial Pan American involvement)

Country	Airline	Date Founded	Pan American Interest			Remarks
			Purchase Date	Initial Interest	Disposal	
Formative Period of Trunk System, 1927-1930						
Peru	Peruvian Airways	4.9.28	16.9.28	50%	25.2.29	Sold to PANAGRA
Dominican Rep.	West Indian A.E.	20.6.27	15.12.28	100%		Incorporated into Pan Am
Chile	Chilean Airways	21.12.28	31.12.28	50%	30.7.36	Non-operating.
Mexico	Cía Mexicana	20.8.24	23.1.29	100%	15.1.68	Sold to Mexican interests
U.S.A.	PANAGRA	25.1.29	25.1.29	50%	8.1.67	Partnership with W.R. Grace; Sold to Braniff
U.S.A.	NYRBA	17.3.29	15.9.30	100%		Incorporated into Pan Am
Brazil	NYRBA do Brasil	24.1.30	15.9.30	100%	30.12.66	Renamed Panair do Brasil; Sold to Brazilian interests
Addition of Feeder Route Systems, 1931-1940						
Colombia	SCADTA	5.12.19	10.4.31	84%		Became AVIANCA in 1940; Sold to Colombian interests
Colombia	UMCA	24.8.31	13.4.32	54%	15.6.61	Dissolved
Cuba	Cubana	8.10.29	6.5.32	100%	23.7.54	Sold to Cuban interests
Guatemala	S.A. de Guatemala	6.6.33	21.6.33	100%	22.6.40	Dissolved
U.S.A. (C.Z.)	Panama Airways	7.11.36	7.11.33	100%	30.4.41	Dissolved
Guatemala	Aerovías de Guat.	10.10.40	10.10.40	40%	30.11.45	Became AVIATECA; sold to Guatemalan Gov't.
Mexico	Aeronaves de Mexico	7.11.34	18.12.40	40%	26.12.59	Sold to Mexican Gov't.
Wartime Expansion of Feeder Systems, 1941-1945						
Venezuela	AVENSA	13.5.43	14.7.43	30%	28.4.76	Sold to Venezuelan interests
Bahamas	Bahamas Airways	36	10.12.43	45%	23.10.48	Sold to B.S.A.A. (U.K.)
Dominican Rep.	C.D.A.	26.4.44	26.4.44	40%	26.7.57	Sold to Dominican interests
Panama	COPA	21.6.44	30.8.44	40%	15.3.71	Sold to Panamanian interests
Honduras	SAHSA	16.11.44	16.11.44	40%	21.1.70	Sold to TAN (Honduras)
Nicaragua	LANICA	17.11.44	17.11.44	40%	8.74	Sold to Nicaraguan interests
Costa Rica	LACSA	17.10.45	17.10.45	40%	14.9.70	Sold to Costa Rican interests

Pan Am's Flying Boats in Perspective

The table on this page summarizes the production of the great flying boats—those with four engines or more—that were promoted as contenders for transoceanic flight. Some were successful, some served even though for much of the time they only stood and waited, and some were disasters. The tabulated numbers are intended to present a balanced perspective of the flying boat era as a whole, and of Pan American's pioneer role. In the space available.

The **(P)** denotes a prototype that never went into service, in contrast to those that did, having served their original purpose and then been refitted as production aircraft. Other numbered references refer to special characteristics of importance, as follows:

The best known examples of the payload-range trade-off were the famous *China Clipper*, the **Martin** type **M-130**, which could carry only a few passengers between San Francisco and Honolulu, and sometimes, bucking strong headwinds, even had to turn back **(1)**; the **Boeing 314** was restricted to a maximum of 30 passengers on this segment, and to 40 on its transatlantic flights **(2)**; while a few of the **Shorts "Empire"** boats, at an early stage of the type development, were converted for transatlantic use (as **S-30s** or **S-33s**). These could carry only a few passengers, even with in-flight refuelling **(3)**.

Of the "giant" flying boats, the most efficient was the **Martin Mars**, which once carried 301 passengers on a short flight **(4)**, beating a 15-year-old record by the spectacular but ponderous **Dornier DoX** which once managed to lift 169 people off the waters of the Bodensee **(5)**. The gigantic **Hughes H-4** Hercules was designed to carry a battalion of troops **(6)** but it left the water only once on a much-publicized short hop at Long Beach. The **Saunders-Roe Princess** was built to carry 100 people **(7)** but was never tested.

Some of the numbers are of interest. One Martin M-156, of the M-130 type, was exported to the Soviet Union **(8)**. Of the Shorts C Class "Empire" boats, no less than 792 of the basic type were built. These were mainly **S-25 Sunderlands**, long-range developments for the Royal Navy during World War II. Some 40 or so were converted to **Sandringhams** (Plymouths in B.O.A.C. service) and a few were produced as civil versions (Hythes) **(9)**.

The **Kawanishi H8K "Emily,"** claimed by some aviation specialists to have been the finest flying boat ever built, were used on Japanese semi-commercial services in the western Pacific towards the end of World War II **(10)**.

Of the 1266 great flying boats estimated to have been built, only one fifth, whether civil or military or in total, were American.

The big boats gave good service after World War II in those regions of the world that had not benefited from wartime airport construction work that laid the foundations—literally—for heavy landplane operations. Thus, in the South Pacific, Sandringhams and Solents were still providing scheduled service until the mid-1970s.

Only two big flying boats are still flying today, Martin Mars, used for fire-retardant bombing runs on Vancouver Island, British Columbia **(11)**.

Country and Aircraft	Year of First Service (or Flight)	Gross Weight (x 1000 lb)	Typical Seating	Normal Range (st. miles)	Numbers Built				First Airline
					Civil	Military	Other	Total	
U.S.A.									
Sikorsky S-40	1931	34	38	900	3	—	—	3	Pan Am
Sikorsky S-42	1934	38	32	1200	10	—	—	10	Pan Am
Martin M-130	1935	52	32(1)	3200	3	—	1(8)	4	Pan Am
Consol. Coronado	(1937)	68	(50)	1500	—	216	—	216	—
Boeing B.314	1939	84	70(2)	2400	12	—	—	12	Pan Am
Vought-Sik. VS-44	1942	57	16	3000	3	—	—	3	Am. Export
Martin Mars	(1942)	145	106(4)	4000	—	7(11)	—	7	—
Hughes H-4	(1947)	400	(600)(6)	3000	—	—	1(P)	1	—
U.S. Total	—	—	—	—	31	223	2	256	—
U.K.									
Shorts S-23 (C Class "Empire")	1937	40	24(3)	800	43 40(9)	709(9)	—	792	Imperial B.O.A.C.
Shorts S-26 (G Class)	1940	74	12	2500	3	—	—	3	B.O.A.C.
Shorts S-45 Solent/Seaford	1947	81	39	2000	15	11	—	26	B.O.A.C.
Saunders-Roe SR-45 Princess (12)	(1952)	330	105(7)	5500	—	—	1(P)	1	—
U.K. Total	—	—	—	—	101	720	1	822	—
France									
Latécoère 300	1934	51	(mail)	2000	4	3	—	7	Air France
Latécoère 521(6)	(1935)	81	20	3500	2	—	—	2	—
Latécoère 621(6)	1947	157	46	3750	9	—	—	9	Air France
French Total	—	—	—	—	15	3	—	18	—
Germany									
Dornier DoX(12)	(1929)	123	66(5)	1000	2	—	1(P)	3	—
German Total	—	—	—	—	2	—	1	3	—
Japan									
Kawanishi H8K "Emily"	1943	72	64	2800	10(10)	157	—	167	Japan Naval Air Service
Japanese Total	—	—	—	—	10	157	—	167	—
WORLD TOTAL	—	—	—	—	159	1103	4	1266	—

The **Kawanishi H8K** flying boat, nicknamed "Emily."

The **Martin Mars,** built for U.S. Naval Air Transport.

The six-engined **Latécoère 621** went into service on the trans-Atlantic route from France to the Caribbean in 1946.

Acker, Edward, chairman, 84
A300 and A310 Airbus, 87
Aeromarine Airways, 2
Aeronaves de México, 24, 88
Aérospatiale, A300 development, 87
Aerovías Centrales, S.A., 24, 50
Aerovías Reforma, 24
Airline Deregulation Act, 82
Alaska Southern Airways, 32
Alaskan Airways, 32
Alemán, Miguel (Aeronaves), 24
American Export Airlines, 56
American Overseas Airlines, 56
AMTORG, Soviet trading organization,
    Buys Fleetster, 23
Atlantic Aircraft Corp.
    Founded by Fokker, 7
Atlantic, Gulf and Caribbean
    Airways, Pan Am foundation, 4
AVENSA (Venezuela), brief summary, 89
AVIANCA, succeeds SCADTA, 22
Aviation Corporation of America (s)
    Pan Am parent company founded, 4
    Purchases UMCA, 23
    Purchases Alaskan lines, 32
Bahamas Airways, brief summary, 88
"Barreiras Cutoff," 48
Belairbus, Belgian Airbus
    subcontractor, 87
Benoist XIV flying boat,
    St. Petersburg-Tampa, 2
Bez, Nick (Alaska Southern), 32
Blöhm and Voss Ha 139,
    German Atlantic surveys, 40
B.O.A.C., competes with Britannia, 64
Boeing 247, compared with DC-2, 45
Boeing 307 Stratoliner, 48-49
Boeing 314 flying boat, 42-43
    Replaced by DC-4, 52-53
    Great flying boat comparison, 89
Boeing 367-80, 707 prototype, 67
Boeing 377 Stratocruiser, 56-57
Boeing 707 family
    Table, 65
    Fuselage cross-section, 81
Boeing 707-121, 65-66
    Jet Age chronology, 67
Boeing 707-321, 70-71
    Last one sold, 86
Boeing 720 and 720B, 72-73
Boeing 727, 74-76
Boeing 737, 76-77
Boeing 747, 78-79
    Fuselage cross-section, 81
Boeing 747SP, 80-81
Boston-Maine Airways, 26
Bouilloux-Lafont, Marcel,
    French Atlantic challenger, 30
Breguet-Nord, explores Airbus idea, 87
Bristol Britannia, 64
Caldwell, Cy, delivers Pan Am mail, 5
Canadian Pacific Airlines, Polar Route, 64
CASA, Spanish Airbus subcontractor, 87
C.A.T. (Mexico), 24
C.D.A. (Dominican Republic), 88

Chambers, Reed (Florida Airways), 4
Chilean Airways, 14, 88
China Airways Federal, Inc., 34
China Clipper, service, flight log,
    and crew, 38-39
China National Airways Corp. (C.N.A.C.),
    Established, 34; DC-2 service, 44;
    aids war effort, 60
C.M.A. (Mexico)
    Founded, 10; Pan Am takes control, 24;
    Early DC-2 delivery, 44; brief summary, 89
C.M.T.A. (Mexico), 10
C.N.C.A. (Cuba), 25
Colonial Airways, Trippe association, 4
Condor Syndikat, sponsors SCADTA, 3
Consolidated Commodore, 20-21
    Helps Chinese evacuation, 44
Consolidated Coronado,
    Great flying boat comparison, 89
Consolidated Fleetster, 23
Convair-Liner CV-240/340/440, etc., 58-59
    Comparison with DC-3, C-46, 61
COPA (Panama), brief summary, 88
Corporación (Argentina), 58
Cubana (Franco-Cuban airline), 25
Cubana de Aviacion Curtiss, Cia Nacional, 25;
    brief historical summary, 88
Curtiss C-46 Commando, 60-61
"Dash Eighty"—Boeing 707 prototype, 67
De Havilland, aircraft manufacturer,
    explores Airbus idea, 87
De Havilland Comet, loses lead to 707, 66;
    jet age chronology, 67
De Havilland Trident, pre-dates Boeing 727, 75
Danske Luftfartselskap, Det (D.D.L.),
    Danish Atlantic plans, 51
Deutsche Zeppelin Reederei,
    Airship v. Flying Boat discussion, 28
Dixie Clipper, 42
Dornier 18 flying boat, German Atlantic
    surveys, 40
Dornier DoX flying boat, Great flying boat
    comparison, 89
Dornier Wal flying boat, SCADTA-Condor, 3
Douglas Dolphin, 35
Douglas Sleeper Transport (DST), 46
Douglas DC-1, prototype for DC-2, 45
Douglas DC-2, 44-45
Douglas DC-3, 46-47;
    Comparison with C-46, CV-240, 61
    Fuselage cross-section, 81
Douglas DC-4, (inc. C-54, R5D), 52-53
    Airliner comparison, 65
    Fuselage cross-section, 81
Douglas DC-4E, 52
Douglas DC-6B (inc. DC-6, DC-6A), 62-63
    Airliner comparison, 65
Douglas DC-7C (incl. DC-7, DC-7B), 64-65
Douglas DC-8, 68-69
Douglas DC-9, compared to Boeing 737, 77
Douglas DC-10—see McDonnell Douglas
Fairchild, Sherman, shareholder in WIAX, 8
    in C.M.A., 10
Fairchild FC-2/FC-2W/FC-2W2
    Carries first Pan Am mail, 5; with
    C.M.A., 10; development, 11; PANAGRA, 15;
    Characteristics compared, 15

Fairchild 71, development, 11; PANAGRA, 15;
    Characteristics compared, 15; Pacific
    Alaska, 32
Fairchild Type 91 (or XA-942A), **50**
Fairchild F100B Pilgrim, 32
Falcon Jet Corporation, 84
Fansler, Percival (St. Petersburg-Tampa), 2
Farman 2200, French landplane,
    Significance on flying boat development, 28
Fleet, Reuben, (NYRBA), 20
Florida Airways, forerunner of Pan Am, 4
Florida West Indies Airways, 2
Focke-Wulf Fw 200 Condor,
    Landplane v. Flying Boat discussion, 28
    Non-stop Atlantic flight, 40
Fokker, aircraft manufacturer,
    Subcontractor for Airbus, 87
Fokker, Anthony, visits U.S.A., 7
Fokker F-VII and F-VIIa/3m, 5-7
Fokker F-10A, 26-27
Fokker Super-Universal, 50
Ford Edsel, buys Stout Metal Airplane Co., 19
Ford Tri-Motor, 16-19
    Fuselage cross-section, 81
Ford 8-AT, 32
Foreign Air Mail Contracts—first four, 2
Frye, Jack, specifies DC-2, 45; record
    Constellation flight, 55

Grace, W. R., Corporation, founds PANAGRA, 14
Gray, Captain Harold,
    First Atlantic mail services, 42;
    Succeeds Trippe as president, 70
Guatemala, Aerovías de, summary, 88
Guatemala, S.A. de, summary, 88
Hammer, Fritz (Condor Syndikat), 3
Hawker Siddeley, aircraft manufacturer,
    subcontractor for Airbus, 87
HBN-100, precursor of Airbus, 87
Hindenburg, German airship establishes
    trans-Atlantic passenger service
Huff-Daland Dusters, foundation of
    PANAGRA, 14
Hughes, Howard, sponsors Constellation, 55;
    rejects Pan Am merger proposal, 56
Hughes H-4 Hercules, Great flying boat
    comparison, 89
Hull, Theodore, (C.A.T.), 24
Ilyushin Il-62, 67

Internal German Service (I.G.S.), 74
Intercontinental Hotels Corporation (I.H.C.), 84
Jannus, Tony (St. Petersburg-Tampa), 2
Jelling, survey/expedition, 40;
    Sequel to, 51
Kawanishi H8K "Emily", Great flying boat
    comparison, 89
Keystone Pathfinder, 8-9
LACSA (Costa Rica), brief summary, 88
LAMSA (Mexico), merges with Aeronaves, 24
LANICA (Nicaragua), brief summary, 88
LaPorte, Captain A. E., inaugurates trans-
    Atlantic services, 42
Latécoère 300, 52; Great flying boat
    comparison, 89
Latécoère 631, trans-Atlantic contender, 40;
    Great flying boat comparison, 89
Lincoln Standard biplane (C.M.T.A., C.M.A.), 10, 50

Lindbergh, Charles,
    Carries mail for WIAX, 8; surveys
    Caribbean, 12; pilots C.M.A. inaugural, 16;
    pilots S-40 inaugural to Canal Zone, 28-29;
    Pacific survey, 31; Atlantic survey, 40
Líneas Aereas Occidentales (Varney), 24
Lockheed twin-engined aircraft compared, 33
Lockheed Sirius, Lindbergh's survey aircraft, 31, 40
Lockheed 9 Orion, 50
Lockheed L-10 Electra, 33-34
Lockheed L-12 Electra Junior, L-14 Super Electra, 33
Lockheed L-18 Lodestar, 33-34
Lockheed Excalibur, Pan Am order, 54
Lockheed L-049 Constellation, 54-55
Lockheed L-1011 TriStar, 84-85
Loening Air Yacht, 25
Long Island Airways, founded by Trippe, 4
McDonnell Douglas DC-10, 82-83; fuselage cross-
    section, 81; Chicago crash, 85; development
    potential, 85
Mallory, William "Slim" (C.M.A.), 10
Marine Air Terminal, La Guardia, 86
Martin M-130, 38-39; Great flying boat comparison, 89
Martin Mars, great flying boat comparison, 89
Mayo, William B., supervises Ford Tri-Motor development, 19
Mexicana—see C.M.A.
Musick, Captain Ed, Commander of *China Clipper*, 39
National Airlines, 1960 lease agreement with Pan Am, 68;
    purchased by Pan Am, 82
New York Airways, 26
New York, Rio and Buenos Aires Line (NYRBA), 20-21, 88
Niña, La, FC-2, of WIAX, 5
Norske Luftfartselskap, Det (D.N.L.)
    Norwegian airline Atlantic plans, 51
North American Aviation, 34
North Haven, Pacifc depot ship, 31
Northrop Delta, 50
NYRBA—see New York, Rio...
Pacific Alaska Airways, 32
Pacific International Airways, 32
Pan Am Building, opened, 70; sold, 84
Pan Am Express, 86
Pan Am Shuttle, 86
Pan American-Grace Corp. (PANAGRA)
    Established, 14; DC-2, 44; S-43, 51;
    brief summary, 88
Panair do Brasil, established, 20; Fairchild 91, 50;
    Sikorsky S-43, 51; brief summary, 88
Panama Airways, brief summary, 89
Peruvian Airways, 14, 88
Philadelphia Rapid Transit Service (P.R.T.), 7
Pickwick Airways, 24
Pilgrim, Fairchild F100B, 32
Polar Route, 64
Post, Wiley, flies with C.A.T., 24
President, Boeing 377 service, 56
Priester, André, hired by Trippe, 4
QANTAS, special Boeing 707, 65
Rand, James (NYRBA), 20
Ransome Airlines, purchased, 86
Republic Rainbow, 54
Rickenbacker, Eddie (Florida Airways), 4
Rihl, George, founds C.M.A., 10
Rowe, Basil, founds WIAX, 9

SAHSA (Honduras), brief summary, 88
S.A.S., Polar Route, 64
St. Petersburg-Tampa Airboat Line, 2
Saunders-Roe Princess, Great flying boat
    comparison, 89
SCADTA, pioneer in Colombia, 3; Trippe
    acquires control, 22; brief summary, 88
SEDTA (Ecuador), German subsidiary, 58
Servicio Bolivariano de Transportes Aéros, 22
"Seven Seas"—Douglas DC-7C, 64-65
Shorts S-23 "Empire" flying boats, 40;
    Great flying boat comparison, 89
Shorts, S-26 "G" Class, and S-45 Solent,
    Great flying boat comparison, 89
Sikorsky, Igor, builds aircraft for Pan Am, 12
Sikorsky S-36, 12
Sikorsky S-38, 12-13; NYRBA, 20; UMCA, 23;
    New York Airways, 26
Sikorsky S-41 (Boston-Maine), 26
Sikorsky S-40, 28-29; great flying boat
    comparison, 89
Sikorsky S-42, 36-37; compared with DC-2, etc., 45;
    great flying boats, 89
Sikorsky S-43 "Baby Clipper", 50-51
Smith, C. R., comments on DC-3, 47
Southeastern Air Lines, and Southern
    Airlines, Pan Am foundation, 4
Spirit of St. Louis, The, carries mail for
    WIAX, 8; surveys Caribbean, 12
Stout, William B., Metal Airplane
    Company, and aircraft, 18-19
Sud Aviation, explores Airbus idea, 87
Sullivan, Captain R. O. D., pilots S-41 on
    Boston-Maine route, 26; inaugurates
    Atlantic passenger service, 42
Syndicato Condor (Brazil), 58
TACA (Central America) confrontation, 58
Tomlinson, "Tommy," T.W.A. high-altitude
    flying, 49
Trans-Pacific Air Route Development (Table), 31
Tripartite Agreement, 30
Trippe, Juan, operates Long Island Airways, 4;
    Forms Pan Am, 4; purchases C.M.A., 10; consults
    Sikorsky, 12; negotiates with Grace, 14; takes
    over NYRBA, 20; gentleman's agreement with von
    Bauer, 22; buys Cuban airline, 25; review of
    acquisitions, 28; plans Pacific route, 31; sponsors
    S-42, 36; M-130, 39; contender for Atlantic, 41;
    attempts T.W.A. merger, 56; succeeded by Gray, 70;
    death, 82
Tupolev Tu-104, first sustained jet service, 67
T.W.A. (Transcontinental and Western, or Trans World
    Airlines), sponsors DC-2, 45; sponsors Constellation,
    55; competes on North Atlantic, 56; 64-65; high-altitude
    experiments, sponsors Boeing 307, 49
UMCA (Uraba, Medellin and Central Airways), 23, 89
United Air Lines, sponsors DC-4E, 52; buys Pan Am's
    Pacific routes, 84
Uppercu, Inglis M., founds Aeromarine, 2
Varney, Walter, competes with Pan Am in Mexico, 24
Vickers, VC-10, 67
Von Bauer, Peter Paul, founds SCADTA, 3; sells to Trippe, 22
Vought-Sikorsky VS-44, great flying boat comparison, 89
West Indian Aerial Express, 8-9, brief summary, 88
Whitbeck, Jack, Pan Am representative in Miami, 5
WIAX—see West Indian Aerial Express
Yankee Clipper, 42
Yerex, Lowell, flies with C.A.T., 24; confronts Pan Am, 58